KATHARINE THE GREAT

DEBORAH DAVIS

KATHARINE THE GREAT

KATHARINE GRAHAM
☆ ☆ AND THE ☆ ☆
WASHINGTON POST

HARCOURT BRACE JOVANOVICH   NEW YORK AND LONDON

The author wishes to thank the following publishers for permission to quote from the sources listed:

Basic Books, Inc. "Despair and the Life of Suicide" from LYING, DESPAIR, JEALOUSY, ENVY, SEX, SUICIDE, DRUGS AND THE GOOD LIFE by Leslie Farber, © 1976 by Basic Books, Inc., Publishers, New York.

Houghton Mifflin Co. THE WASHINGTON POST by Chalmers Roberts, © 1977 by Houghton Mifflin Co. Reprinted by permission of the publisher.

Alfred A. Knopf, Inc. EUGENE MEYER by Merlo Pusey, © 1974, and LETTERS OF THOMAS MANN, selected and translated from the German by Richard and Clara Winston, © 1971 by Alfred A. Knopf, Inc. Reprinted by permission of the publisher.

William Morrow & Company, Inc. FELIX FRANKFURTER REMINISCES by Harlan B. Phillips, © 1960 by William Morrow & Company. Reprinted by permission of the publisher.

Psychiatry Magazine. Excerpts from "Distance and Relations" and "Guilt and Feelings" by Martin Buber in *Psychiatry*, volume 20, no. 2, May 1957. Reprinted by permission of the publisher.

Simon & Schuster. ALL THE PRESIDENT'S MEN by Carl Bernstein and Bob Woodward, © 1974 by Simon & Schuster. Reprinted by permission of the publisher.

State University of New York Press. THE LETTERS OF LOUIS D. BRANDEIS, edited by Melvin I. Urofsky and David W. Levy. Volumes II and III, © 1973, volume IV, © 1975 by State University of New York Press. Reprinted by permission of the publisher.

Set in Linotype Times Roman
Printed in the United States of America

LIBRARY OF CONGRESS CATALOGING IN PUBLICATION DATA
Davis, Deborah, 1949–
Katharine the Great.
Includes bibliographical references and index.
1. Graham, Katharine, 1917–
2. Women publishers—Washington, D.C.—Biography.
3. Washington Post. I. Title.
Z473.G7D38   070.5'092'4 [B]   78-22248
ISBN 0-15-146784-6

First edition
B C D E

To my grandmother,
who did not live long enough

Special thanks to Gene Stone, Tom Stewart, Elaine Markson, Sheryl Dare, Marcus Raskin, Debra Garrin, Charlie McConney, Lori Mollichelli, Peggy Brooks, who was very helpful to me in the early stages of the book, and to Phil O'Neill, without whom this book would not have been possible.

KATHARINE THE GREAT

A biography is considered complete if it merely accounts for six or seven selves, whereas a person may well have as many as one thousand.

VIRGINIA WOOLF

Some are born great, some achieve greatness, and some have greatness thrown upon them.

WILLIAM SHAKESPEARE, *Twelfth Night*

☆ **1** ☆

Katharine Graham

Katharine Graham came to national prominence during the Watergate scandals, when the *Washington Post*, which she owns and publishes, ran a daring series of stories on political corruption which ultimately led into the Nixon White House and which caused President Nixon to resign from office. The Watergate stories established Mrs. Graham as a publisher of conscience and courage, and of legendary power—she was the woman who brought down a president.

Washington is in many ways Katharine Graham's town. She was raised there; her father bought the *Washington Post* at auction in 1933; she married and gave birth to four children there; and there she nursed her erratic husband, Philip, through years of well-publicized mental illness, which jeopardized the stability of the newspaper that her father had given him shortly after their marriage. When her husband committed suicide in 1963, Katharine inherited the *Post* and by harsh, efficient management built it into a news vehicle that is both economically and journalistically dominant in the capital city. As in all cities, that dominance means that the publisher has close social relationships with the city's important politicians, and that they influence her newspaper, just as her newspaper

KATHARINE THE GREAT

influences them. When her husband ran the paper, there were working arrangements with officials in the Departments of State and Justice, the intelligence agencies, and the president's office. She supported the Vietnam war because of her friendship with Lyndon Johnson, and had it not been for what happened between her and Nixon, she most likely would not have sponsored the two years of Watergate stories, which she suspected would implicate him.

Nixon came to Washington as president in 1968 with a hatred for the press (and the *Washington Post* in particular) that he had developed as a congressman twenty years earlier. He had been a calculating, effective witch-hunter on the House Un-American Activities Committee and later in the Senate, which had earned him the reputation as the brightest and hardest-working of the young Republicans. He came to despise Philip Graham, not because Graham opposed the spirit of his campaign against domestic Communists, but because the *Post* had accused him of "excesses" in performing an important service. When Nixon landed the vice-presidential slot on the Eisenhower ticket in 1952, Graham printed a story about illegal contributions to his campaign, and Nixon was forced to deliver the humiliating Checkers speech (he had also received other gifts; did the people want him to give back his dog Checkers?), which assured his enmity for the *Post* forever afterward.

Katharine supported Nixon for president in 1968, when antiwar candidate Eugene McCarthy did well against Johnson in the Democratic primaries. After Johnson announced in March that he would not accept the nomination for another term as president, she looked to Nixon for a solution not so much to the war as to the intolerable problem of dissent. When the antiwar displays continued, and intensified, during Nixon's first year in office, Katharine ran an editorial objecting to the movement's attempt to "break" a president.

In exchange for her support, she expected Nixon's friendship and received instead his unprovoked attacks. Spiro Agnew announced publicly that the *Washington Post* and its subsidiary news companies, including *Newsweek* magazine, "all grind out the same editorial line . . . powerful voices harken to the same master," by whom he meant Katharine. In the privacy of her office, John Ehrlichman read off a list of media sins, and she was beside herself trying to elicit from him exactly what it was that the president wanted to see in print.

Their mutual dance ended abruptly in June 1971, when the *New York Times* published the first of its stories based upon the Pentagon Papers, the classified Defense Department documents that revealed misjudgment and deception in the conduct of the war. Once published, the documents became a matter of journalistic competition; the *Post* obtained a set, and when a Nixon administration official telephoned executive editor Benjamin Bradlee to ask that he not publish them, Bradlee said, "I'm sorry but I'm sure you understand I must respectfully decline." Nixon's attacks became more bitter, his threats more serious; in June 1972, Katharine and Bradlee seized the opportunity to cover the arrest of the Watergate burglars.

Katharine did not, much as she enjoyed the acclaim that Watergate brought her, want the taste for scandal to alter permanently the practice of journalism; she became concerned, after it was over, that reporters' disrespect for the men in public life had gotten out of control. Several months after Nixon's resignation, she wrote an essay entitled "The Press after Watergate: Getting Down to New Business,"* in which she complained that the "dedicated public servants" Nelson Rockefeller and Henry Kissinger, who were both her friends, did not "entirely understand" the new requirements for disclosure. She disliked the breakdown in authority and felt that scrutiny of political behavior was not the proper way

* *New York* magazine, November 4, 1974.

to determine a man's fitness for office. To judge a leader, one must look beyond his actions into his "character." Her message was that Richard Nixon had been an exception. Reporters should now, again, simply report the news.

Her fame brought unwanted attention to her own power. There were several flattering "authorized" portraits, all reiterating the same few themes, as she provided them: the eccentric, dynamic family, the education at Vassar and the University of Chicago, the marriage, her husband's suicide, having to learn to run the newspaper "from the top down." There were also unauthorized articles, which examined her ruthless labor policies, her enduring support for the Vietnam war; which speculated that a relationship with the CIA might have had something to do with Watergate. It did.

These are the questions that go to the heart of Mrs. Graham's life as a publisher. She is not comfortable with them, has not cooperated with any efforts to analyze them, and wishes they would stop. "I have called a halt to all articles and books about me," she told this author. When she wanted a book, she would ask one of her own writers to do it. I continued to work and she told her friends not to speak to me, as she feared the book would be a "hatchet job." Recognizing the tendency of the rich and powerful, as well as the poor and powerless, to be suspicious of those whom they do not know, I was nevertheless struck by the arrogance implicit in her attitude: that unless she can control what is being written, it is neither legitimate nor reliable. What is the elusive wisdom of the people who own the means to shape the flow of information to us; how do their attitudes determine what we know?

One who writes about Katharine Graham's life is led unavoidably to a study of the political uses of information, a phenomenon that I have called mediapolitics, a discussion of which the reader will find woven into the narrative. A political treatment of her life and work, as she would agree, is more interesting than a book that might attempt merely to humanize her, to penetrate the legend and reduce her mystery with anecdotes, which explain nothing at all. Her legend is about her political power, and that is the reason that she is an important and worthy subject.

☆ **2** ☆

The Legend

It was a sweet, sunny spring morning when Katharine Graham had a breakfast for Robert Redford on the veranda of her Georgetown mansion. The meeting was a prelude to his making a film about her newspaper, a detective story in which two *Washington Post* reporters uncover political crimes that implicate the president of the United States. It would be a true-to-life account, ending when seven of the president's closest aides are indicted. Their plans were extraordinary in that even as they spoke, the Congress was preparing three articles of impeachment against the president himself, and he would resign from office in less than five months.

Seated with Redford and Katharine on her black and white tiled porch, at several small round tables, was a group of young men all nervously eyeing one another: Dustin Hoffman, Redford's co-star; Carl Bernstein and Bob Woodward, the Watergate reporters, the authors of *All the President's Men*, just submitted for publication, which would be the basis for the movie in question; and Donald Graham ("Donny"), Katharine's son, a Harvard graduate, Vietnam veteran, former member of the District of Columbia police force, and heir to his mother's fortune and to her publishing empire.

Donny was with his mother that day because the *Washington Post* was a family newspaper, the Grahams' claim to being a great American family. The family, that was the central thing, the reason and the spirit of Katharine's publishership. Her determination was a legacy from her husband, Philip Graham, who had killed himself in 1963. Her sense of mission in publishing came from her parents—millionaires, social servants, art patrons (modern art and Oriental masterpieces dominated the living room, where the breakfast guests drank their final cups of coffee)—who had bought the *Post* in 1933 with the intention of building it into an influential political force. The Watergate stories had been the culmination of that effort, the proof of the family's power in media, its facility with politics, its good name, its right to command deference; and Robert Redford's calling on Katharine symbolized all of that, although she was surprised to find herself only mildly flattered. Before Watergate she would have been thrilled at his interest in her; now, having played her tense, dramatic role in bringing down a president, having achieved her place in and around and above the political life of the nation, her family itself at last a medium for political communication—now, Robert Redford's world, a world of images devoid of substance, seemed by comparison silly and frivolous and small.

Arising at seven on the morning of the mediapolitics breakfast, Katharine had put on a good casual dress and gold chains and had gone downstairs to consult with her servant. They decided on scrambled eggs and sausage set out in silver chafing dishes, fruit, little rolls; Katharine had thought that it would be more gracious if she served the food than if her woman did it, that it would allow everybody to feel more at home.

The legend that surrounded her seemed to inhibit conversation, just as she had been afraid it would. Redford was awkward, Hoffman nearly speechless; Woodward joked with Bernstein feebly. In such situations the solution was light gossip, an art that Katharine perfected after her husband's death, when she was forty-six years old. Telling short, funny stories that illuminated the human side of politics would help to break the ice; one of her favorites was about Henry Kissinger, Nixon's national security adviser and war architect, who in spite of a hatred of the press equal to the president's had persuaded Katharine that he was her friend. Back in 1970, Katharine told the actors brightly, Kissinger was trying to negotiate an end to the Vietnam war and was exhausting himself shuttling back and forth to the peace talks in Paris. Then Nixon let the country know about the Cambodian invasion and said that the United States had been bombing Cambodia secretly for a year. Suddenly there had been a great outcry against Kissinger; he was called a war criminal, accused of genocide; and in addition to his other concerns, he began to worry all the time about that. He became so preoccupied with the war criminal stigma, Katharine went on sympathetically, that when he took her to the movies, as he did every time he returned to Washington, he would sit through the entire show thinking about why he was misunderstood. And now she came to the point of the story, at which the guests laughed politely: that on one of these occasions, when the movie ended, Kissinger was unable to remember the plot.

It is true that personal alliances of this sort are the small pieces out of which the riddle of history is woven, and Donny proudly thought that the story displayed his mother's virtuosity in politics. Yet Carl Bernstein must have wondered. Kissinger worked closely with Richard Nixon; their ideas not only about the war, but about necessary measures regarding opposition to the war (infiltration, wiretaps, other political intelligence), were indistinguishable. How could the woman who had been appalled at Nixon's political crimes admire his colleague in these matters? Had she not learned since Watergate that men in government are capable of many things, that political behavior should not be overlooked just because a man takes her to the movies?

Katharine had always said that Watergate was simply good journalism, not the result of her political views. For Bernstein it had been different: all his life he had associated Nixon with McCarthyism and the persecution of his parents, and he did not believe that as president Nixon was any less villainous. The Watergate burglars were arrested in June 1972; since the day that Bernstein and Woodward traced the slush fund that paid the burglars to John Mitchell, Nixon's campaign counsel, in October, Bernstein had been convinced that this was the moment in history when Nixon was going to be exposed for what he was. In anticipation he contracted with Simon and Schuster to write a psychological study of two of Nixon's men, Mitchell and Gordon Liddy, the finance counsel of the Committee to Re-elect the President (CRP), who had been indicted in September for paying the burglars. The book (working title: *The Worst and the Dumbest*) was put together haphazardly over the next six months, between newspaper stories; by the spring of 1973 a manuscript was in private circulation. Redford, it seems, obtained a copy, for one day he telephoned Woodward, whom he had never met, to say that the structure of the book was wrong, that it should be the story of their investigation, that they, not the president's men, should be the protagonists.

Woodward waited a month before telling Bernstein about the actor's call; it was difficult enough being journalists without thinking of themselves as heroes in a drama of their own creation. But they rewrote the book Redford's way over the next year, and he paid them almost half a million dollars for the film rights. He cast himself as Woodward and asked Dustin Hoffman, who had also tried to obtain the property, to portray Bernstein. After all of these arrangements had been made, and Redford had rented an apartment in the Watergate apartment complex, where he and his wife would live during the location shooting (the FBI building, the Library of Congress), he asked Woodward to introduce him to Mrs. Graham. Katharine thought, since it was her newspaper that he was going to exploit, that the request came rather later than it might have, but she agreed, graciously.

Finally, on Katharine's veranda, the conversation drifted to Redford's plans for the production. He would need photographs and measurements of the newsroom, her office, Ben Bradlee's office, in order to build accurate sets (when Bradlee visited the duplicate of his office, he felt dizzy; even the same books were on the shelf); he would want to ship their trash to the Burbank studio; he and Hoffman would have to spend several weeks in the newsroom observing real reporters at work. He would want to feature the *Washington Post* prominently, use real names, engage a major actress to play Mrs. Graham's part; Lauren Bacall was mentioned. Katharine gave her consent.

The filming was well under way before Katharine changed her mind and had her lawyers see what could be done to prevent Redford from finishing. It turned out that she was not able to prevent the contracts that he had signed with the reporters and with Warner Brothers from being fulfilled, but her attitude did deeply anger him, and he cut her out of the movie and deleted all references to her, except for one unflattering remark by John Mitchell.

The movie, *All the President's Men*, had its international premiere in Washington in 1976; Katharine, as it happened, loved it and forgave Redford for their past differences. It was exhilarating to see one's triumph reenacted on the screen. It was proof of her greatness; it secured Katharine's place in the national consciousness.

THE FAMILY

☆ 3 ☆

The Father

In the beginning was the father, Eugene Isaac Meyer, who was born on October 31, 1875, into a cultured Jewish mercantile family in the pioneer village of Los Angeles. He was the fourth of eight children and the first son. In a patriarchal family, that made him the most honored child.

Eugene Meyer's father, Marc Eugene, had come to Los Angeles in 1860 from Strasbourg, the capital of Alsace, France, fleeing anti-Semitism and poverty and seeking adventure. His new town was predominantly Spanish in culture. The land had belonged to Mexico until a decade earlier; official records were kept in both English and Spanish, and merchants posted bilingual advertisements. It was a wild town of only five thousand, where American gunfighters and Mexican bandidos often terrorized the citizens, but Marc Eugene quickly felt at home among the French Jewish settlers who spoke French as well as English and Spanish, if less so with the Prussian Jews, who spoke Polish. The Jewish colony was largely responsible for the town's developing industry and business; nearly all were merchants, and by the time Eugene Isaac was born, his father had become one of the most prominent of them. He was at once the consular agent for the

French government, an agent for imports and exports of fine fabrics, a fledgling banker, a gold speculator, a real estate investor, and a director of the crude system of wooden pipes known as the Los Angeles City Water Works. "Mr. Meyer," a contemporary wrote of Marc Eugene, "was a man of fine physique, handsome appearance and with a great measure of personality." He belonged to one of the most outstanding Jewish families in Europe.

Jewish religious leaders then were also the political leaders of their people. Marc Eugene's father, Isaac, had been a rabbi and the secretary of the Jewish Consistory, the civil governing body of Strasbourg. His grandfather Jacob had been a member of the Congress of Jewish Notables convoked by Emperor Napoleon I for the consideration of Jewish rights. And his brother-in-law, the eminent Zadoc Kahn, served as the Grand Rabbi of France from 1880 until 1905, acting as a liaison between wealthy Jews and early immigrants to Palestine, who were beginning to create settlements in the Holy Land in response to the pogroms of Eastern Europe.

When Marc's father died, his mother refused help from wealthy relatives, and she and her two daughters and son were forced to make a living selling flour in Alsace. Marc had to drop out of the *Gymnasium Protestant* at the age of fourteen. Rather than wait until he was old enough to work in a relative's business, Marc Eugene left for an unknown new life in 1859, at the age of seventeen, sailing four months around Cape Horn to the gold-rush town of San Francisco. He carried a letter of introduction to his cousin Alexander Weill, the San Francisco representative for the Lazard brothers, investment bankers whose past ventures in the New World included financing for the Revolutionary War and the French and Indian War and soon would include the Civil War. The Weills, Lazards, Kahns, and Meyers had all intermarried many times, as was the custom among wealthy European Jews, and the families took care of one another.

Weill immediately feared that his teenaged cousin would fall into bad ways—drinking, prospecting, or worse—and put him to work in his dry-goods store, where Marc Eugene was introduced to the rudiments of business. The store was a frontier bank of sorts. Many of Weill's customers paid in gold dust, which he would then ship to the Lazards in France. Others left bags of dust for him to hold in his safe, which he did free of charge, as a service. He might not see the depositor again for a year, when he would come in again from the mines with another bag of dust for the safe and a smaller bag as a bonus for Weill. Soon he was lending money to other businesses and to real estate developers, and Marc Eugene found that despite his intention to break away from the family business, to work in Weill's dry goods was to learn banking.

The young Meyer left Weill after a year to go to the more exotic village of Los Angeles. Again he had a letter of introduction, from Weill to cousin Solomon Lazard, who had also become the banker in his territory, holding money for Basque shepherds. Here Marc Eugene decided to settle and began to take an active part in the life of the town.

Lazard, one of the most civilized of the townsmen, was a lieutenant in the Los Angeles Mounted Rifles, a voluntary military company that patrolled the hills surrounding the city to protect against bandits, Indians, and an anticipated invasion of Mormons, said to be migrating there from Utah. Meyer too joined the Rifles and, to prove himself, another vigilante group as well; he also belonged to the Hillcrest Country Club and to the Hebrew Benevolent Society, which gave money to fledgling charities. He worked faithfully for Solomon Lazard & Company and in 1864, at the age of twenty-two, was made a member of the company; in 1868, a year after he had married sixteen-year-old Harriet Newmark, whose older sister Caroline had married Solomon Lazard (the tradition of intermarriage continuing in the colony), he became a principal partner.

15

The Newmarks had welcomed the ambitious young man like a son. "Dear [Marc] Eugene brought [Harriet's] bridal dress from San Francisco, that is to say, the material," wrote Harriet's mother to another daughter. ". . . Everybody said she was the prettiest bride they ever saw. I can assure you, dear Eugene is not a little proud of her. He was dressed very nicely, all in white, black swallow-tailed coat and white necktie, and embroidered bosom shirt. . . . I feel very happy as she has a very nice young man for a husband. She could not have done better had she been very accomplished."

The ceremony was performed by Harriet's father, Joseph, a lay rabbi. Newmark was a learned man who had been a kosher ritual butcher in Poland and had founded no fewer than four synagogues in America: two in New York and one in St. Louis, as well as the one in Los Angeles.* He carried out the service in Hebrew, then hosted the wedding feast in the Bella Union Hotel, where "a colored man cooked the poultry," according to a contemporary account, and tables were set with pies, jellies, and chicken salad. One floor below was a funeral for a man who had been killed in a gunfight.

The couple moved into a one-bedroom house that neighbors and relatives had furnished beautifully with horsehair chairs and sofa, walnut and marble-top tables, a rosewood piano, hat stands, lace curtains, scarlet draperies, and carpets imported from Brussels by Alexander Weill, who had also supplied the material for Harriet's wedding dress.

Marc Eugene's marriage secured his place in the tight Jewish community. In 1868 he was asked to join the board of directors of the Los Angeles City Water Works, a private company of which Solomon Lazard was the president. Dr. John S. Griffin and a merchant, Prudent Beaudry, who had once sworn that he would drive every Jew in Los Angeles out of business, were his partners. The company had been formed

* This exists today as the Wilshire Boulevard Temple.

to buy the contract to modernize and manage the city's water system from Don Louis Sainsevain, who had been unable to fulfill his promise to the city to replace the primitive wooden system with a network of solid iron pipes. The three men completed that task, then applied in 1869 to lease the Los Angeles River water for fifty years, in return for which they offered to establish a complete distributing system for domestic use, to cancel several claims against the city, to place fire hydrants on downtown corners (a number of buildings having been lost to fire), and to construct an ornamental fountain in the plaza, at a total cost of about $200,000. The company received instead a thirty-year contract, which was sufficient to give the board of directors very special standing indeed until the turn of the century.

The French government, at about this time, approached Meyer through Lazard to ask that he be France's consular agent and work with French bankers who wanted to begin investing in the American West. He consented, but found that affiliation with France drew him into the events that were shaking Europe. Anti-Semitism was becoming a virulent force in politics; in 1868 Meyer organized a Los Angeles chapter of the Paris-based Alliance Israélite Universelle, a defense society that had been founded in 1860 in response to the Mortara case, a bizarre kidnapping of a Jewish child by the Papal Guard. The alliance was dedicated to the political and physical protection of European and Middle Eastern Jews; the Los Angeles chapter, with Meyer as president, raffled rifles and cigars to raise money to send to Paris headquarters.

Meyer's alliance lasted only two years, until 1870, when the Franco-Prussian War broke out and the French, Polish, and German Jews in Los Angeles found themselves unable to cooperate on anything, even charity. The Newmarks and other Poles raised money for war relief for the Prussians. The Germans, caught in shifting European political loyalties, supported the Prussians; whereas the French, Marc Eugene among them, already in conflict with his new family, sent money to France. These frontier Jews still felt themselves to be loyal citizens of their respective homelands. "Two well known citizens, one of Prussian and the other of French birth," reported the local newspaper, "discussed the war yesterday afternoon with such emphasis that they came to blows." The Pole was a man named Moritz Morris; the Frenchman, Marc Eugene.

His marriage to the Polish Harriet somehow survived the Franco-Prussian War, and the family prospered. By the time Meyer had bought out Solomon Lazard's store in 1873, they had three daughters; then, in 1875, Harriet gave birth to Eugene Isaac, the father of the subject of this book. He grew up alternately proud and contemptuous of his immigrant parents. There were later two more sons and three more daughters.

The boy spent his early years in school and at the old Lazard store, which his father had renamed Eugene Meyer & Company. The townspeople called it the City of Paris. Meyer supplied not only settlers but country merchants throughout the lower California coast, and as far inland as Tucson, and his store soon became the largest and most magnificent in the Southwest. The retail salesroom was 125 feet long and 80 feet wide, with counters 120 feet long. Along each counter were forty cushioned stools for customers. The stock, many tons in cloths and clothing, was organized by departments: silks, calicoes, carpets, oilcloths, mats, and ready-made hats, boots, shirts, and shoes. There was a private room for wholesale transactions. Behind the main store was a warehouse in which were stored hundreds of bales of grain.

The town did not offer much for a spirited and wealthy youngster. Every night Eugene and his parents and sisters visited relatives, which after a generation of intermarriage included most of the Jews in town. These well-to-do families all lived within twelve blocks of the center of town.

It was then common in wealthy houses to have a nurse-

18

governess, an upstairs maid who during meals was the waitress, a parlormaid, a full-time cook, a private tutor, and, in times of illness, a medical nurse. In addition, there was a seamstress who visited several times a week, another woman who did only mending, a laundress, a music teacher, a cabinetmaker, and a woman who made the rounds of the families to shampoo and comb everybody's hair—the combined salaries totaling not even $100 a month.

Eugene was taken from this narrow life at the age of nine. His father, Alexander Weill's former stockboy, was asked to take over Weill's position as San Francisco representative for Lazard Frères (Weill wanted to return to Paris), and Marc Eugene sold his department store and moved the family into a spacious Victorian mansion on the 1700 block of Pine Street, in downtown San Francisco. Here the boy saw a city teeming with Irish, Chinese, Czechs (micks, chinks, bohunks, he learned from the other boys), and gold miners and Basque shepherds, who staged bloody public cockfights on Washington Square.

Marc Eugene now directed all West Coast investments of the Lazards' London, Paris, and American banks and relished the international banker's life. He dressed his wife and daughters in a manner befitting their affluence, attended cultural events, and belonged to the boards of social welfare groups. He wore long double-breasted coats and bow ties, and he required his son to wear starched Eton collars, which, Eugene objected, caused bullies to pick on him. His father did not relent on the collars, but he paid for boxing lessons with James J. "Gentleman Jim" Corbett, a fighter who was on his way to becoming heavyweight champion of the world. Eugene became, consequently, something of a bully himself, running around in his starched collars mocking and taunting his teachers, provoking his classmates, tormenting his sisters and little brothers, unafraid because a champion fighter had taught him to box.

19

The once rebellious Mr. Meyer started to worry about his oldest son's education. "You don't work enough to suit me," he told him after a bout of bad behavior, and arranged with a professor of German from the University of California to tutor him three days a week in Greek, Latin, ancient history, and mathematics. Eugene was made to read his father's financial journals from New York, London, Berlin, Frankfurt, and Vienna and to learn French and German from them, as well as finance. He read briefs in a lawsuit against Lazard Frères for alleged faulty maintenance of military roads on federal lands in California and Oregon. Soon he appreciated how completely was his father absorbed in the world of business. Even card games with friends, to which his father took him, became forums for the discussion of politics and finance. Meyer was, his son realized, one of San Francisco's dominant financial minds.

The Meyers could have become one of the great San Francisco families. Cultured, educated, civic-minded, they also became connected with the Levi Strauss fortune in 1892, when their oldest daughter, Rosalie, married Sigmund Stern, the bachelor Strauss's nephew and heir. In 1893 their second daughter, Elise, married Sigmund's brother Abraham, and there was the possibility of Lazard Frères financing mining and industrial operations with Levi Strauss supplying the clothing for the workers, the two clans together controlling much of the wealth of California and the Northwest. But political and financial events intervened—the Panic of 1893, a crisis of confidence in U.S. currency—and Meyer, one of Lazard Frères' most versatile men, was called to New York, where Lazard occupied a pivotal position in America's investment banking network. The Meyers, minus the two married daughters, piled their belongings onto a train in May 1893 and rode across the country to a new life in the East. The most memorable part of the trip for Eugene was passing a tribe of Apaches as they were being relocated by U.S. troops. The Meyers, with the three boys and three girls, first stayed in the elegant Savoy Hotel in New York City and then found a townhouse to buy on East 72nd Street.

The Panic had been caused by the European bankers' response to the Sherman Free Silver Act of 1890, which required the U.S. Treasury to purchase $4 to $8 million worth of western-mined silver each month and to mint the equivalent in silver dollars. The rest of the world was on the gold standard, and bankers in Europe did not believe that the silver dollar would have equivalent market value. They began to withdraw their money from American industry, especially from the railroads, which they had financed through an American who sat with them on the Court of the Bank of England, J. P. Morgan. The railroads were the principal instrument of industrial development in the United States, and Meyer's job, as Lazard saw it, was to persuade the bankers to leave their money in and allow the crisis to burn itself out. Meyer persuaded Morgan, Morgan's example influenced the European bankers, the Free Silver Act was repealed late in 1893, and the Panic ended as quickly as it had begun. But the "Jewish banking fraternity," as the Populists called it, became hated for suppressing financial populism, even though Lazard, a Jewish banker, had been one of the first to move capital into the West and had been instrumental in keeping it there.

Eugene had been taken out of the University of California in midyear when his family went east and had been put to work that summer as a messenger in the Lazard office, for which he was paid $12 a week. He spent endless days in a stuffy cubicle and on weekends desolately wandered the slums of the Lower East Side, where everywhere was the living evidence of anti-Semitic agitation in Europe. By the time he went to Yale that fall, as planned, he had become quite self-consciously Jewish as he had not been in California; he did not live in an official Yale residence, where Jews were not welcome, but shared a room in a rooming house with another

21

Lazard Frères son. He studied the full range of subjects: logic, ethics, psychology, Spanish, English literature, German, French, and political economics; he was interested primarily, though, in European politics, an interest heightened in 1894 by the Dreyfus affair in France.

Alfred Dreyfus was a wealthy Alsatian Jew, a captain in the French army, who was accused of promising to pass military documents to Germany, which France hated and feared: Germany had annexed Alsace-Lorraine in the Franco-Prussian War. He was charged with and convicted of treason and sentenced to "degradation and deportation" for life on Devil's Island, a barbaric penal colony for political prisoners off the coast of French Guinea. In 1896 the army's chief of intelligence discovered that the real traitor had been one Walsin Esterhazy, but the military suppressed this evidence. In 1897 Dreyfus's brother made the same finding, and the army held a court-martial for the accused; but he was acquitted within minutes, and Dreyfus remained on Devil's Island in solitary confinement. The next year an army colonel was proved to have forged the papers that incriminated Dreyfus. The colonel committed suicide and Esterhazy fled to England, but in a third court-martial in 1899 the court was unable to admit error; Dreyfus was again found guilty but his sentence was reduced from life to ten years. The Dreyfus case divided all French political actors, on every conceivable issue, into Dreyfusards and anti-Dreyfusards, the nationalists, royalists, and militarists aligning against Dreyfus; the republicans, anticlericals, and socialists, including Georges Clemenceau, the future premier, coalescing around him, less concerned with the Dreyfus cause than with discrediting the rightist government. The left wing came to power as a result of the Dreyfus case in 1899, but Dreyfus was not completely cleared until 1906.

The country, as well as Dreyfus, was weakened by the long political crisis. Engaged in an arms race with Germany since the 1870s, the purpose of which was one day to win back Alsace-Lorraine, the French nationalists and militarists so lost credibility that the new pro-Dreyfus government cut military spending and reduced the influence of the army in government. The Triple Alliance, which Germany had formed with Austria and Italy after the Franco-Prussian War, could therefore commit itself to commercial and colonial expansion without fear of French reprisal. France had signed a mutual aid treaty with Russia in 1894, partly to ensure completion of the trans-Siberian railroad, which ironically had been financed in 1891 by the Jewish Rothschilds; but the French-Russian alliance did not neutralize the Triple Alliance. Rather, it fed the fever of shifting political affinities throughout Central, Western, and Eastern Europe and made France part of a network of countries that were pulled into World War I when Archduke Francis Ferdinand of Austria-Hungary was assassinated by a Serbian nationalist in 1914.

Eugene had finished Yale in 1895, having taken a double load to get out early because he had been eager to go to Europe. His ostensible reason was to study, and he enrolled at the University of Berlin, but he spent most of his time in France with his father's brother-in-law, Zadoc Kahn, the Grand Rabbi. Kahn was one of the most ardent and vocal defenders of Dreyfus. The writer Émile Zola, a famous and fascinating man, was working closely with Kahn at that time, producing pro-Dreyfus pamphlets. The most inflammatory of these came to be "J'Accuse," published in 1898, in which Zola charged the judges with obeying orders from the war office in their acquittal of Esterhazy.

Eugene had been very much affected by the case while at Yale and had wanted to see firsthand his uncle's legendary commitment to justice. Kahn arranged for him to meet Alexander Weill, the man who so long before had employed Eugene's father as a stockboy in gold-rush San Francisco. Weill was by then the manager of Lazard Frères in Paris. The old man learned that Eugene was interested in finance and asked him if he would go to the London office, marry a Lazard daughter, and eventually become head of the English branch. Eugene politely refused. "I think you're going to have a war here" was what he told Weill, "and I'd rather live in a country that won't be involved in that war."

But he had other reasons as well. Lazard had become a conservative, unexciting house. Other bankers were making history: J. P. Morgan financing arms manufacture in France, Great Britain, and Russia, the Triple Entente countries, helping them prepare to fight expansionist Germany; the Rothschilds floating billions of rubles' worth of Russian bonds in France to pay for the trans-Siberian railroad; Jacob Schiff of Kuhn, Loeb and Company dramatically refusing to aid Russia because of the czar's oppression of Jews (and later contributing to the czar's overthrow by financing Japan in the Russo-Japanese War of 1904, later still financing the Kerensky regime); the Rothschilds and Schiff financing settlements in Palestine. The Lazard house, maddeningly, opposed Zionism on the theory that French Jews ought to remain loyal to France.

Eugene could have forgiven the provincialism, the indifference to political currents, and the lack of historical understanding—and he would have, had the company not been treating his father so badly. The European partners had finally promoted Marc Eugene Meyer to managing partner of the New York office, but they extracted high service fees for every piece of support work they performed for him and made it clear that they would not renew his five-year contract if he complained. Eugene returned to his clerk's job in New York after his year in Europe and absorbed what he could about finance. He learned arbitrage, the buying and selling of foreign currencies, from Lazard partner George Blumenthal, who had opportunely, Eugene thought, married his sister Florence.

But it would be only a matter of time until he formally broke with the Lazard company; he began looking around for something else to do.

Eugene's raw instinct for making money was as fine as any man's. While he was in Europe, he came into the $800 that his father had promised him if he would not smoke until he was twenty-one. He invested the money in Northern Pacific common stock, his first venture in the stock market, and let it earn dividends until he learned all he could on his job; by 1900 his initial investment had yielded $5,000. He protected this money by putting part of it into gold certificates, a hedge against a presidential victory by free silver advocate William Jennings Bryan; he used the remainder to buy options on one thousand shares of what he considered to be the best railroad stock, at guaranteed prices. When William McKinley, in whom the bankers had confidence, defeated Bryan, Eugene exercised his options on the railroad stock; prices shot up, as he had predicted, and by January 1901, two months later, its value had increased tenfold—and he had $50,000. He then told his father that he was leaving Lazard.

"I've worked all my life to make a position for you in the firm," Marc Eugene exploded, wounded. "You know I've had you in mind in everything I've done. What sort of ungrateful son are you?"

"You've done everything a father could do for his son," Eugene replied calmly, "and a good deal more besides. I owe everything to you. But now you've done enough. You can't deny me the one thing you had."

"I've denied you nothing."

"You've denied me the chance to make my own way in life."

Meyer was alarmed enough to notify Alexander Weill, who came to New York. Weill offered Eugene a small partnership in the New York office, but it would have had to come out of his father's share, and Eugene, again, refused him. He left the company, and soon afterward his father and his brother-in-law, Blumenthal, followed him.

Fifty thousand dollars was precisely the cost of a seat on the New York Stock Exchange. Eugene bought one that was available as part of an estate and began to operate on the floor, finding, immediately, that his international training put him at a distinct advantage on all the crucial matters of finance: not only arbitrage, but interest rates, foreign exchange rates, and how to use the time difference between New York and the financial centers of Europe. He affiliated with several correspondents in Paris and London and planned his actions on the floor on the basis of their reports of monetary movements there. In his first year he capitalized on a ferocious stock fight for control of several railroads between J. P. Morgan and E. H. Harriman, Wall Street's two railroad giants, and came away with half a million dollars. He used that money to found his own brokerage house, Eugene Meyer Jr. and Company, in 1903.

Eugene's tiny firm contributed to the financial world the idea of statistical research. He produced reports (and sent them to Morgan, Harriman, other legendary financiers, just to let them know that he was also on the Street) that evaluated companies by geographical location, climate, access to natural resources and croplands, proximity to transportation and to other industry. His methods enabled investors to judge stock values accurately, on the basis of fact rather than rumor; within five years they had enabled him to achieve several substantial financial coups. Other brokers began telling each other to watch out for Eugene Meyer, that pretty soon he was going to have "all the money on Wall Street."

Eugene was an iconoclastic young millionaire. Profoundly independent, he lived happily with his parents in their Upper East Side townhouse. Though a consummate businessman, he preferred the company of left-wing intellectuals and activists

like the people he had known in France. During the few years
in which he was earning his first fortune, his steady lady friend
was Irène Untermyer, daughter of the eminent leftist attorney Samuel Untermyer, who was involved in some of the
most important litigation in the country, part of his continuing
effort to reduce the power of bankers. Untermeyer campaigned
against the bankers' stranglehold on the nation's credit (and
eventually headed a congressional investigation of J. P. Morgan, the worst offender); he wanted government control of
the stock market; he demanded government regulation of the
railroads; he blamed bankers for profiting from the wave of
Jewish immigration by building shoddy slum housing. The
Untermyers introduced Eugene to the founders of the Henry
Street Settlement, Lillian Wald, a nurse, and Mary Kingsbury
Simkhovitch, a social economist. These women had raised the
money to buy a seven-story brick Georgian house for their
project in 1900, and the old mansion had become a center
for artists and union organizers, as well as a makeshift school
and hospital for the poor. Eugene spent evenings and weekends at the house and donated funds to pay the salary and
expenses of a full-time nurse. These activities did not make
him popular with his Wall Street colleagues. Nor would
they like him any better when, in 1918, he left Wall Street
for the War Finance Corporation, an agency through which
the government provided money for economic recovery from
World War I. They would also dislike his efforts in 1931,
when, as head of the Reconstruction Finance Corporation,
he designed legislation that reduced the power of private
banking and empowered the government to lend money to
industry and take capital risks that bankers would not in
order to bring the country out of the depression; and again in
1946, when he was the first president of the World Bank,
which lent money on the world market for the public good,
not for profit. Wall Street respected Eugene Meyer, even
idolized him, but did not like him.

27

His failure to marry Irène Untermyer was explained by his unwillingness to enter into one of those incestuous family alliances that characterized New York Jewish society. He remained uninterested in marriage until the age of thirty-two, when in an art gallery he saw a woman, wearing a tweed suit and gray squirrel hat, looking at Japanese prints and decided that she was the one who was going to be his wife. "That's the girl I'm going to marry," he told his companion, the sculptor Gutzon Borglum (the man who later carved Mount Rushmore).

"Are you serious?"

"Never more so."

"Then you'd better speak to her or you'll never see her again."

A week later Borglum telephoned Eugene to say that he had met "that girl" and had arranged a party for them to get acquainted. The meeting turned out to be rather awkward; she was not interested in his money, which surprised him, and not particularly impressed with his achievements. She had her own life to worry about. She had, she told him, saved $500 and was about to go to Europe to study. She did not want any entanglements. It had been very nice meeting him. He loved her wildly.

☆ 4 ☆

The Father
and
the Mother

The mother was Agnes Elizabeth Ernst, a slim German beauty, a member of the inner circle of the 291 Club, within whose modest walls one could meet such artists as Alfred Stieglitz, Georgia O'Keeffe, and Edward Steichen (and on whose walls hung some of the first Picassos and Matisses ever to be seen outside Europe). Agnes was also, at twenty-one, the first female reporter to be hired by the influential *New York Sun*; she taught Bible classes to youth gangs; she was a heavy-handed but determined sketcher and a student of Oriental painting and sculpture. And she was a successful and cruel flirt, in whose diaries were recorded tales of amorous advances by men such as Auguste Rodin, whom she rejected with just the right balance of firmness and grace, so that their intellectual relationship would not be sacrificed. These were tales that she inflicted on the rich Eugene Meyer, who insisted, to her amusement, on seeing her again and again.

"This morning I had a note from Rodin saying that next

Sunday, when I am going out to see him, was too long to wait," she notified him in 1909 from Paris, where she had gone, defiantly, on her $500 a few months after they had met. "Would I not come sometime Thursday, rue de Varime, to look at the drawings once more? . . . Of course I have to go. But it means that he expects 'gratitude.' You need have no fears for me, however; tactful self-defence has become my second nature of late, and I shall do my best to carry off the situation—and the drawings. . . . The whole thing is an awful circus. Only:—Rodin has not been my only complication of late, and sometimes I get a bit tired of the game. I yearn for mountains, fresh air, and the elimination of the male element."

Eugene went about this courtship methodically. Agnes sent him several Rodin sketches, as evidence of the artist's feeling for her; Eugene responded with a check for $400, ostensibly as payment for the drawings, but he wanted her to keep it. She protested—"The idea of sending me $400 was mad. You are a sweet child to think about it but please consider me quite spoiled enough"—but her $500 had long since been spent and she did not send Eugene's money back. He sent her other checks on other pretexts, making possible her prolonged stay in Europe. He visited her in France, where he met Rodin, of whom, Agnes was startled to discover, he was not jealous. The sculptor was asked to join Eugene and Agnes for dinner. Rodin liked Eugene, accepted his claim to Agnes though she did not, and drew a "French interpretation" of Eugene and Agnes together.

Eugene also introduced Agnes to his sister Elise, who was then in Paris, and when he went back to New York, Elise entertained Agnes on his behalf. Eugene visited Agnes's parents in the Bronx on Christmas Day, then wrote Agnes about the meeting, hoping she would then tell them more about him. All Agnes wrote her mother was "Mr. Meyer, isn't he a brick?" She thought him solid, reliable, boring, generous, tough, and lonely. She also felt that he needed her, as other men did not. "And now I am going to scold," she once wrote him. "I heard from some one that you were not looking well because you were working so hard. And you tell me to take care of myself. I wish you wouldn't do such things or I shall have to come home and lead you astray." Unwillingly, that year in Paris, she came to rely on his money and to expect his visits. When was his steamer coming in? She demanded in the fall: "HURRY UP." He thought her petulant, brilliant, sophisticated, confused, lonely, desirable, and unloving. She frequently was able to enrage him, despite his efforts to be calculating.

His trip produced an argument within the first few hours; he went angrily to his hotel and did not telephone her for a week. Finally Agnes repented and had a messenger deliver a note: "I wish to send you just a little scrawl so that we may meet like nice sensible children when you come back. . . . I have come to realize that I have been expecting from you the resolution and the work of two will-powers,—even more at times when mine was almost deliberately working against yours. Knowing me as you do, the recognition of un-fairness needs no added promises, *n'est-ce pas?*" She was the most fascinating woman he had ever met; since he did not yet know her or her family well, he did not understand the depth of her unhappiness.

During Agnes's childhood, the Ernsts had lived in a large, solid house thirty miles from New York City, in Pelham Heights, a well-wooded community with one village school and three churches. There were three older brothers, maids, and cousins, all of whom spoke German and loved Martin Luther, father of Lutheranism. They were not simply Ger-mans, but Hanoverians, immigrants from the northwest prov-ince, the seat of German science, technology, medicine, music, art, and education. They hated the militaristic Prussians, descended from Teutonic knights, whose conquests of other

German provinces enabled them from the late 1800s on to dictate the tone of German national life. Agnes's father's father had been the personal clergyman to the last king of Hanover. The king refused to support Prussia in the Austro-Prussian War, and as a consequence he fell to Prussian forces in 1866, and his kingdom became a Prussian province. To build a stronger army, Prussia developed a government-controlled economy and obedient central bureaucracy. All the young men were conscripted for military service. Agnes's grandfather, deploring the "vulgarization of life," sent his six sons out of the country. The youngest, Agnes's father, went to sea at age fourteen. Some years later, in New York, he married Agnes's mother, also a refugee from Hanover, and studied law at night. They built a harsh Hanoverian home life—worship of Luther, Wagner, cold baths, long walks in the winter, sacrifice, and discipline. They had three boys, the oldest of whom, Carl, ran away from home at an early age and never saw the family again. Agnes was born on January 2, 1887. She was her father's darling; she was preoccupied with him for the rest of her life.

She remembers her father as having "soft curls." He was physically undemonstrative; there never was the "slightest caress, but many loving looks and perfect mutual trust and understanding." He woke her at five in the morning to take walks in the forest, reciting poetry. She loved him unquestioningly and forgave him the occasional beatings he gave her. Even late in life, after she had long hated him, the sweet memory of his worrying over her, a girl of five, as she was prepared for brain surgery, was untainted by the thought that the bullet, fired by a playful brother, had come from her father's carelessly placed gun; it was his irresponsibility that had nearly killed her.

Frederick Ernst had an affair with a widow, and his daughter's happy life began to deteriorate. He neglected his work, needed money, and sold their beautiful country home. He demanded that Agnes go to secretarial school instead of to Barnard, where she had been admitted at the age of sixteen. Her mother encouraged her education, but Agnes, never close to her, grew away from them both. Only years later, when Agnes's own daughter, Katharine Graham, asked about her mother's family, did Agnes begin tᵒ wonder about it. In 1968, when in her eighties, she began to correspond with Lucie Schmidt, a cousin who had grown up in her parents' house, asking about "my story." Lucie, who had become a governess about the same time millionaire Eugene Meyer married Agnes, was living in a Lutheran deaconry in Bernardsville, New Jersey, in the company of "twenty old women," she said, "who are still up and about." Her room had two large windows which, as in Pelham Heights, overlooked trees. Agnes supported her with $200 a month and urged her to accept the "welfare checks," probably Social Security, that were mailed to her at the deaconry.

At the age of ninety-two, Lucie Schmidt began to write Agnes, eighty-five, about the family of her mother, Lucie Schmidt Ernst. Mrs. Ernst, like her husband, was born in Hanover. "Jurgen Schmidt was our grandfather," Lucie Schmidt wrote, "a sailor who died in his middle years of Yellow Fever somewhere at sea, where he had nursed some of the young sailors who had caught it from the natives when they went ashore against rules. He must have been an unusually fine man. People still talked about him when I grew up. One of the things that impressed me most was that they had been fine German folk dancers, that he and his wife could dance on a wooden plate."

Jurgen was buried at sea. When the ship got home, his wife learned she was a widow with seven children, of whom Agnes's mother, Lucie, was the oldest girl. Fortunately, Mrs. Schmidt owned some land and the little white house built for her when she had married Jurgen. The boys went to America, and later Lucie went, too. After she had married Frederick

33

Ernst and had established a house, Lucie sent to Hanover for her nieces, of which Lucie Schmidt, Agnes's aged cousin, was one. And that was all Lucie could say.

Agnes, possessed of both "theoretical and practical genes" from her scholarly and seafaring ancestors, defied her father and attended Barnard on scholarship in 1903. She lost her scholarship the following year because of what one of her professors termed "insolence" and paid her own way until she graduated. She tutored high school students in geometry and algebra for her out-of-pocket expenses, which included bringing money home to her mother and father. During the summer, to earn the $150 fall registration fee, she became the principal of a Baptist high school in Hell's Kitchen, where at the age of seventeen she made peace between two rival gangs.

At Barnard she belonged to the Alpha Phi sorority. Like all the Barnard sororities, Alpha Phi excluded Jews, and Agnes began to cultivate members of this mysterious group, who she felt had more cultural depth and more "brains" than the general student population. One of these girls, Judith Bernays, told Agnes that she had an uncle in Vienna who wrote "the most extraordinary things"; his name was Sigmund Freud. Agnes read some of the obscure man's writings, the groping early experiments with the subconscious that would develop into the science of psychoanalysis, and she was "revolted." Freud's theory of the Oedipus complex shocked and upset her; it was, she thought, a description of her relationship with her father, with the sexes reversed. But whatever complex there was vanished shortly afterward, when Agnes landed a job on the *New York Sun*; she was the first woman that the newspaper had ever hired, and her childish father said, "A reporter? I would rather see you dead."

One of Agnes's first assignments for the *Sun* was to interview a photographer named Alfred Stieglitz. Vice-president of the amateurish New York Camera Club since 1896, he had founded, under its auspices, the Photo-Secession movement, which endeavored to elevate photography to a fine art. In 1905, with Edward Steichen, who was famous for having taken the first good color photograph, he opened an attic studio at 291 Fifth Avenue, which he called "291"; there they exhibited their own works, and those of Picasso and other progressive European artists. This caused the Camera Club to expel him, a news event in the art world. When Agnes went to interview Stieglitz, she remained for six hours, talking about art theory, and wrote an enthusiastic story that ran on page one. Art collectors started coming to 291, and buying.

Agnes became involved with the group, which included the painters John Marin, Max Weber, Marsden Hartley, Katharine Rhoades, after whom she would name her third daughter, and Georgia O'Keeffe, who married Stieglitz in 1924. (Stieglitz took photographs of old New York that looked like paintings; O'Keeffe painted flowers with an intricacy and attention to detail that gave her paintings the appearance of photographs.) Early in the association, Agnes sat for a portrait by Steichen, which is now hanging at the Museum of Modern Art in New York. It is a back view, showing only the right side of her face, in which she wears a high draped hat, a white blouse open halfway down her back, a dark shift, and a wide sash, looking for all purposes like the perennial Gibson girl. Later she tried to learn to draw from Stieglitz, who published one of her thick-limbed attempts in the short-lived *291* magazine, in the same issue that carried the enigmatic comment "Marriage without license, religion without god."

In those years Agnes was not at all interested in marriage. She was an unattached young woman whose friends were the most exciting group of men in the country; and that was exactly what she wanted. When she overheard Meyer and Borglum talking about her in the American Art Galleries in February 1908, she attributed it to her hat, the success of hats at that time being measured by the number of compliments they evoked from strange men. When she later met Eugene Meyer, she thought him a good man, but he did not excite her. She soon left for Europe, inspired by Stieglitz to be present at the birth of French modernism. She visited an aunt in the German town of Lesum and was disturbed by German hysteria and hero worship. Then she found a small apartment in Paris and made the rounds with introductions from Stieglitz: Matisse and Rodin, whom she adored, as she unsparingly informed Meyer when he continued to pursue her; Gertrude Stein, a "magpie" whom she did not like, because she was "ugly" and "masculine" and "offended my aesthetic sense . . . [as she was] enveloped by a monklike habit of brown corduroy."

Eugene was a source of security for her while she was in Europe, but little more, as her letters to him revealed. "Very intelligent but there's no love in them," Eugene said to Borglum. When she returned to New York, they continued to meet for lunch and the theater, but she as often as not took along a poor male artist friend, and Eugene ended up entertaining them both. After several months of this behavior, he quietly bought two first-class tickets on a steamer to the Orient, then met Agnes for lunch at a French restaurant. She had been talking lately about going back to Europe; she talked about it then. "I'm going away myself for a while," he said indifferently.

"For how long?"

"Six months at least."

Agnes was suddenly overcome with a sense of loss. "I'm going with you," she almost begged.

"I know. I already have your ticket."

After the quiet Lutheran wedding, on February 12, 1910, which was attended by the 291 artists, the Ernsts, and the senior Meyers (Orthodox Jews, all of whom said that it wouldn't last), Eugene gave the wedding feast at the Plaza

Hotel. When it had ended, early the next morning, the couple took the train to Seven Springs, Eugene's farm in West-chester County, which Agnes was thrilled to find was close to her childhood village of Pelham Heights. They stayed there two weeks, getting acquainted, and then left for San Francisco, where they would board the ship to the Far East. Agnes, who days earlier had been earning $40 per week writing free-lance newspaper articles (the *Sun* never put her on salary), now traveled with a full-time maid in attendance. Eugene bought an entire railroad car for their privacy.

When they reached Chicago, Eugene wrote to Agnes's mother, claiming to be a poor substitute for Agnes, who wanted to sleep late: "Liebe Mutterchen [dear little mother]," it began, "In Washington we saw the sights. . . . We also were introduced to the President [Taft]—who congratulated us—and sounded a big laugh from the bottom of his big chest. . . . Agnes seems to be happy still and joins me in sending you our love. Your dutiful son Eugene." In San Francisco they found that the maid was not to Agnes's liking, so they let her off and found another, who accompanied them across the Pacific. In the Orient, Agnes "was released," she believed, "from the bondage of seeing myself as the center of my private universe." This had been to her a problem of great significance; it paralleled "that wider egotism which has isolated the Western mentality from the magnificent cultural achievements of the Orient."

Back in New York, the Meyers began married life in a townhouse on 70th and Park. Agnes began to have dresses made for her by Gunther's—tweed, jersey, simple designs and good fabric—for $1,000 apiece. She bought a $60,000 string of pearls from Tiffany and a $24,000 diamond necklace from Cartier. Eugene set up a large fund for her use, and notes started to pass between them regarding finances: "Please pay this as it is correct"; "Please give [Agnes's secretary] Miss Meyer [no relation] $10 and I will pay you back in cash—

do *not* attach my account." Their early years together were a surprise to both. Eugene turned out not to be adoring, but a stiff taskmaster, breaking Agnes in to the maze of social and housekeeping requirements, making her feel that, by contrast, her artist's life had been selfish and irresponsible. Agnes did not, however, submit to being tamed. She continued her Bohemian friendships; she did not come home to nurse their new baby, Florence, who had been conceived during the honeymoon, because she did not like the baby to bite her nipples. She offended Eugene's business associates; she did not, she insisted, have to do anything she did not want to do.

As a rich married woman, Agnes became less an artist and more a patron of the arts. "Agnes and her new husband Eugene Meyer," notes a contemporary art book,* "commenced a regular pattern of purchase and outright financial subsidy to the circle of American painters Stieglitz had begun to support through exhibitions at Photo-Secession Galleries. . . . the Meyers supported painters Marin, Weber, Hartley, and Walkowitz, who became mainstays of Stieglitz's stable of American artists." The book also remarks upon Edward Steichen's working "to develop a vivacious portrait style to support himself; his clients were rich Americans like the Meyers and the [George] Blumenthals [of Lazard Frères]." The artists themselves assigned her this new role; she was no longer Agnes but "Mrs. Meyer," the arbiter of their disputes.

"Our future as a group is now in full discussion," wrote the Cubist Marius de Zayas to Agnes, then twenty-eight years old, in July 1915, "and I believe you ought to know our different points of view and give us yours forthwith. . . . I don't think that Stieglitz at heart is really interested in taking any definite attitude or in doing any particular thing. . . . At present it is in the power of Stieglitz to make of New York the world center of the best elements of modern art. But to do it he

---

* Weston J. Naef, *Fifty Pioneers of Modern Photography: The Collection of Alfred Stieglitz* (New York: Metropolitan Museum of Art/Viking, 1978).

would have to take a business attitude which for personal reasons and lack of capital he refuses to take. . . . I suppose you are now giving your attention to something far more important than art and its evolutions. But I also believe you are still interested in knowing. . . ."

Stieglitz, aware of the dissatisfaction and wounded by it, defended himself to Agnes in letters written in thick, open script: "The Marin that you want is yours. No one else is to have it. You are to make your own price. . . . I regret deeply that both you & De Zayas should feel that I have not been frank with you. . . . I regret most though that you should feel that 291 has lived solely in your imagination— that it was an illusion.—I'm truly sorry. . . . Personally I see many other things to be done by 291. . . . And many of those things will be done whether at 291 Fifth Ave. or on the street."

The Meyers became one of the most important and remarkable couples in New York. They had five children in ten years and, depending on their fortunes (which were, in any case, considerable), moved the family into the St. Regis Hotel, into apartments on Central Park West, East 55th Street, and Fifth Avenue, and back and forth between New York and Washington, where they finally bought a vast mansion and stayed, interrupted by world trips, for the rest of their lives.

In the first years of their marriage, Eugene was preoccupied with stock sales and bond flotations that helped to create new American industry. His investment firm, Eugene Meyer Jr. and Company, though prominent, was small. His statistical reports had helped J. P. Morgan to sell stock in United States Steel, the nation's first billion-dollar corporation, and in International Harvester. Despite his success, though, or because of it, Morgan and the other financial powers were reluctant to work in partnership with him. His ambitions to finance great projects were, as a consequence, frustrated, until he became involved with the creation of Allied Chemical Corporation and Anaconda Copper, both of which became crucial to America during two world wars.

Anaconda began as a small venture that produced low-grade copper ore; it became an international giant largely as a result of a unique mineral separation process. Eugene had found its inventor working in a London basement; during the First World War Anaconda supplied the Allies with copper wire for its communications network. Allied Chemical also started in a makeshift laboratory; a German-trained chemist, in response to the German boycott of American textile manufacturers, was cooking dyes in pots and pans in a garage in Brooklyn. This chemist was acquainted with the Blum family of Alsace, France, which included the socialist leader Léon Blum, who had entered politics as a result of the Dreyfus affair. Eugene knew Henri Blum, whose father, Nathan, was a silk merchant who had first suggested to Eugene's father that he emigrate from France to the United States. Henri Blum asked Eugene to put up money for the chemist's work in February 1915, and within a year and a half the company was employing two hundred researchers in a $2.5 million plant. It supplied all the blue dyes for the U.S. Navy; by 1931, during the depression, Eugene's stock in Allied Chemical was worth $43 million. These companies, which grew wealthy from America's effort to counter the rising militarism of Germany—blue dyes for uniforms, copper for wire— brought him international fame as a financier and gave him the power and financial independence to exert extraordinary influence in government. His government service, however, was slow in coming.

When the United States entered World War I in 1917, Eugene offered his services to Bernard Baruch, another lone Wall Street operator who had gone to Washington to run the National Defense Council's Raw Materials Committee, which was to coordinate the military's raw material needs with industry. Baruch considered Meyer to be his principal rival, however, and did not answer his letters. Eugene then wrote to his friend Louis Brandeis, associate justice of the Supreme Court, offering to "give my time and work to the service of the country," and Brandeis found him a job for a dollar a year on the Advisory Council's Committee on Finished Goods, where he lasted three days. He was fired when he accused the director of conflict of interest in choosing a manufacturer to supply the United States armed forces with shoes.

Eugene Meyer and Louis Brandeis had an unlikely friendship. They were very different men in style, personality, and political views, Eugene believing in the power of money to alleviate social ills, Brandeis blaming the great money trusts for those problems and working to control Wall Street for most of his early life. In important ways, though, they were not so different. Both were idealists, men of great character, who were not fully accepted in their respective fields, but whose own methods revolutionized established practice. Both were pioneers in the use of hard economic data, Meyer at his investment firm, Brandeis in briefs that he wrote in support of social and economic reform legislation. The most famous of these was the "Brandeis brief," a legal document written to uphold maximum-hour legislation, which did not cite a single case but for the first time presented statistical, economic, physiological, and medical information to prove that women who were forced to work sixty or seventy hours each week, or lose their jobs, were becoming sick, or dying.

Brandeis also opposed monopoly in the transportation industry and worked with Samuel Untermyer to control J. P. Morgan. Like Untermyer, and Meyer, he was extremely concerned with the Lower East Side ghettos in which Jewish immigrants were living and working; by about 1912 Brandeis had become the leading American Zionist. In this capacity he was always asking Jewish millionaires, his ideological enemies, to contribute time and money to help their people. In 1915

41

he approached Meyer, whom he barely knew, and suggested, since Meyer was not a Zionist, that he assume the presidency of an innocuous educational organization, the new University Society at Harvard. Brandeis hoped that Meyer and his intellectual wife would eventually draw thinkers, professionals, businessmen, and artists into the society, and that it would become an intellectual home for the American Zionist movement. After their initial talk, Brandeis was, he recorded, "strongly convinced, as is [Felix] Frankfurter," another Harvard-trained labor-reform lawyer and Zionist, "that he would be an excellent choice." A few days later Frankfurter also "talked with Eugene Meyer and he is very receptive. . . . He has a fine sense of wanting to 'back up Mr. Brandeis,' but feels his inadequacy for that leadership. I urged on him the opportunity of fitting himself for leadership. I can land him, I'm sure."

Eugene accepted the assignment after long deliberation, and though he never acknowledged membership in a Zionist organization, he remained intimately involved with Zionist efforts for the next several years, mainly because of his admiration for Brandeis. Brandeis cast him in the role of persuading his rich associates "to ease their swollen fortunes," a task he was unable to perform himself because he had alienated most of the rich Jews in New York, particularly after publication of his book, *Other People's Money, and How the Bankers Use It,** which attacked Jacob Schiff, the Guggenheims, and others whose support he now needed. Eugene was able to elicit hundreds of thousands of dollars for the movement from these families, although some, like Untermyer, felt that the movement was dictating to them what to do with their money and resented it. These people, Brandeis told him, were to be "humored" by giving them a limited voice in Zionist executive committees.

* New York: Frederick A. Stokes Company, 1914.

Meyer, of course, gave generously, and he backed Brandeis, head of the Provisional Executive Committee, in his factional disputes with the other major American Zionist group, the American Jewish Committee. The Provisional Committee believed that the movement ought to be as widely understood as possible and used Meyer's University Society as its tool; the American Jewish Committee, though, with its subfaction, the Workmen, wanted to work out policy in secret among the leadership. Its leader was, like Meyer, a member of a prominent New York family: a young man by the name of Cyrus Sulzberger.

Eugene also did more technical work for the movement. He advised the Anglo-Palestine Company, which transported hard-won funds from London to the Palestine settlers. This money was distributed carefully, according to the Zionist ideal. "The utmost vigilance should be exercised to prevent the acquisition by private persons of land, water . . . or any concession for public utilities," Brandeis wrote to Chaim Weizmann, his counterpart in Europe and later the first president of Israel. "These must all be secured for the whole Jewish people. . . . the possibility of capitalistic exploitation must be guarded against. A high development of the Anglo-Palestine Company will doubtless prove one of the most effective means of protection." With Meyer's help, Anglo-Palestine became the largest bank in Israel, the instrument for financing industry, agriculture, and a socialistic government.

In 1916 Brandeis was appointed to the Supreme Court by Woodrow Wilson and turned over his Zionist work to Felix Frankfurter, who had also become friendly with the Meyers. Eugene and Agnes were by then going to "cellar meetings," as Agnes said, participating in the most sensitive negotiating of the movement, deciding how and from whom to buy guns for the early Palestine army, the Haganah. If such associations were unusual for a banker, they were natural for Zadoc Kahn's nephew, who had spent an intense year in France at the time of the Dreyfus affair. They were natural also for Eugene's brother Walter, a wealthy attorney, who later became a founder of the Hebrew University in Jerusalem, and for his sister Aline and her husband, Dr. Charles Liebman, through whom Eugene channeled his contributions to the underground once he had moved to Washington and started working in government.

Brandeis was sorry that Eugene lasted only three days on the Advisory Council and spoke to President Wilson about using his talents to better advantage. A month later, in late spring 1917, Wilson named Meyer to a commission that was to go to Russia to establish relations with the Kerensky regime, which, Wilson hoped, would not pull out of the war against Germany. Meyer's appointment was considered a victory among Zionists, who thought that Kerensky, a socialist, would be a friend to the Jews and their socialistic movement. Meyer was their man on the commission: "The President has appointed Eugene Meyer on the Russian Commission," Supreme Court Justice Brandeis wrote to another Zionist; "the thing now is to select the best aides to go with him."

Eugene also told the president that he would like to pay for the commission to take along two doctors and enough serum to vaccinate the Russians against the typhus epidemic that threatened the population. Meyer believed strongly in preventive medicine; as the lay chairman of the pathology laboratory committee at Mount Sinai Hospital, an institution created by the wealthy New York Jewish families, he had sent medical teams into Mexico and Serbia with the same vaccine; the vaccine had indeed been developed at Mount Sinai. But his offer, to his amazement, was rejected. Wilson, it turned out, had changed his mind about including him on the commission at all; the new Kerensky regime, for which Jacob Schiff had floated bonds for billions of rubles, had decided that Jewish financiers were the world's archetypal oppressive capitalists. Meyer was to them a villain.

After his second disappointment in Washington in less than two months, having no desire to return to New York, Eugene wandered one day into Bernard Baruch's office. Baruch's Raw Materials Committee was a loose organization intended to coordinate wartime production of all essential industries. Baruch was a terrible choice for the job; he was notoriously disorganized himself and had not, as Eugene noticed, even put together a filing system, but was running his office from notes scribbled on pieces of paper. Eugene returned to Baruch's office every day until he had organized Baruch's files. He continued to come in, Baruch grudgingly saying nothing because he needed him, and performed other services—answering phones, writing letters. Finally, Baruch said that he might as well take over as head of the Metals Unit, where he would supervise the manufacture of copper, lead, zinc, aluminum, and silver. He naturally outshone Baruch, just as Baruch had feared, and Wilson soon made Meyer the director of the new War Finance Corporation, which provided government loans to war industries. This function, performed in all previous wars by private investment bankers, did not endear Eugene to his Wall Street colleagues, and he warned Agnes, who had shown a remarkable ability to spread around his professional secrets, that "*you* must be *very careful* not to discuss what I tell you."

The War Finance Corporation was the beginning of Eugene's decades of government work; after 1918 he and Agnes lived and worked principally in Washington, although they maintained an apartment in New York, where Eugene went frequently to attend to business affairs. His government work kept him in touch with Brandeis and Frankfurter, who remained lifelong friends; Agnes wrote and lectured on art and education and continued to donate money for Israel, including, in the 1960s, $1 million for Hadassah Hospital.

The Meyer family lived in a large apartment in Northwest Washington, at 2201 Connecticut Avenue, and later moved into a mansion, which their children remember as home. There were eventually five of them: Florence, who had been named after Eugene's sister; Elizabeth, after a cousin of Agnes's; Eugene III, whose nickname, Bill, was the name of Agnes's favorite brother; Katharine, after the artist Katharine Rhoades; and Ruth, after another of Eugene's sisters. On May 2, 1926, all of the children were baptized to please Lucie Ernst, Agnes's mother. Agnes was Lutheran, but the children were baptized Episcopalians. Later that month the parson wrote to Agnes asking that she "look at them [the children] 60 years from now" and think of him. "On that day," the parson said, "Eugene [Bill] won't be so chippy, nor the blessed Ruth quite as pretty, Florence will have lost weight, Elizabeth some of her wisdom, Katharine none of her joy."

☆ **5** ☆

Miss Katharine Meyer

Katharine was born in New York City on June 16, 1917. She was a pretty and happy baby, rather moon-faced, with fat cheeks. Her parents and brother and sisters lived at 820 Fifth Avenue, uptown from the 291 Club, where Agnes had met the painter Katharine Rhoades.

On June 29, thirteen days after her birth, Katharine Rhoades wrote the new baby a letter. "Dear Namesake Katharine, will you accept from me as a token full of affection and joyous wishes for you, this little necklace which I have loved for many years, and which I wore very very often when I was younger and wiser. . . . it goes to you with all my early hopes & joys strung together with the little pearls." Miss Rhoades was a feminist whose best-known work was an untitled drawing that had illustrated an article in *291* magazine, "Motherhood a Crime." The story described an unwed mother who took her life with a bullet; the drawing, if held upright, looked like the head of a rooster, with an egg at the top of the page and a sperm at the bottom; but if turned on its side, it became a pistol: thus, life and death. Rhoades was one of the most promising of the 291 artists, but she abandoned art for religion and became a secretary to museum

47

curator Charles Freer; Katharine never learned much about her from Agnes, except that she had been a legendary beauty whom Katharine could never hope to equal.

The baby grew up amid extraordinary wealth and power. Her father was a multimillionaire. During her infancy, when he was director of the War Finance Corporation, he was one of the pivotal figures in Washington. The WFC had been essentially Eugene Meyer's creation: he had drafted the enacting legislation at the request of President Wilson, and he decided which companies it subsidized for war production, for what products, and for how much money. Politicians and businessmen, consequently, courted him; he testified before Congress; he worked grueling hours while the war was being fought. After the Treaty of Versailles, which imposed heavy war reparations on Germany (a provision that Eugene opposed, predicting, correctly, that Germany would refuse to pay them), he was invited to the Supreme Economic Council in Paris, where in 1919 financial ministers from every European nation were meeting to set policy that would aid the economic recovery of the Continent.

After meeting the ministers, Eugene persuaded Wilson to retain the WFC, which could make postwar loans to American companies so that they would be able to increase their exports to Europe. His plan was to administer $1.5 billion in revolving credit, one of the first times that this concept was used. He remained director of the WFC until 1925, through the presidency of Warren Harding and into the term of Calvin Coolidge, who disbanded it in 1925. He then administered loans for the Farm Loan Board until 1929, when, disillusioned with public service, he went back without enthusiasm to the investment business (making money was no challenge to him); but he returned to government during the depression, when Katharine was fourteen.

Katharine's mother, too, was a busy, distracted parent. When Katharine was five and her sister Ruth was still an infant, Agnes devoted most of her time to writing *Chinese Painting as Reflected in the Thought and Art of Li Lung-mien*,* a study of Oriental "selflessness." Sometimes she accompanied her husband on trips and left the children in the care of their governess, who sent them with the chauffeur to Potomac Elementary School every morning and did their lessons with them at night. Agnes tried to compensate for their absences by taking the children on summer pack trips ("horrible events," Katharine remembered, the entire family climbing mountain trails preceded by servants, who set up camp for them), but the children's letters show them to have missed their parents' participation in their daily lives. "K got your cable to-day," wrote sister Elizabeth to their father, on the occasion of Katharine's seventh birthday. "It was from Paris, and we thought that you were already in London."

Katharine and her siblings spent their winters in Washington and their summers at the Mount Kisco farm. The Washington home, Crescent Place, was thought of as her mother's house; she had wanted it, and it reflected her taste: an imposing building with columns, a circular driveway, and a front yard with a fountain over which was the cement head of a lion. The house had three floors and a basement. On the first floor was an enormous foyer with a fifteen-foot ceiling from which hung a huge crystal chandelier. The floor was white marble with black insets. On the left wall was a seven-foot-high Oriental statue from the fifth century, worth, at the time, $120,000, that was Agnes's most prized possession. Immediately behind that wall was a reception room, where guests deposited their calling cards or invitations; to the left of that was the drawing room, where the Meyers entertained their guests before dinner. To the right of the foyer was a flower room, stocked twice a week with fresh flowers grown in Agnes's garden at Mount Kisco and shipped down to her.

* New York: Duffield and Company, 1923.

Adjacent to that was an office for Agnes's secretary, paneled in wood, with its own bathroom. At the back end of the ground floor was the dining room, which seated forty and was covered wall to wall with an antique Oriental rug. Off the dining room was the pantry, which contained a walk-in safe where the Meyers kept their silver and their liquor. On one wall was a dumbwaiter that carried food and dishes to the kitchen in the basement. Near the back stairs was a buzzer system that told the maids where they were to bring refreshments; lights went on in a box on the wall, each light having the appropriate label: South Porch, Entrance Hall, Stair Hall, Reception Room, Dining Room, Library, Drawing Room, Office, Mr. Meyer, Mrs. Meyer, Mrs. Meyer's Dressing Room, Miss Ruth, Miss Elizabeth, Miss Katherine (with her name misspelled), Miss Florence, Sitting Room, Second Floor Hall, Loggia (lounge), Mr. Wm. A, Mr. Wm. B, Sewing Room.

The second floor was the family's living quarters, and the third floor was for servants. During the winter the house had a full staff of twelve, including a butler, pantry maid, parlormaid, governess, chauffeur, and a series of personal maids for Agnes, although Eugene never had a valet. The house was set on two acres on a small hill, on a residential block in the middle of the city. Eugene built tennis courts in the yard, after the children repeatedly demanded, "Are you going to put in tennis courts or not?"

During Washington's steamy, oppressive summers, the Meyers moved up to Mount Kisco, which was considered Eugene's home; he had owned the property before he and Agnes were married and had planned and built the house shortly afterward. Sometimes they drove up with the chauffeur or, after they had bought an airplane, sent him up alone and had him pick them up at the local airport. The Mount Kisco home was much larger than Crescent Place and was furnished even more lavishly. There were marble floors and fireplaces and thick velvet draperies. On every wall hung valuable

Oriental and modern paintings, many of which they had bought from Cézanne and Picasso directly when they were still considered to be artistic wild men. The grounds were wooded; there were tennis courts, a thirty-thousand-gallon swimming pool that was filled from its own storage tank, stables for horses, including Eugene's favorite, Buddy, and Florence's, Sir Hercules. There was pasture land for their cattle, and they employed a butcher who killed the cattle and cut premium steaks. During the winter these steaks were shipped to the family in Washington.

The Mount Kisco estate became legendary among great artists and politicians. Agnes spent many hours writing letters of invitation, arranging visitors' schedules, and, when she had succeeded in assembling a group of eminent people, such as Alfred Stieglitz, Constantin Brancusi, or, later, Eleanor Roosevelt, Adlai Stevenson, directing their activities and conversations as if they were children. Katharine remembers these occasions without fondness. Her mother displayed Florence and Elizabeth as the beauties and Ruth as the sensitive artist; ignored, Katharine felt like a "plodding peasant" and spent a lot of time playing tennis with her brother.

The visitors did not always enjoy Agnes's posturing. Thomas Mann, the German writer, whose work contained the recurring theme of the artist in conflict with society, told her after an extended stay that her "good children" were right to complain that she sacrificed them to her writing, a comment that only confirmed Agnes's view of herself as an artist. Years later, another guest having made a similar observation, she actually left a houseful of visitors, in a rage, and flew to California, where, in a few days, she received a conciliatory telegram: WE THE . . . UNDERSIGNED . . . DO HEREBY DECLAIR [sic] OUR INDEPENDENCE OF MATRIARCHAL DOMINATION [and] WILL BE GLAD TO WELCOME YOU BACK ON A COOPERATIVE BASIS . . . IF AND WHEN YOU RETURN TO SEVEN SPRINGS FARM YOU SUBSCRIBE TO PROGRAM OF FULL

COLLABORATION SIGNED . . . MEYERS [and the Edward] STEICHENS. Agnes also poured herself into a number of park and school projects in Westchester County, an exercise in political muscle (she was the county supervisor's personal emissary) that prompted Eugene to write teasingly, "I have just been reading an article on 'The Finance of Tyrant Governments in Ancient Greece.' Under the heading of 'Public Works' it says: 'Nearly all the more noted tyrants were famous for their many and costly public works.' . . . Very truly yours, Eugene Meyer."

Father was an even less accessible but a more benevolent figure. Though his frequent absences once provoked a rather comical show of parental concern from Agnes, in the form of a long letter to all their children explaining their father to them, Eugene had a very real understanding with them. Their dinnertime political debates were the foundation. Eugene asked a question; each child would be required to state his or her position; he pointed out the disparities; they argued more and more vehemently, until all of them, and Eugene—everybody except Agnes—had deteriorated into laughter. He was a man who appreciated intellect and was largely bored by his children's other preoccupations: tennis, horseback riding, swimming, social ritual. Katharine was his favorite. "You watch my little Kay," he had said to a friend when she was only five. "No matter how many times she's knocked down, she'll always come up straight." There was a seriousness and depth to her that set her apart, that made it difficult for a self-centered person like Agnes to be comfortable with her thoughtfulness and distance.

Katharine followed her sisters to the elite Madeira School, one of the oldest and finest girls' preparatory schools in the country. Lucy Madeira had founded the school in 1906 and ran it out of a modest building in the city. By the late 1920s, after the Meyers had sent their oldest daughters there, the school had grown too large for its quarters and Lucy Madeira wanted to move it, but because of the depression there was no available money. The Meyers then owned several hundred acres of vacation property on the Potomac River in northern Virginia, and since they "never used it anyway," as Agnes said, they donated it to Lucy Madeira's cause. The school put girls through a rigorous routine of language, economics, science, and philosophy, as well as regular afternoons learning about life; in ninth and tenth grades, Katharine was an assistant in a hospital; in eleventh, a messenger for a congressman on Capitol Hill. She graduated in 1934 and in September started at Vassar, like Elizabeth (Florence went to Radcliffe); but unlike Elizabeth, who spent most of her time riding horses, as her father noted, "Kay plans to be a student, not an athlete."

Katharine Meyer, class of '38, intended to specialize in German and economics, but her father suggested that she concentrate on literature and economics, as she was already fluent in one foreign language from the family's French tutor and could "always do the German over in Europe." She lived in one of Vassar's dormitory houses, as Vassar had no sororities. She was among the girls chosen for the Daisy Chain in her sophomore year, their single function being to appear draped in flowers at that year's commencement.

Vassar, like Madeira, had been founded to promote the somewhat radical cause of women's education. It was established in 1865 by a brewer, Matthew Vassar, who wanted to do something worthwhile with his fortune, and was set in New York's rich Hudson River Valley about fifty miles north of Mount Kisco; its reputation grew steadily until its board of trustees could claim at the turn of the century that a Vassar education was "in a fair degree comparable" to that which could be obtained at men's colleges. When Katharine enrolled there, the campus had the charm it had had for seventy years. The grounds, enclosed by high stone walls, were crossed by narrow dirt paths. The buildings were Gothic. On the far end was Vassar Lake. Across the street were shops that catered to the students: skirts and sweaters, hamburgers, cosmetics. Many of the faculty were feminists who had devoted their lives to women's education when it had been thought a useless luxury, aging radicals who held lectures on the facts of life for new students.

Katharine's more formal clothes were custom-made, and even at college she corresponded endlessly with her mother about fittings and other details. One dress in particular was "too tight under the arms," Katharine told her, "too short waisted & the skirt just not at all. Was too long & too narrow. I wore it last year & looked like the original scarecrow in it." She had left the dress, a brown two-piece with silver buttons, with her dressmaker, Clyne, who had told her it could be fixed. Katharine suggested that Agnes write to Clyne's about it, because she thought it was pretty and that with alterations it could still be worn. The matter was handled by Agnes's secretary, Miss O'Hara, who suggested to Clyne that the dress be remade for Katharine's sister Ruth. Agnes also wanted to know whether a blue satin dress was something Clyne "is trying to force on you. It looks like a good useful dress." She ordered Katharine's coats from her own dressmaker, Gunther's; during the depression, in 1937, she bought Katharine a full-length mink, immediately insured it, and insisted that when Katharine was not wearing it she lock it up.

Katharine was not mainly interested in clothes, however. She was a good student and, more important, quickly showed a strong interest in politics. Her parents approved of this and encouraged her to be moderate in it. "Why don't you write to Walter Lipman [sic] at the Herald-Tribune," suggested Agnes in 1935, "and tell him what the situation is at College, and that those of you who believe in a practical program for the progress of democratic thought and organization are creating this liberal club to combate [sic] the emotional trend toward communism amongst the girls." They did not anticipate that

Katharine's liberal club would grow and merge with a powerful national movement. In December 1935 she went to Ohio to the founding convention of an organization called the American Student Union, whose goal was to coordinate progressive activities on the major American campuses. There she was elected to the National Executive Committee, in such company as executive secretary Joseph P. Lash, a recent graduate of Columbia University and professional organizer, and James A. Wechsler, also from Columbia, who became the founding editor of ASU's publication, the *Student Advocate*. Her inclusion on the national board brought her new status among most of her classmates, who had thought her to be "an observer rather than a joiner." She was objectively a good choice for the board, an intelligent and diligent worker, but there were some who suspected that she was chosen for her money (movements need benefactors) or because her famous and idealistic father had less than two years earlier bought a newspaper in the capital city (movements need platforms), the economically weak but highly visible *Washington Post*.

Meyer bought the *Post* at auction in 1933, for $825,000, only a few weeks after he had resigned as governor of the Federal Reserve Board, the latest and most problematic of his government positions. He had left government once before, in 1929, but this time he vowed never to return to public service, where, he felt, he had been ill treated. One of the most skilled and prescient of the country's financial managers, a lone operator of whose success the big Wall Street houses were envious, he was also one of only a small number who were willing to sacrifice their own interests, spend their own money (it cost Meyer $70,000 to run the War Finance Corporation), to help the hopelessly mismanaged government agencies control the power of private capital. For his pains he was repeatedly hauled before congressional committees and accused of making money off the government; forced to submit his judgments for approval by politicians, who said that he was Wall Street's attempt to run government; while at the same time resented by other bankers for setting up economic mechanisms for the public that had always been the bankers' prerogative.

After resigning from the Farm Loan Board in 1929, for these sorts of reasons, he did not want to stay in government or go back to Wall Street. He was making a fortune from Allied Chemical and other investments, did not want or need more money (any more Wall Street success and he would have become a billionaire), toyed with the idea of buying a bankrupt railroad and revitalizing it, but after having worked for the public interest knew he could no longer be happy in purely private financial pursuits. He decided instead, at age fifty-four, to retire temporarily from life in the East; he bought a ranch, sight unseen, in Jackson Hole, Wyoming, and planned to "run a few cattle." Louis Brandeis tried to persuade him at this time to head a delegation that was going to Palestine for a year to study economic and industrial problems of the settlers, but Meyer wanted a vacation, he said, and refused. He and Agnes and the children left for Jackson Hole in the early fall of 1929; they had not been there a month when the stock market crashed. President Hoover appointed Meyer the governor of the Federal Reserve Board and ordered him back to Washington.

The depression, however, was a crisis of small and medium-size banks, and of corporations, none of which were eligible for Federal Reserve funds. Hoover therefore asked Meyer to draft legislation for a Reconstruction Finance Corporation that would lend money to businesses, and Eugene modeled it after his earlier War Finance Corporation. With Hoover's backing, the RFC legislation was enacted by Congress in January 1932, with initial funds of $2 billion. Eugene, still the governor of the Federal Reserve ("the Governor," his family now called him), was appointed director of the RFC as well, making him the single most powerful financial manager to work in the government since Alexander Hamilton. Within ten days of its establishment, by the second week in January 1932, the RFC was receiving loan requests from trust companies, agricultural associations, and insurance companies at the rate of a hundred a day; in six months Meyer had lent $1.3 billion to more than five thousand companies and institutions. He made credit available, and interest rates dropped almost to the level at which they had been before the Crash.

Meyer's framework for stimulating economic activity was expanded during the New Deal, when the RFC financed construction and operation of factories, lent money to foreign governments to buy American products, insured business against damages in the event of war and disaster. But it was done without him. Eugene resigned from government finance in May 1933, when Franklin Roosevelt, newly elected on a platform of economic reform, began to circumvent him in making policy, a violation not only of faith but of law; the president is legally required to act in concert with the Federal Reserve governor in economic matters. Just after resigning, Eugene heard that the *Washington Post*, the poorest and worst of the Washington newspapers, for years the toy of the McLean family, had gone bankrupt, and he decided instantly to buy it. As in his other successful efforts, he acted on instinct, but immediately after he had won the bidding and received title, he understood that the *Post* would be his way to remain in public life while retaining his political independence. It would be this personal, powerful voice in government that would sound above debates in Congress and arguments in back rooms, that would finally earn him a permanent place in the capital city and give his family, for the first time, a focus, a common purpose, an identity as people who were more than famous, more than wealthy, but who would be a great American family in the classical sense, dedicated to the public good.

It was from the beginning a family operation. Agnes wrote articles for the *Post* on education, refugees, art, and foreign affairs, for which she received wide notice even from the other Washington papers, which implied that she was so far left that she was probably a Communist, and from the *Daily Worker*, which produced long, wordy editorials criticizing her capitalistic point of view. These attacks distressed her more than they might otherwise have because she had been worried about her son's revolutionary politics, which were causing his schoolwork to suffer, but had not been able to bring herself to talk to him about them. (She did begin to write a letter, decided that it was too preachy and might drive him farther away from her, and instead sent him motherly advice about taking care of himself. He was losing his hair; she would talk to him about that: "The woman who takes care of my hair is the best specialist on that subject in New York. . . . She is sending you one bottle of tonic and one little box of grease, and she guarantees that new hair will grow." Meanwhile she mailed the *Daily Worker* attacks to the moderate Katharine and asked *her* to forward them to Bill at Yale "after reading them yourself. . . . As they must have had my articles before them when they wrote it, they might at least have copied the name correctly. I am afraid sloppy thinking such as this is typical of the Communist.")

Family relations improved when Bill came down the next summer to report for the paper. Elizabeth, who had left Vassar to go to Hollywood as a scriptwriter for David Selznick, did not want to write for the *Post* herself, but she recommended that her father hire a former classmate, "a girl very much worth your notice, called Mary McCarthy. She works for the 'Nation' . . . a very brilliant girl. She was at Vassar when I was, and I knew her slightly. After I left, she joined our 'group.' "

As a student in the depression, Katharine was interested primarily in history and economics and in causes. Her "liberal club," as Agnes had called her group of activist friends, had gone by bus to Albany in the fall of 1935 to campaign against a bill then before the New York State legislature, the Nunan Bill, which would have required loyalty oaths of all public school students. That trip had brought her together with Betty Welt, who was the editor of the Vassar *Miscellany News*, and by that December, the same month she was elected to ASU, her name appeared on the masthead as an apprentice editor. Soon she became known for her "crisp, accurate, nononsense copy" and by the following spring was on the regular editorial staff. Most of her articles were unsigned, but her name appeared on a "Contributors' Column" in February 1936 in which she demonstrated a sophisicated understanding of the relation between media and politics:

. . . the censorship of Sinclair Lewis' novel *It Can't Happen Here* proves that Hollywood means to dedicate its technological advance to the cause of reaction. Under the control of dictators such as Williams, Hays and Hearst, the vast potential mastery of the movies promises to play an actively anti-social role. . . .

According to Lewis' statement in the *New York Times*, February 16, his novel, which deals with fascism but is propaganda only for an American democracy, was banned by Will Hays for fear of "international politics and fear of boycotts abroad.". . .

Lewis, in his reply to the ban, said that the book had been read more than any other novel in the United States this month because it dealt with something in the public mind. "In describing the forces which eventually rallied against fascism," he went on, "I made the anti-fascist leader a Republican supported by many Democrats, and if Mr. Hays thinks an anti-fascist feeling can be interpreted as anti-Republican, that ought to interest a lot of Republicans." In answer to the suggestion that it might create foreign complications, Lewis said, "Mr. Hays is saying that a film cannot be made showing the horrors of fascism and extolling the advantages of a Liberal Democracy because Hitler and Mussolini might ban other Hollywood films from their countries if we were so rash." . . .

The best the movies seem able to accomplish in the way of artistic, socially conscious production is a milk and water liberalism marred with attempts at broad appeal, resulting in such a production as *The Informer.* . . . When they tire of this, they go in for frank assaults on behalf of the Right wing, as in *Red Salute.* A Hollywood picture with a genuine Left wing tendency is obviously impossible.

The widespread appeal of *It Can't Happen Here* proves that it is Hollywood, not America, that is evidencing Fascistic tendencies. Similar strict censorship has not been seen in the press or radio. An occasional social significance is inserted in British movies, but America backs down rather than follow such a lead. In filming *A Farewell to Arms*, Hollywood complied with Italy's requests and made the rout at Caporetto resemble an Italian victory. In accordance with Turkey's wishes, *The Forty Days of Musa Dagh* was not filmed at all.

The same forces in the motion picture business that bring about such censorship will hinder progress that might otherwise be made. Any progressive leaning, any fundamental truth will be eliminated in order not to diminish a picture's box office appeal, annoy a foreign or Fascist government, or encourage disagreement with the status quo which is after all the faithful watch dog of the movie interests.

Katharine Meyer was one of several progressives to control the *Miscellany News* in 1936, and the only one from Vassar to be elected to the national board of the American Student Union. The *News*, consequently, promoted her as an important political force. In March she went to Washington with Constance Dimock, a fellow reporter and activist, and two other Vassar students to "demand passage," as the *News* said proudly, of the American Youth Act, a New Deal social program that would provide relief, education, and vocational training for youth. "Meyer, Shedden, Liebman, Dimock Represent Vassar," said the *News* headline. They submitted a polemical report "for the record" to the Senate Committee on Labor and Education, which argued, as ASU's James Wechsler had earlier argued, that students and workers were all laborers, "whether by hand or by brain," and that they therefore felt solidarity with labor, made labor's struggle their struggle, and demanded, like labor, that the government recognize them as a political constituency.

The national ASU board decided shortly after its formation in December 1935 that its first major activity would be to organize a nationwide peace strike for the following spring, an action that would put ASU effectively in command of the growing student peace movement. The movement suffered during the depression, when student liberalism seemed to many students to be a selfish indulgence. Communists were the exception. The Vassar Communist Club wanted, in 1932, "a new social order, based on production for use and not for profit"; and an outraged Vassar alumna demanded in reply to this, in an incoherent but alarming letter to a wealthy trustee of the college, "What is Fascism? What IS it but the Christian's answer to Jewish Communist? As for me, the weal of my country comes first. . . ."

The original ASU platform had outlined the group's position on four issues of the day: Peace, Freedom, Security, and Equality. The union opposed American war preparations, wanted the abolition of ROTC, and supported the Oxford Pledge, an oath by which students vowed never to fight in a war. It defended academic freedom for students and for teachers, including their right not to sign loyalty oaths. It favored an increase in federal student aid and advocated passage of the American Youth Act; it demanded "adequate social security legislation" of all sorts. And it advocated universal educational opportunity and condemned persecution of Negroes or any other minority group.

Peace was the priority, and the springtime peace strike, the second annual Student Strike Against War (the first had been an uncoordinated venture in 1933), was joined by five hundred thousand students nationwide, affiliated with various peace groups or unaffiliated, who boycotted classes for half a day, most of them with their professors' blessing. At Vassar, ASU Peace Council chairman Betty Bliss told the student body that "the purpose of the strike is to make it clear to those who form government policy that American students . . . do not want another World War. The re-armament of the Rhineland, the border disputes between Russia and Japan, the Italo-Ethiopian dispute, and our billion-dollar armament program testify to the timeliness of such a demonstration. If we wish to prevent war, we must signify this desire now." And Katharine Meyer of ASU's national board, speaking on a CBS radio program, said that "at Vassar, the administration has been wholeheartedly behind the student peace movement. This year we hope to have the student body one hundred percent present as every college organization is co-operating in managing the strike. . . . The support of [an expected] three hundred thousand students, by way of the strike, will be given to those fighting for peace by legislation such as the Nye-Kvale Bill to abolish compulsory ROTC," the first step, in her view, toward doing away with student military training altogether.

In Washington, Katharine's parents listened to her strike day radio show and spoke glowingly of their daughter's performance on a "national hook-up." The strike had been fomented by his radical son Bill, Eugene joked. Elizabeth, hearing about it a week later in Hollywood, informed her father indignantly that "I feel I should have been notified."

Katharine continued to be active, bringing the movement to the Vassar campus. In May, less than a month after the

Strike Against War, and while only a sophomore, she spoke at a conference on undergraduate life. She upset many parents with her defense of student political activism; while other panelists addressed such eternal Vassar issues as weekend leaves for juniors and seniors, the "implications of social maturity," and the value of having one's own banking account, "Miss Meyer pointed out," as the *Miscellany News* reported, "that extra-curricular activities are an important part of a college education because they . . . bridge the gap between college life and the outside world, and give the individual a chance to apply her ideas." Katharine was at this time one of the most prominent women on campus, one of the richest, most outspoken, and, it seemed, politically fearless. Her classmates idolized her; her professors cited her example. But Katharine was bored with the isolation of a women's school, and at the end of the year she transferred to the University of Chicago, which was the intellectual center of the thirties radicals.

☆ 6 ☆

Kate

Katharine broached the subject of changing schools to her father while working with him at the *Post* the summer after her sophomore year. "Kate put up the proposition that she should go to the London School of Economics this year instead of to Vassar," Eugene wrote to Agnes in August 1935 at their Wyoming ranch, where she and Ruth were hiking and fishing. Katharine's friend Connie Dimock wanted to go, too. But Eugene vetoed the idea of London; he felt that what his daughter needed at that stage of her education was information, facts, not to become caught up in the powerful ideologies and emotions that were creating so much tension in Europe. He agreed with Katharine, however, that the Vassar faculty did not have anything to offer that was worth two more years of her time, and so he gave her permission, as she had thought he would, to transfer to another college in the United States. She chose the University of Chicago.

Katharine had become interested in the University of Chicago through a colleague in the ASU whom she had met at a national convention. It was, he had said, the most daring and innovative university of the day, as well as one of the most rigorous. Its president, Robert Maynard Hutchins, who had been dean of the Yale Law School at the age of twenty-eight and became president of Chicago at thirty, had developed a system of undergraduate education called the Chicago Plan, an interdisciplinary course of study in philosophy, history, culture, and language which collectively Hutchins called "the history of ideas." Katharine told her father that she wanted to "do" history and philosophy with Hutchins and economics with Professor (later Senator) Paul Douglas, who was then well known for his left-leaning theories of wage controls and social security.

Eugene telephoned Hutchins personally to arrange his daughter's transfer. Hutchins referred him to Dean Works, who asked Katharine to write to Vassar for approval. "Later," Eugene told Agnes, "Kate asked me what I thought of Connie Dimock going out there with her, or did I think Connie was too radical, which was her [Kate's] suspicion of me. I told her I thought that if Connie wanted to go it would be all right, but that I did not think she should urge or persuade, because if it did not turn out satisfactorily she would be taking more responsibility than she should. There the matter rests as far as Connie is concerned."

Eugene took Kate to Chicago by plane near the end of August to meet the dean and find housing; then they returned to Washington for another week—Eugene was worried about *Post* advertising and circulation and still had not achieved coordination among his news and editorial writers—before joining Agnes and Ruth in Mount Kisco for Labor Day.

The University of Chicago in 1936 was widely known as a hotbed of radicalism, a logical result of having been founded in 1890 as a "great experiment," one aspect of which was the radical ideal of equality of education for women. The only reservation that the school had about this, as an early yearbook noted, was "Were they physically strong enough to stand the mental strain of intellectually competing with men?"

The campus was enormous, compared to Vassar's. The buildings were Gothic, like Oxford's, with high arches and the heavy white stone blocks characteristic of the Chicago School of architecture. The atmosphere was intensely intellectual, electric. In the International House, where Katharine lived— "the best place to be," she thought—political debates broke out spontaneously over meals, in the lounges, at the front desk where residents collected their mail. Though she had been one of the most politically sophisicated women at Vassar, Katharine was overwhelmed. At I House were refugees from countries that had been ravaged during World War I. There were Spanish refugees from the Civil War who had lost their families to the Fascist revolution. There were Jews, victims of nazism. There was a young Nazi named Heinrich Pagels who was confronted and said, "I am glad and I am proud that I'm a Nazi." He justified National Socialism on the grounds that the Treaty of Versailles had been unfair to Germany; he left after a Jewish resident produced evidence that Pagels was reporting the activities of I House exiles to Hermann Goering's secret police, who used the information against their families. There were fraternities that displayed the Nazi flag and hung Adolf Hitler's picture out the window, claiming later that it had been done as a joke.

International House was a large, rambling structure at 1414 East 59th Street, at the southeast edge of the campus. It had a dining room and four lounges, where the students engaged in the popular pastime of smoking ("digestion proceeds more smoothly . . . alkalinity is increased . . . when you make Camels a pleasant interlude in dining," advised the ads in the university's newspaper, the *Maroon*), and eight residential floors with long corridors, accessible by a self-service elevator and carefully segregated by sex. There were thirty rooms on each floor, and a common bathroom with showers and an ironing board that stood under a sign reading "Do Not Iron in the Bathroom." At the far end of each floor was a private "bath suite," where two students who could afford twice the normal rate had two bedrooms behind a locked door and their own bathroom. It was in one of these that Katharine lived, with an heiress from the wealthy northern Chicago suburb of Lake Forest. Tayloe Hannaford was physically the opposite of Katharine, short and blond, expensively dressed, polite, shy, and not as bright as Katharine, as a housemate remembers, but more sociable.

Katharine was "very happy and interested in her work," her father reported to Agnes. She enrolled, her first year, in President Hutchins's History of Culture 201, 202, and 203, the Great Books course, under the auspices of the Committee of the History of Culture, which expected each student to master "the political and social history, the literature, art, science, philosophy and religion" that pertained to his or her chosen field. Hutchins was a passionate and elitist educator. He believed firmly that vocational training and similar efforts to make schooling "pay off" would be the ruin of Western civilization; he taught by means of the "classics of the Western world." And that is what Katharine studied: Homer's *Iliad* and *Odyssey*, the Old Testament, Plato's Dialogues, Aristotle's *Ethics*, Virgil's *Aeneid*, Plutarch's *Lives*, the New Testament, St. Augustine's *Confessions*, Dante's *Divine Comedy*, Machiavelli's *The Prince*, Cervantes's *Don Quixote*, Shakespeare's plays, Swift's *Gulliver's Travels*, Spinoza's *Ethics*, Fielding's *Tom Jones*, Rousseau's *Social Contract*, Freud's *Outline of Psychoanalysis*. The class met once a week, on Tuesdays at four. During that year Katharine studied and wrote constantly, preparing so that she would be able to speak at the discussion sessions, which visiting professors often attended. Sometimes her father would sit in, when he was in town on business, and on those afternoons she really put on a performance. "We require a little more from you because we expect to do more for you than most parents," he would tell her. Katharine earned A's and passed her comprehensive examinations. Hutchins told the Meyers he was surprised to find that their daughter was so "nice."

The Great Books program, however, began to fall out of favor with students who were impatient with its benign, disinterested approach to urgent social and political problems, all of which would supposedly give way to enduring truths. Other professors, unlike Hutchins, were advisers to the government on New Deal social programs and believed, to the students' satisfaction, that these things could not wait. Katharine acceded to her father's wish and took Economics 201 in her winter quarter, a survey course taught by a conservative; but in the spring, while still studying under Hutchins, she took Economics 240 from Paul Douglas—labor economics, because she wanted to get a leftist point of view.

Douglas had written parts of the Social Security Act of 1935, a crucial part of Roosevelt's New Deal legislation, ensuring for the first time federal assistance for the aged and unemployed. When Katharine took his course, he was working on the Fair Labor Standards Act, which would provide a minimum wage of forty-four cents per hour and a maximum work week of forty-four hours; it was enacted into law the following year, in 1938. Douglas, too, was a passionate thinker and teacher, every bit as passionate as Hutchins; but whereas Hutchins was a snob, Douglas was a champion of the working man. The impressionable Katharine Meyer took much of what he said to heart. In May 1937 she went with a small group to the Republic Steel plant in South Chicago to demonstrate in support of strikers; the confrontation was so violent that it came to be called "the Memorial Day Massacre."

The picketing at Republic had been staged by the American Student Union, which was far more active at Chicago than it had been at Vassar and was developing a more militant strategy. The ASU was able to capitalize on converging pressures of the New Deal, the war, the momentum of activism itself, until the "item" at Chicago was "Did you belong to the ASU or didn't you?"

At first the question at I House, among the poorer residents, was whether Miss Katharine Meyer belonged; the consensus was that she probably paid dues but didn't participate. But Katharine did not broadcast her activities to people not her friends; particularly, and prudently, she was close-mouthed about her political work. In October 1936, a month after she arrived, the local ASU chapter asked for nominations to its executive committee. Her reputation had preceded her, and when she volunteered, the ASU accepted her at once. The *Maroon* carried the names of the five women and three men who were the new executive board, Katharine's name among them, and the new leaders quickly sponsored a production of the left-wing play *Black Pit*, a story of life in the Illinois coal fields, which was praised as a "muscular" and moving play, a fine work in the tradition of revolutionary art.

The ASU executive board then formed a committee called Material Aid for Spain, which appealed to students to contribute clothing, shoes, canned food, and blankets "to relieve distress among Spanish government troops" fighting General Francisco Franco, whose army in exile was supported by Hitler and Mussolini. The committee raised $135, most of that coming after ASU arranged with I House to show the film *Spanish Earth*, in which a solemn-voiced Ernest Hemingway told of the suffering of the people of Spain. ASU did not directly sponsor, but encouraged, other leftist programs as well: trial attorney Clarence Darrow in the Oriental Room on "Crime and Punishment" (education is the only way to deter crime; punishment is irrelevant to it); William O. Douglas, then an attorney at the Securities and Exchange Commission, on "Capitalistic Waste."

Aside from its campus programs, the board was concerned that fall with the second national ASU convention, which was to be held at Chicago in December 1936, exactly a year after the first convention in Ohio. As hosts, Katharine and her colleagues arranged for meeting rooms in churches and did what they could to find out-of-town delegates free places to sleep.

The four-day convocation became the forum for a number of unrelated political struggles. On Monday, James Wechsler, editor of ASU's *Student Advocate*, read a speech by John L. Lewis, organizer of the United Mine Workers and the Congress of Industrial Organizations. Lewis thanked the ASU for its solidarity with labor and asked that students picket with him at the gates of a local steel mill at five-thirty the following morning, which forty delegates did, distributing leaflets and getting pushed around by police. After Wechsler came a woman named Loh Tsei, "the Chinese Joan of Arc," who, reported the *Maroon*, led off with "a smashing attack on Japanese aggression in China" and asked American students to support China against Japan. Joseph P. Lash, ASU's national secretary, then asked for mass support for a student pilgrimage to Washington to advocate passage of the American Youth Act.

On Tuesday there were round tables, and Tuesday night a banquet and a speech by Spanish Catholics urging support of the Loyalists against Franco and "war on Fascism wherever it appears." On Wednesday the delegates argued hotly over the Oxford Pledge, adopted during its first convention, which committed ASU members to refuse to participate in any war. This was a position attractive to the pacifists but increasingly difficult to reconcile with concern for the Spanish and for the abominations of nazism.

The Oxford Pledge was retained, barely, and on Thursday the delegates once more heard of the evils of capitalism. "There is too much emphasis on the discrepancy between our culture and that of pre-revolutionary Russia," reported a Yale professor. He had witnessed the Bolshevik Revolution, "but I never felt more personal terror and horror than when I visited some of our own 'peace-time' coal counties."

With the confusion and glory of the convention—the pacifism and antifascism, the sympathy with labor and wariness of communism, the opposition to an embargo against Spain and advocacy of an embargo against Japan—the ASU attracted an increasingly conflicted membership. By the winter of 1937, Chicago had the largest ASU chapter in the country, with 425 paid members, and many of them wanted ASU to become more militant. While the *Maroon* begged for ASU's return to "study" of various problems, especially that of academic freedom, and Robert Maynard Hutchins attacked them, the ASU prepared for their spring action: another Strike Against War. For this they coordinated with the prominent Socialist Club, headed by George Reedy, whose ambition much later landed him a job as adviser to President Lyndon Johnson.

The executive board now included Katharine's closest friend, Sidney Hyman, an I House resident whom she urged to take charge of ASU's Committee on International Affairs. Hyman was one of Chicago's most prominent intellectual activists; he had once been co-editor of the campus literary magazine *Comment*, now controlled by an anti-Communist named Charles Tyroler, who eventually formed the Committee on the Present Danger, which in 1979 was still agitating about the Communist menace. Tyroler's most famous essay was an editorial on the noted anarchist Emma Goldman, who had been Agnes Meyer's friend in the 291 Club days: "an atheist, anarchist, free-love advocate . . . who would be in jail if the law were enforced." Breaking with Tyroler's views, Hyman left *Comment* to become editor of the left-wing magazine *Phoenix*, his position when Katharine and he served together on the ASU. She too could have worked on *Phoenix* but instead founded a weekly ASU bulletin that carried activity notices and articles by guest columnists—her first venture as a publisher. The bulletin kept her involved, while safely uninvolved, during the Strike Against War, after which her name no longer appeared in the *Maroon* in connection with ASU. This may have been because of the growing domination of the club by the Communists, which caused many moderates to drop out, or because her schoolwork had suffered. That summer she was obliged to repeat economics.

In her senior year, weary of political battles and disenchanted with Hutchins, she devoted herself to European history, her major, and to a clique of people at I House who were the most intelligent and interesting of the European exiles. They would sit together at a round table, Kay, Tayloe, Sid Hyman, a White Russian, a Bulgarian, Elizabeth Mann and her husband, the famous anti-Fascist professor Giuseppe Borgese whom her father, Thomas Mann, had not wanted her to marry. "At the age of fifty-seven," he had complained jealously, Borgese "probably no longer expected to win so much youth. But the child wanted it so and brought it off. He is a brilliant, charming, and excellently preserved man. . . ."

It was common at I House for groups to linger at the tables after dinner, their conversation open to anyone who cared to join, but this group was an exception: one did not sit with them unless invited. The refugees appreciated Americans with money and position and accepted Katharine readily, although she did not have much to say to them and usually just listened appreciatively. Several times a week they went for beer to Hanley's Buffet, the campus hangout, Katharine in her plain blouse and plaid skirt, her low shoes, and "forever modest," Sid Hyman remembers, "grateful for small kindnesses." Hyman was the son of a rabbi and her constant escort, although "going out with Jewish boys is a thing that queers a girl with the clubs faster and more completely than anything else," as a *Maroon* story once noted. Katharine was horrified at this petty, clubby anti-Semitism on the eve of the Holocaust.

Most of her friends were poor, and though the beer at Hanley's was only a dime a glass, and nobody could have more than two (Joe Hanley's orders), Katharine would quietly pick up the bill when it came and pay it. Sometimes she would take them driving in her big black Buick, her brother's car, which he had decided was a symbol of capitalism and no longer wanted. Summers and holidays she brought them to Mount Kisco, always fighting her fear that they would be put off by her parents' ostentatious display of wealth.

Her friends of course knew her father from his frequent visits, when he would take them to dinner and talk politics, encouraging them to challenge his thinking, liking them better the more they did. Agnes was a different case. Once or twice a year she would appear at the house in her heavy, fitted, brocaded clothing, wearing pearls or diamonds, and speak to no one, but sit sternly in a straight-backed chair waiting to take Katharine to meet a politician or diplomat. Katharine, upstairs, nervously bit her lip while dressing, and then slunk down the back stairs in her long dress, trying to avoid being noticed by her friends. Naturally they did notice, and the consensus was that Agnes was the bane of Katharine's existence. This idea was confirmed when Agnes did not show up for Katharine's graduation in 1938 (neither did Eugene, but more is expected of mothers) and instead sent a note signed by her secretary, who spelled Katharine's name incorrectly. Katharine read it and burst into tears.

Armed with an A.B. in history, experienced, she felt, in politics, and knowledgeable about foreign affairs, Katharine set out to be a reporter. Eugene arranged a job for her on the *San Francisco Daily News*, and she went to California to live with Rosalie and Sigmund Stern, Eugene's oldest sister and her husband, the nephew of Levi Strauss. Living among high society of that lovely city where her father's father had begun life in America, where Jews were a much more visible part of city life than in Washington, she covered dockworkers' strikes and paid dues to the American Newspaper Guild, founded only five years earlier, in 1933, as part of the nationwide union movement. The work was easy enough, but she was unhappy at first. Male reporters ridiculed her, treated her offhandedly, did not respect her education, and she wanted to go to the *Post*. Her father suggested that she stick it out for a year. But he soon regretted his advice; within a few months she had gotten a better beat, the Treasure Island navy base, had had some professional recognition, and had no thoughts of returning to Washington at all. Her father then pleaded that they needed her on the *Post*. She went home, moved into Crescent Place, and had not been there six months before she married a thin, nervous law clerk named Philip Graham, a *protégé* of Felix Frankfurter's who had earned some of the highest grades in the history of Harvard Law School.

☆ 7 ☆

A Fortunate Marriage

Katharine came home to live with her wealthy, prominent family in a cliquish, power-conscious city. She was twenty-two years old, and her style was University of Chicago. She wore skirts, not dresses; and she expressed her political opinions with a stridency that was offensive to men who worked with real problems of government and who liked women to be demure rather than intelligent and, more importantly, beautiful, in the traditional way.

She had a natural inner beauty, a softness and generosity that went quite beyond her youthful bravado, but somehow in Washington it went unnoticed, while her younger sister, Ruth, the only other one of them still living at home, got the attention, the compliments, the invitations to society affairs. Ruth had many friends in Washington, including the brightest and most exciting young men working in government, whereas Katharine knew hardly anyone. She was not home more than a month or two when she had to endure Ruth's lavish debutante party, which their parents held at Crescent Place during Christmas week of 1939. Even at that, an occasion on which she should have been thinking of her sister, she felt insecure and envious; this party was so much nicer than hers had been.

On the night of the party she saw a tall, thin young man in an inexpensive suit hovering nervously in the hallway. Katharine approached, he said something about Ruth's good looks, she retorted sharply that that girl was four years younger than herself. "And you're getting along in years too," Phil mocked. He liked her sharpness, her lack of polish, and before he left that night he had asked her out to dinner. There was an electricity between them; they laughed, they argued politics. He was Philip Graham, a Supreme Court law clerk, a passionate New Dealer who was beginning, like other New Dealers, to forget his commitment to social welfare as he became caught up in the excitement of the war in Europe. Katharine was a pacifist, but she had been disillusioned when Russia and Germany signed their nonaggression pact and attacked Poland; he blamed the student peace movement for America's unpreparedness to join the war. Katharine liked a man who knew what he wanted.

Since her return from San Francisco, Katharine's father had been grooming her to take over the paper eventually. She wrote articles, sat in on editorial conferences and helped decide editorial policy, worked in the advertising and circulation departments, and every night mechanically assembled the pages, writing headlines and placing stories where they would have the proper degree of impact. A few days after her dinner with Phil Graham, he telephoned her at the *Post* at six-thirty, just before deadline, while she was pasting up the front page, and commanded her to meet him at Harvey's restaurant for drinks. Katharine said that she would like to but she was busy, and Phil commanded her to bring the pages with her and they would work on them together. Katharine liked a man who took charge.

Phil knew very well that laying out the front page of the *Post* was no small opportunity for an ambitious young lawyer, nor was having drinks at a place like Harvey's, among powerful businessmen and politicians, with the publisher's daughter.

Katharine could not be much more flattered, for her part, than to be seen with a Supreme Court clerk. They sat at a table together, attended by a waiter in a red jacket, trying not to get the layouts wet from Scotch, laughing and arguing, on the eve of another world war, and suddenly realized that they had fallen in love. On their next date Phil told her, perhaps too abruptly, that they were going to be married. And that he hoped she wouldn't mind having only two dresses because he wasn't going to take a lot of money from her father. Katharine said that she would not mind at all.

Katharine was a society girl and her family had been a subject of interest in Washington and New York since before her birth; Phil was in awe of Katharine's father, a banker, a leader in government finance, who had bought a bankrupt newspaper, housed in a building that his own reporters described as a "rat-infested shell," in order to have an independent voice in government. He had made himself president of the Washington Post Company, which was actually worthless, and had made his eccentric wife, whom Phil did not especially like, the vice-president. Meyer's only son was interested in medicine, not journalism, which meant, as Phil was aware, that at the age of sixty-four he had no male heir for the *Post*.

The Meyers did not know as much about Phil. He was an enigma, vaguely thought to be a country boy who had excelled at Harvard, and was accepted on that basis by the New Deal crowd. He dressed Ivy League but did not have the manners of an Ivy Leaguer; he was nervous, volatile, almost frenetic, and loved to talk about feelings and personalities, as well as ideas. He was a gossip; he gave the impression of openness; his charm drew people to him, though he rarely said much about himself.

Phil was part of an elite group of Harvard Law School graduates who had been carefully selected by their professor, Felix Frankfurter, to become clerks of the Supreme Court.

This group, called the Frankfurters, lived together in an old Virginia mansion called Hockley Hall, set on a hill overlooking the Potomac River, where, assured of bright futures, they luxuriated in the bachelor life. The house was modeled after Frankfurter's own bachelor quarters when he had been a young lawyer in Washington before joining the Harvard faculty in 1914. Frankfurter had called his home the House of Truth. "How or why I can't recapture," Frankfurter later wrote, "but almost everybody who was interesting in Washington sooner or later passed through that house. The magnet . . . was exciting talk, and it was exciting because talk was free and provocative." Hockley never quite lived up to Frankfurter's example. There was intellectual talk, but it was "like a southern plantation," as people remember, "something out of *Gone with the Wind*, with black houseboys to bring mint juleps" to the guests during weekend parties. On weekdays a butler served tea every afternoon at four. Professor and Mrs. Frankfurter did not have children, and the Hockley men were like sons to them. The young Joseph Rauh became an eminent lawyer and founder of Americans for Democratic Action; Hedley Donovan later published *Fortune*; John Oakes went with his family's business, the *New York Times*; Carl McGowan became a judge. But the most outstanding, Frankfurter's favorites, were Philip Graham and his closest friend, Ed Prichard, whom everybody called Prich. Phil was from Florida, Prich from Kentucky, both country boys who reached great heights and fell to early ruin.

Phil arrived in Washington with the distinction of having been president of the Harvard *Law Review,* the top honor in the top law school in the country. The competition at Harvard was brutal. Six hundred students were admitted to the first-year class and at the opening convocation the dean told them to "look at the man on your left and the man on your right. At the end of the year one of you won't be here." Harvard admitted students from every background and let them fight one another for the right not to be one of the lower third of the class that was annually flunked out. There were one or two suicides during Phil's first year. Harvard was also "the most democratic place in the world," as Frankfurter insisted; you rose or fell strictly on merit, not connections, not social rank. At the end of the first year the top sixteen or seventeen students were invited to join the *Review*. They worked on the *Review* during their second year and then voted one of their number, "the best man for the job," to be president while they were in their final year.

Phil entered Harvard Law in 1936. He did not strike the Harvard crowd as the academic type, but "contrary to appearances," recalls a classmate, "I thought he was a great man." His friend met him at the start of their second year, when they had both made *Law Review*. "Phil looked like a playboy, he came from the University of Florida, not Ivy League. People on the *Law Review* were grinds, and Phil went out with women, screwed around, drank a lot. He worked harder and played harder. I would hear stories about him having parties at his apartment, girls staying overnight, but I was jealous, I wasn't going out yet with women, and for all I knew they may have been nice girls from Radcliffe."

On the *Review* Phil was now part of a great tradition, and the editors realized that despite his casual manner, he had unusual brilliance and talent. The men on *Law Review* were the school's aristocrats, not bound by ordinary rules, a role that Phil enjoyed. They rarely went to class; they worked on the *Review* until early morning, seven nights a week, went to an all-night cafeteria at three or four for some kind of meal, worked again until eight or nine in the morning, slept, and started again at five. To stay on the *Review* they had to keep up a B-minus average, which the *Review* made easy to do. There were class notes on file in the offices, canned lecture notes for each course, and right after they put to bed the June issue, the editors spent two or three days doing a year's worth of studying. At the end of his second year, Phil found himself in a fight for the presidency with an editor named Ted Tannenwald, who was number one in the class. Phil was tenth. The second-year editors got together and eliminated each other, one by one, until only Phil and Tannenwald were left. The few Jews on the *Review* wanted Tannenwald, but Phil was the better man. "It was hardly unanimous," he later told Katharine.

As president and editor-in-chief, Phil solicited articles from leading professors and legal scholars and personally edited them. Additionally, he supervised the production of case comments, the analyses of recent court decisions for which the *Review* was famous. The process of "commenting" consisted of assigning the editors to read hundreds of pages of fine-printed advance sheets on federal and state opinions and then, for cases they wanted to publish, doing "prelims," preliminary checks of other journals to see whether the subject had already been treated. The editors would then meet with the note editor, who was Ted Tannenwald, and he would approve comment topics, which would take four or five weeks to write. "You learned a hell of a lot of law that way," Phil had said, "almost as if we were running a school for ourselves." Phil upheld the tradition of the presidency. He worked at Gannett House under a burning light, his head bent over his work, writing, smoking, his tired figure visible through the window, as *Law Review* presidents, in the middle of the night, always were. But he worked harder than most, and his colleagues had the sense "that it wouldn't take very much. He always looked as if he needed sleep, and he was so damn skinny, and nervous."

Frankfurter was one of the dominant figures at Harvard in those years, a prominent legal scholar, radical thinker, but more than that a man of great energy and presence who, if he liked a person, was an extraordinary friend, looking to know all about him, to become a guiding force in his life. Frankfurter taught courses in administrative and labor law and public utilities regulation, but his best-known one was Federal Jurisdiction, a seminar on that week's Supreme Court decisions, which was open only to members of the *Review* and a few others whom Frankfurter approved.

His influence extended well beyond Harvard. Since he came to the law school he had placed many young lawyers in government, particularly for the reform agencies of the New Deal. He found the law clerks for Benjamin Cardozo, Stanley Reed, Louis D. Brandeis, and Oliver Wendell Holmes, all of whom wanted clerks only out of Harvard; and in this way he created an elite that influenced American politics for years afterward. The clerks he selected were unmarried, with no other demands upon their time, men who could be not just lawyers, but companions to frequently lonely old men. "I used to pick up my justice in the morning," remembers one, "have breakfast at his house, be available for every kind of errand."

Frankfurter himself was appointed to the Court in 1939, in large part for his contribution to the cause of individual liberty. In 1910 he helped W. E. B. Du Bois organize the National Association for the Advancement of Colored People; in 1920 he formed the American Civil Liberties Union with Jane Addams, Helen Keller, and Norman Thomas. The ACLU was Frankfurter's vehicle for the defense of Sacco and Vanzetti, two Italian anarchists, a shoemaker and a fish peddler, accused of bank robbery and murder, whose case was a political *cause célèbre*; their defenders said that they were on trial for their anarchism. Frankfurter campaigned for their release from the time of their arrest in 1920; when they were executed in 1927, he wrote a book called *The Case of Sacco and Vanzetti*, which argued that justice had failed.

Frankfurter's own first law clerk on the Court was Ed Prichard, Philip Graham's best friend, who was less a researcher, as were most clerks, than a statesman-companion, a young friend with whom the justice could test his knowledge of the issues before the Court. Phil worked for Stanley Reed his first year out of law school and went with Frankfurter in the summer of 1940, when Prich's term had ended. Both Phil and Prich were fascinated by Washington's social and political workings; they knew not only lawyers, but top men in government like Speaker of the House Sam Rayburn and presidential assistant (later Secretary of Defense) James Forrestal. They spent many evenings at Frankfurter's house, entertaining the justice and his wife, Marion, who was semi-invalid. Prich was the one with the unusual wit; he was a mimic and great storyteller. Phil always had something to say about people; he had humor; he could characterize them in a few well-chosen words, devastate them with a remark.

During their engagement, Katharine and Phil frequently visited the Frankfurters together. She had known them through her parents but now became an especially good companion for Marion, who, like herself, had been a newspaper reporter. Frankfurter thought that Phil and Katharine were a "most compatible couple" and promoted Phil to his friend Eugene Meyer, assuring him that Phil was very, very bright. Eugene was well aware of that fact and told Frankfurter he was sure that Phil would make a fine son-in-law. He and Phil had had their first political argument the day Katharine brought him home to dinner. Roosevelt's Court-packing plan had just failed, and Phil the young lawyer told Meyer the banker that the Supreme Court was the "old enemy" that had to be controlled for the survival of social welfare legislation. "Life has taught me that there are three elements to success," Meyer answered: "know everything there is to know, work harder than anybody else, and be absolutely honest"; and that while he didn't doubt the young man's integrity, he suspected that even the clerk to Justice Frankfurter, who had been a friend of his for years, didn't know everything there was to know about constitutional law. Court-packing was, clearly, unconstitutional. Phil asked him slyly whether it was true that Meyer's loans to banks and large corporations in 1932, when he had been the director of the Reconstruction Finance Corporation, had made necessary a lot of these government welfare programs. Meyer answered that no, his policies created deliberate inflation, which pulled the country out of the depression faster than handouts ever could.

Once Phil had decided to marry, he wanted to do it right away. The place was to be Mount Kisco. The date was set for June 5, 1940, guest list drawn up, flowers and food and liquor ordered, announcements placed in the Washington and New York newspapers. Then Phil began to worry: suppose his marriage interfered with his Court duties. He was scheduled to start with Frankfurter that summer, and Felix, as Phil called him, needed constant companionship, attention. He was driving the justice home from Court one night, the question churning in his brain, the car weaving from lane to lane on the deserted street. Phil finally blurted out that he was planning to marry Kay Meyer, not knowing that Frankfurter had helped maneuver Eugene into accepting him. "Can I do it? Can I still work for you on the Court?" Phil's driving was getting wilder, and Frankfurter in the best of circumstances hated cars. Phil was heading right into one of those hundreds of statues that rise up from the streets in Washington when Frankfurter told him to go ahead and marry her, but to watch the road in the meantime.

The *Post*'s competitor, the *Washington Evening Star*, printed a detailed account of the wedding, particularly of Katharine's clothing:

Seven Springs Farm, the country home of Mr. and Mrs. Eugene Meyer at Mount Kisco, N.Y., was the scene of the wedding of their daughter, Miss Katharine Meyer and Mr. Philip Leslie Graham of Hockley in Arlington, Va., son of Ernest R. Graham of Miami, Fla. The ceremony was performed by the Rev. Dr. Carl

Kretzmann, pastor of the Lutheran Church of South Orange, N.J., officiating at 5 o'clock, in the garden which nature at its loveliest made a beautiful setting. Mr. Meyer escorted his daughter and gave her in marriage. She was attended by her sister, Miss Ruth Meyer, and Mr. Edward F. Prichard, Jr., of Paris, Ky., was the best man. The bride was dressed in a period costume of heavy silk in ivory shade made with long fitted sleeves, the close-fitting bodice buttoned with small silk buttons to her throat where it was finished with a narrow turned-down collar of the silk. The skirt was very full and long and had bands of the silk wider as they were nearer the hem, from two to four inches apart. About her shoulders she wore rare old lace and on her head a wreath of orange blossoms and she carried a spray of white orchids. . . . The informal reception which immediately followed was for only the members of the two families and intimate friends. . . . Mr. and Mrs. Graham left later for a wedding trip to Bermuda, the bride wearing a light gray and yellow print frock with light gray coat and hat and yellow accessories.

When they returned from Bermuda, the Grahams bought a modest two-story house on 37th and R streets in a run-down section of Georgetown, directly opposite a high school. Phil could not afford a nicer house on a better street, and he would not allow the Meyers, parents or daughter, to offer him money. Katharine was already beginning to see the sorts of sacrifices she was going to have to make for the sake of his pride, and she would say ruefully, when letting people know their new address, that "we will definitely have to change it someday."

Katharine immediately proved herself to be a most unobtrusive, good-natured wife who was happy just to be married to a man she thought so much smarter and more worldly than herself. Phil made it clear from the start that he still needed his time with men. He stayed out frequently after Court discussing great issues with the Hockley crowd, and Katharine would come downstairs in a bathrobe to greet them when Phil invited them in around midnight for a last drink.

In the early 1940s the Supreme Court was hearing a great many tax and labor matters; they were called "mop-up cases," technical questions left over from the vast amount of New Deal legislation: how much violence should be tolerated during strikes; could unions compel worker membership; should the Court uphold certain taxes? These sorts of cases, business cases, really, did not interest Phil, and although he did what research was necessary for Frankfurter, his heart was not in issues of the private bar. He saved himself mainly for matters of the Constitution, individual rights, the permissible powers of Congress, which had been tested during the New Deal and were once again important with the United States about to enter the Second World War.

The most controversial case while Phil was with the Court was *Minersville* v. *Gobitis*, known as the flag-salute case, in which two Jehovah's Witness children were compelled to salute the American flag against their religious principles. Most of the justices on the Court by 1939 were civil libertarians, appointed by Roosevelt, and the Court's decision against the Jehovah's Witnesses was a shock. Frankfurter, incredibly, wrote for the majority: "A grave responsibility confronts this Court whenever . . . it must reconcile the conflicting claims of liberty and authority. But when the liberty invoked is liberty of conscience, and the authority is authority to safeguard the nation's fellowship, judicial conscience is put to its severest test." Frankfurter, like many immigrants, was an ardent patriot (he would walk the halls of the Supreme Court whistling "Stars and Stripes Forever"), and he felt, quite simply, that government had a right to instill patriotism in its citizens, especially during times of war. "National unity is the basis of national security," his opinion continued. "To deny the legislature the right to select appropriate means for its attainment presents a totally different order of problem" than such free speech issues as the right to distribute handbills. The decision foreshadowed a change in the country and was the beginning of Phil's consuming war fever. National security was now valued above civil liberties, as it was throughout and then after the war, and national security remained Phil's priority during all the years that he published the *Post*.

His time with his wife was spent traveling, playing tennis at Crescent Place, at dinners with her family (she dressed casually, he wore a suit and tie), at Washington social functions. A fellow law clerk recalls that Phil began to move, with the Meyers, in the "stratospheric heights" of society, a level far above that of the other Harvard lawyers, who, though ambitious, were for the most part not yet political and social beings, but merely lawyers. The conspicuous exception was Ed Prichard, who considered himself Phil's intellectual equal or better and was comfortable not only with the Meyers but with every other powerful person in Washington. Prich appreciated Katharine's gentleness and she believed, as did others, that he would someday be president of the United States.

But it happened one November in the early 1940s that Prich was caught stuffing ballot boxes in Kentucky and was indicted for, and subsequently convicted of, election fraud. It was not an indication of the man; Phil still believed in him. So did Joe Rauh, and so did four Supreme Court justices, who liked him so well that they felt they would be biased and refused to hear his appeal. Thus Prich entered the Federal Correctional Institution at Ashland, in July 1950, where he remained until President Truman, responding to Phil's and Joe Rauh's pleading, granted him Christmas clemency five months later. His government career was ruined, and he stayed in Kentucky in private law practice, where he is to this day. Katharine did not condemn Prich, nor did she understand why Phil feared so for himself.

"I've been reading up on the history of Scottish Grahams," Katharine's oldest son once wrote to Agnes, his grandmother, thirty years after his parents' marriage, "—a lot of backers of lost causes." Several generations ago, the Grahams had migrated from Scotland to Canada and then down to Michigan, where Ernest Graham, Phil's father, was born. Ernest might have been called a drifter: for much of his youth he wandered through Wisconsin, Minnesota, the Dakotas, and Montana, working the gold mines in the mountains, a victim of the mining fever that drove the Indians ever westward. In South Dakota, around 1910, the same year Eugene Meyer married Agnes Ernst, Ernest Graham married a pioneer woman named Florence, whom he found teaching school in the Black Hills. They had two children, Mary and Philip. The family went briefly back to Michigan, where Ernest bought a general store, with which he went bankrupt. In Michigan he met an executive of the Pennsylvania Sugar Company (Pennsuco), who then promised that if he would go to Florida he could manage a Pennsuco experiment with growing sugarcane in the Everglades. It sounded fine, and in 1921 Ernest took his family to live on a houseboat in the Florida swamps.

Pennsuco was a wealthy company, the owner of lucrative contracts to process sugar from the two largest sugar plantations in Cuba, at a time when Cuban sugar was in demand, the sugar beet crop in Europe having been destroyed during World War I. Because of Cuba's political instability, however, Pennsuco wanted to grow sugarcane in Florida and thought it could be done cheaply. The experiment failed. Mud, burning heat, alligators, mosquitoes, and malaria plagued the men who tried to work the seven thousand acres of swamp, and costs rose. Pennsuco did not want to pay the taxes on the land, and in 1932 the company gave the entire seven thousand acres to Ernest Graham. Then, in the Florida swamps, he started a dairy farm.

Through eleven years of sugarcane farming, Philip and his sister Mary lived among Mikosukee Indians, a people who had once fiercely fought the white man's encroachment but who now lived with them in harmony, hunting and fishing among the water reeds in slim canoes. The Mikosukee wrestled alligators for sport, and Phil's best friend, one of a number of Mikosukee males called Charlie Tigertail, taught him to turn them on their backs by twisting their necks, to tickle their stomachs to put them to sleep, and to wake them up by whistling the alligator mating call. Later, Phil would tell this story as a comment on his humble beginnings, sometimes nostalgically.

Ernest had Phil cutting cane, and after he started the dairy farm and the family had moved onto the land, when Phil was already at the University of Florida, he insisted that he take a year off school to drive trucks. Phil's mother was a schoolteacher, the opposite of her husband; she subscribed to the *New Yorker* in Phil's name and repeatedly told him that she wanted him to go to Harvard. When Phil was a sophomore she died of cancer, demanding on her deathbed that Ernest send Phil to Harvard to study law. His grades at Florida were not high, and he was an excessively nervous, high-strung boy who often talked to himself and did not seem to be in the best of health, physically or mentally. After his mother's death, his father immediately remarried and had two more children, William and Donald Robert. Phil would still drive home from college on weekends to help on the farm but would weave down the road recklessly, almost as if he did not want to get there, and he acted distant from his strange new family, almost feeling as if he no longer had a home.

In his senior year he applied to Harvard, which did not accept him, and if his father had not become rich from the increased value of his farm, so close to Miami, and acquainted, as a rich man, with U.S. Senator Claude Pepper, he never would have gotten in. Pepper, as it happened, knew the Harvard dean and wrote him a letter to persuade him that rejecting Phil, a "most brilliant" young man, had been a serious mistake. If not for Pepper, and for his mother, he would not have become president of the Harvard *Law Review*, would not have been living in Hockley Hall in 1939 and clerking for Felix Frankfurter in 1940. He would not have married the eligible heiress Katharine Meyer, and it would not have been said of him, as it was said by many important men, that "Phil is the most flawless human being I have ever met."

Phil finished clerking in June 1941 and started work in the Lend-Lease Administration under a man named Oscar Cox, who had discovered a statute written in 1879 by which Roosevelt could claim authority to lend and lease military equipment to the Allies before the United States itself entered the war. For this reason Cox was one of the most influential men then in the administration, and Phil, obsessed with fighting Hitler, thought that to have maximum impact, he ought to be in Cox's office. Lend-Lease, however, was a temporary creation that soon lost ground to the Office of Emergency Management, an optional part of the president's 1939 Reorganization Act, which, when war against Japan was declared, developed into the department primarily responsible for the war effort. When Phil was at Lend-Lease he met OEM's director, Wayne Coy; shortly afterward Phil got himself transferred to Coy's department. Coy had already hired Joseph Rauh and Ed Prichard, and their assignment was to push industry leaders and, indirectly, the president toward fighting Hitler and away from what Rauh called their "pillow fights" over such old issues as social welfare and taxes.

War was more urgent than Roosevelt's social programs, and Phil became the "cutting edge," as Rauh remembers, of all their efforts, "the most brilliant, vibrant legal mind," the most effective at moving Roosevelt toward the goal, for despite his contingency war agencies, Roosevelt was vacillating and did, in the opinion of the Hockley men, need to be pushed. Phil bothered the president with memoranda. A *Time* magazine story noted that the Russians had lost more arms fighting the Nazi invasion than the total number the United States had on order, and Phil sent the article to Roosevelt. He took it on himself to look into certain industry practices, and when he found that gasoline production was low, for instance, that oil companies were saving money by producing low octane when the military needed high octane, he sent Roosevelt a note through Coy asking that the president grant him, at age twenty-six, the authority to require high-octane production. Roosevelt granted permission, Phil ran around issuing orders, and gas output rose. He wrote an article for the April 1942 issue of *Atlantic Monthly* entitled "Teamwork in Washington: Conversion to War"—he wrote it, but Wayne Coy got the byline—which urgently drove home the point: "We now have a better working government than France or England had at the start of the war," Phil said; "it is better than we ever had in the last war. In fact, if it continues as it is, it will probably be the best government that ever lost a war." The piece helped Phil win his campaign for $8 billion in government loans to defense factories, a strategy reminiscent of Eugene Meyer's at the War Finance Corporation during World War I. Phil had once accused Meyer of contributing to the depression by aiding business at the expense of the little man; now with that government money came industry conversion to war production on a large scale, and Phil understood the power of capital and that Meyer had been right.

Meyer was usually right. He knew politics, finance, felt a social responsibility and acted on it, was acquainted with everybody Phil might meet or could hope to meet. Yet marrying into a wealthy, prominent, and well-connected family posed problems as well as opportunities for Phil. He resented his tie to the Meyers even as it helped him. Agnes, he soon found, was arrogant and presumptuous. "I know how hard it is coming into a rich family with no money of your own," she had told him, wanting him to understand he could have anything, that what was theirs was his; humiliating him. Katharine, in her shoulder-length hair and red lipstick, was without conceit, yet she had the easy, superior air of the privileged, the fluency in French and familiarity with German, the plan for graduate work in American history at Harvard (or economics at the London School, which her father and Professor Hutchins had had in mind for her), or a real newspaper career, all of which she had given up to marry him. Phil went into the management and budget office one day and showed around a few new hundred-dollar bills, grinning widely, asking boyishly, "Where do you think I got these?" Coy had given him half the fee for writing the article in *Atlantic*, and his friends were struck by the irony: why is a man married to a woman worth millions still excited about a few hundred dollars?

The United States entered the war in December 1941, and Emergency Management was suddenly taking orders from the War Department. Young men were drafted. Philip Graham, exempt because he was already in government service, but with what he called his "ghastly weakness for action, movement, and go," wanted desperately to join the army, to be part of the fight, to capture some of life's romance. Within a week after the Japanese bombed Pearl Harbor he asked Felix Frankfurter to recommend him for the Army Air Corps, and regardless of how the Meyers may have felt about it, Frankfurter gave Phil his letter on December 19. "I deem it a patriotic duty no less than a source of deep personal pleasure to write in support of Mr. Philip L. Graham's application to enter the Air Corps. I cannot imagine that any applicant would bring to the service of this country a stronger combination of character, resourcefulness, and those indefinable qualities of personality by which men are endowed for leadership. . . . He early showed powers much beyond his years and he naturally became the leading man in his [law school] class. . . . He has shown zeal, intrepidity, complete devotion to the task at hand, the capacity to arouse confidence in other men, and that sparkling humor. . . . Among the literally thousands of young lawyers I have known there are very few about whom I could be as confident that they would give a good account of themselves. . . ."

In the spring of 1942, Phil entered the air corps as a private, turning down a commission because he wanted to see combat. He was sent to a training camp in Sioux Falls, South Dakota, his mother's state, where he lived with Katharine for the rest of the summer and fall. The air corps was the place to be in this war, the first war to use modern fighter planes, and it was Phil's chance for heroism; unfortunately, though, his first year of service was anything but heroic. He apparently was injured on the base: "Time has been working away at my once raw wounds with all the efficacy of the sulfa drugs," he wrote to Frankfurter in December 1942. "Kay's very helpful Lt. has by now started on the tortuous path to Washington the following: an application from Pvt. G. . . . for a waiver of the defect under a War Department Regulation which the Lt. discovered; a statement of the Flight Surgeon that my 'calcified lesions' are 'of no present or future clinical significance.' . . . Our Lt. is hopeful that the papers may be approved and back here by mid-January for the next OCS [Officer Candidate School] shipment but . . . frankly I am grown convinced that God intended me for Sioux Falls."

While still a private, Phil was asked to join the Sioux Falls teaching staff, but he declined. In January 1943, still waiting for his medical clearance to join OCS, which he now thought was his only way to get out of camp, he learned that the clearance would probably come through that month but that he ought to consider cadet training, commission in four weeks, instead of OCS, commission in thirteen weeks. He accepted cadet school and the flight surgeon approved him for "general military service." He was promised combat. But Phil never made it to the New Haven cadet training school. Whether by mistake or intention, the army deciding for itself how to use this highly intelligent man, he was sent instead to the Army Intelligence School in Harrisburg, Pennsylvania. Katharine went with him, to her parents' pleasure: they had not been sure that she would make a good army wife.

At Harrisburg Phil had an instructor named James Russell Wiggins, a former editor of the *St. Paul Pioneer Press-Dispatch*, who knew East Coast newspapers and had heard of the Meyer family. He made a special effort to know Katharine, a publisher's daughter, and it might then have occurred to Phil that the intelligence community is interested in newspaper people. He told Wiggins he was going to stay with law, but Wiggins, who later became the *Post*'s managing editor, did not believe him. He "just always assumed that Phil was the *Washington Post*."

Phil completed intelligence training and was assigned to the air intelligence staff of General George C. Kenney, commander of the Army Air Corps in the Pacific, directly under General MacArthur. The Japanese had taken the Philippines in December 1941, and in 1943 MacArthur was still arguing with the Joint Chiefs over Pacific strategy. He wanted to attack the Philippine islands and in so doing destroy the Japanese fleet; the Joint Chiefs insisted that he push through Japanese lines to Formosa, which would give the United States the advantage of having its B-29 bombers under the protection of Chiang Kai-shek.

In this long and difficult debate, Phil Graham became an expediter, assuming a role similar to the one he had created for himself in the Office of Emergency Management. MacArthur's plan was supported without question by Kenney and the other Pacific generals, and Phil undertook to get Roosevelt's personal approval, for which he needed adequate intelligence on the Philippine islands: Could they be taken? How strong, actually, were the Japanese ground forces and fleet? How safe was MacArthur's grand strategy? An intelligence pilot finally reported that the middle islands were the "vulnerable belly of the imperial dragon," and with that information, which Phil carried to Roosevelt from General Kenney, MacArthur won permission to execute what historians have said was the most brilliant "strategic conception and tactical execution of the entire war." The Americans made their first main landing on October 29, 1944, followed by the battle of Leyte Gulf, "the greatest naval engagement of all time," in which American naval forces completely destroyed the Japanese fleet. Following that, in January and February 1945, was a bloody fight on Luzon island for Manila Bay and protracted mop-up operations until June.

For his role in the Leyte and Luzon campaigns, Phil was made a commissioned officer and received the Legion of Merit, the fifth-highest award in the armed forces, for "exceptionally meritorious conduct in the performance of outstanding services." His medical problems continued to keep him away from battle, but with his commission he rose rapidly to the rank of major and was sent for a time to do high-level intelligence work inside the Pentagon.

One man who served with Phil in the Pacific was Pare Lorentz, the documentary filmmaker who had married Katharine's sister Elizabeth in June 1943. Lorentz had been head of the United States Film Service when it produced such left-wing films as *The Plow That Broke the Plains*, *The River*, and *The Fight for Life*, documentaries on war and depression that had been shown widely in American movie theaters. Lorentz had a sharp wit and could see through Phil rather easily. "Phil is in good physical condition and has a clear picture of the confusion," he wrote to Eugene in August 1945, six days after the atomic bomb had been dropped on Hiroshima. "Thank you again for the Scotch; with seven bottles of Haig & Haig used judicially Phil should be a Lt. Col. very soon. . . ."

When Phil was first shipped overseas, Katharine had returned to Washington, and their marriage, at least for her, regained the aura of wartime romance. She felt purposeless without him; she waited; she worked on the *Post* but without interest. "I was pregnant"—her first pregnancy the previous year had resulted in a miscarriage—"and Philip was away and I was just looking for a mindless job to make the time go faster," she told one woman who had known her as a pacifist at Vassar. Her "mindless job" was in fact not mindless but quite demanding, a weekly column called the "Magazine Rack," which summarized articles from major magazines. The column was well written and popular, and she became one of the most widely read of the many Washington feature writers.

Her baby was born in 1944, with difficulty, danger, and pain. She named the child Elizabeth, after her sister. With her husband gone, Katharine became closer to her parents than she had been since childhood; Agnes even took care of the baby for her or, when she couldn't, gave her to a "very good maid." Phil occasionally came home on leave to see her and the baby; during one visit Katharine conceived again, and their first son, Donald, was born in April 1945, another hard birth. "Kay and the baby couldn't be better," Agnes wrote happily to Eugene, who was away on business. "I was over there yesterday and shall . . . bring Kay home on Tuesday in the car. The baby is a strapper and I think looks more like Phil. . . . He is lighter in coloring than Elizabeth and may yet turn out to be blond. Kay and I grow happier every day about his being a boy."

Throughout the war years, Katharine took an active part in the social life of the capital city. Parties were inevitably gatherings of the people responsible for the war effort, and she had the idea of using the *Post* to publicize these occasions as patriotic events. She shared her thoughts with Felix Frankfurter, who was appalled. "In order that the morale of the country should be right," he scolded her, "the dominant atmosphere of Washington must be austere. Now the fact of the matter is that the influence of trivial and frivolous 'so-called social life' has always been bad in creating the right atmosphere in which Government moves. . . . It is bad enough to have this so in peacetime. In wartime it is indefensible." Frankfurter himself liked good company, lively talk, but he enjoyed even more his eternal role as teacher. "There are not many influences stronger than the seductions of publicity— silly as it may appear to you—for taking people's thoughts and time and energies in to frivolities like cocktail parties and dinners and whatnot. . . . And then, of course, there is the encouragement to snobbery, which, to put it mildly, should be discouraged when a life and death struggle for democracy is going on."

Needless to say, Katharine dropped the notion of publicizing Washington parties, although "to stop publicity," as Frankfurter said, "is not going to make little men big and frivolous women serious." She concentrated on her babies, did some work with her mother on her Committee on the Reorganization of Community Services, with her father on a refugee committee, and waited for Phil's return. On September 2, 1945, the family received a letter from Pare Lorentz saying that Phil would be coming home soon. "I suppose old Graham is in Tokyo Bay," he remarked. That was where MacArthur was, in Tokyo setting up a new government for the Japanese, writing them a constitution patterned after that of the United States, and Phil had a way of being at the center of events. Pare had gotten to know Phil as men get to know each other during war, and he liked him. He did think him a bit taken with himself, though, and ended his note with a goodhumored warning: "He will be unfit to live with for a while after he gets back."

☆ **8** ☆

Half German, Half Jewish

Katharine suffered from the war, while Phil was gone, in another way. She had a Jewish father whose relatives were persecuted by Nazis, and a German mother who was ashamed and bitter that her country could let the Nazis take power. Katharine was the only one of the Meyer children then living in Washington, and she saw the war pull her parents apart. It tore at her as well.

A cable arrived for Eugene from London on June 25, 1940, only twenty days after Katharine was married, which suddenly made the war very real to her. "ZADOC KAHNS DAUGHTER SUZANNE DREYFUS AFTER NARROW ESCAPE OUT OF ST MALO NOW IN LONDON WITH TWO GIRLS AGED 18 AND 14 YEARS NEPHEWS AGED 17 AND 15 STOP WOULD YOU BE PREPARED TO SPONSOR THEIR COMING IN USA STOP IF SO COULD YOU BE SO GOOD CABLE ANSWER TO GALERIES LAFAYETTE REGENT ST LONDON AND ALSO HAVE THE CONSULATE GENERAL INFORMED AND INSTRUCTED STOP ALINE LIEBMAN [Eugene's sister] KNOWS ALL PARTICULARS OF THE ABOVE SAID STOP WITH ALL OUR ANXIOUS HOPES AND DEEPEST THANKFULNESS = SUZANNE DREYFUS."

Suzanne Dreyfus was Eugene Meyer's first cousin, whom

he had met only once, in 1896, when he had gone to Paris and Berlin to study after graduating from Yale. She was the daughter of his uncle Zadoc Kahn, the Grand Rabbi of France. The Kahn and Dreyfus families had grown close during the ten-year Dreyfus ordeal, and the man whom Suzanne had married, Adolph Dreyfus, appears to have been one of Captain Dreyfus's nephews. Suzanne and her children were at a French summer resort when the Germans occupied France in early 1940; they hid on a Belgian coal barge that was sailing for England, and when they contacted Eugene Meyer, their rich American cousin, from London, they had no money with which to leave Europe.

Eugene cabled Joseph P. Kennedy, the U.S. ambassador in London, asking for visas for his relatives. Kennedy replied that the law required Meyer to assume responsibility for their maintenance and support and to guarantee in writing that they would not become public charges; he promised to do so. Meyer also contacted the American Express Company in New York, which sent a message to its London office: "EXERT EVERY POSSIBLE INFLUENCE TO ASSIST IN SECURING TRANSPORTATION FOR MADAM SUZANNE DREYFUS AND CHILDREN . . . ON FIRST AVAILABLE BRITISH STEAMER TO UNITED STATES OR CANADA STOP THIS CLIENT FRENCH NATIONAL AND AMBASSADOR KENNEDY GREATLY INTERESTED ACCOUNT OF EUGENE MEYER IMPORTANT WASHINGTON CITIZEN AND FRIEND OF OUR HIGHEST OFFICIALS."

Kennedy was a dominant figure in London society in 1940, an enthusiastic host, a loyal friend. And he was an advocate of Prime Minister Neville Chamberlain's policy of appeasing Hitler, which some of his critics felt to be a result of his business interests. He nevertheless obtained the visas for Eugene in less than a month, and by August 1940 the Dreyfuses were "living in your house," as the oldest of the Dreyfus boys, Bertrand, wrote gratefully to Meyer later, "drinking your wine, smoking your cigars, and using your tennis court."

The three younger children were placed in the right schools by Agnes's brother Frederick Ernst, who was the deputy superintendent of the New York City school system. Bertrand, of high school age, was enrolled in the program for advanced high school students at the College of the University of Chicago; Eugene asked Robert Maynard Hutchins to reserve him a room in the International House, where Katharine had lived only a year before. He then wrote Hutchins with a change of plans: "I have conferred with our mutual friend Katharine, who suggested that International House is so full of foreigners that it might be better for young Dreyfus to live in a dormitory." Kay may have felt that Bertrand would become Americanized faster if he lived with American students, but Bertrand told Eugene, after one year, "The fellows were awfully nice, very familiar . . . but, on the whole, they were too childish and rather uninteresting." He moved over to I House, which "reminds me of Paris' Quartier Latin," and eventually earned a Ph.D. in nuclear physics.

After the children were settled, the Meyers undertook to get the rest of Eugene's relatives out of France. They secured a visa for Suzanne's husband, Adolph, who arrived in New York with a request that the Meyers help his brother Jacques, stranded without money in Casablanca with his wife, Madeline, who was Suzanne's sister, and their daughter, Catherine. The Jacques Dreyfuses had sailed from Marseilles to Casablanca expecting to leave from there for America on a reserved steamship. But the United States was in the process of changing its immigration quotas, and officials in Casablanca suspended the Dreyfuses' visas until the new quota was known. They were there for five months, savings dwindling, before they were able to sail.

For the support of the two families, Eugene established the tax-exempt Fund for Assistance to French Relatives, which paid their passage, immediate expenses, and a stipend of $800 a month per family. His sisters and brother contributed several thousand dollars, but he bore the bulk of the cost, which amounted to $31,275 after four years, at which time he spoke to his business manager, Floyd Harrison, about the Dreyfuses trying to become self-supporting. He refused, however, any efforts at cash repayment; four years earlier he had insisted that Adolph reverse his instructions to make him beneficiary of a life insurance policy. "This is not merely a formal request, but one which I mean definitely. . . . In connection with my helping you. . . . it is not my purpose to put you under any obligations. . . . Should the war be over some day . . . I am willing that you should repay the amount in your own good time [but] should you be unable to do so . . . the matter will not affect me or my family's welfare so far as I can now see."

The ordeal of the Dreyfus family dramatized the meaning of the war for Katharine: it was a war against Jews. Germany had defeated France three days before Katharine's father received Suzanne Dreyfus's telegram; in the months that the Dreyfuses remained at Crescent Place, telling their sad stories, France established the Vichy government, which showed, Germany felt, amazing "understanding" of the Jewish problem. Marshal Henri Philippe Pétain, the German-appointed head of Vichy, established laws that discriminated against Jews and consented to the German plan that France be given top priority in "combing Europe from West to East" to "resettle" Jews in the depths of Eastern Europe. Jews were to be deported even if they had only one Jewish parent, even if they were baptized Christians.

Katharine was not raised as a Jew and knew little of her father's thinking on the subject. He rarely spoke about Jewish issues, not even the central role that Jews as scapegoats were playing in the politics of Europe. He "spared" his children the emotional and political torments of Zionism, but in children's eyes reticence can make a parent seem secretive, ashamed. Katharine's mother was a more vocal person; she made no secret of her sympathies with the Jewish cause, giving freely to Jewish charities and discussing Zionism with certain guests; but Agnes had many causes that her children could see: education, Oriental art, social welfare, the Democratic party. She had not raised them to be Jews; she had baptized them. Katharine grew up in a city where people were suspicious of the Jewish influence in finance, government, and the news, and the Meyers lived through several periods of "rejection," as Katharine said, when there was a feeling in Washington against Eugene Meyer's inordinate power, a Jewish power. She had seen anti-Semitism at Chicago, where girls "queered" themselves by dating Jewish boys. Her closest friend there, her steady date for two years, had been Sidney Hyman, a Jew, but she had married a Scottish Methodist.

Her father's Jewishness was a liability in running the *Post*. Washington was a Protestant town, dominated, when Meyer bought the *Post*, by *Times-Herald* publisher Cissy Patterson, who was openly anti-Semitic. She was related by marriage to both the Hearsts and the McCormicks, the two most powerful newspaper families in the country, and she had wanted, with their backing, to buy the *Post* herself, to publish the *Times-Herald* in the evening and the *Post* in the morning. When Meyer got the paper, he declared that it would be independent, a slap at her, with her obvious political ties and effort to dominate the news. He probably did not know that she owned the syndicate that distributed the *Post*'s four best comics, "Andy Gump," "Winnie Winkle," "Dick Tracy," and "Gasoline Alley," but he found out soon enough, when she tried to cancel the *Post*'s contract to run them. He sued, she fought it; two years later the court decided in his favor. She sent him a package of raw meat with a note saying, "Take your pound of flesh."

Jews themselves expected special treatment from Meyer. In 1942, while Katharine was visiting her husband at his army camp, Meyer was confronted by a man named Peter

Bergson, chairman of the Hebrew Committee of National
Liberation, who demanded his support in print for a Hebrew
Palestine Army to fight the "disastrous event occurring to the
Hebrew people of Europe." Rumors of the Holocaust were
just beginning to filter out of Eastern Europe, and they were
not universally believed; perhaps Meyer did not yet believe
them. Neither would he publish Bergson's argument that
Zionists were cooperating with the British Colonial Office to
restrict immigration to Palestine. "The *Washington Post* is
not a Jewish paper," he told him simply. But Bergson would
not let the matter drop. He kept after Meyer for two more
years, writing lengthy letters, blaming mistaken interpretations on "your managing and city editors [rather] than [on]
personal sinister intentions on your part," badgering him,
until Meyer printed Bergson's charges and refuted them, on
the editorial page, at length. "The Jewish Agency," not Bergson's committee, "represents the people of Palestine," the
editorial said. It was a risky statement, a victory for Bergson
in that it forced Meyer to take a position different from the
official American position, a position as a Jew. United States
policy was to support British control of Palestine and not to
acknowledge separate Jewish liberation efforts. Rich Jews,
including Meyer, gave money to the Jewish Agency through
underground channels, money that bought arms and medical
supplies, that paid for the ideal of Zionism, but they did not
talk about it, let alone say it in print. Meyer had been working
to be accepted as a patriotic American; he had once gone so
far as to telephone Secretary of War Henry Stimson (who
made a transcript of the conversation and classified it Secret) to tell him that "I would like, if it seems that the *Post*
can be helpful in a major way, to make it so. . . . I have
in mind that we could do a campaign [on military training]
both in the news and in the editorial department." The Jewish
issue compromised his credibility, his independence.

In the spring of 1944, Katharine's father learned from

Adolph Dreyfus, who by then was living in New York, that his cousin, Dr. Leon Zadoc-Kahn, had been taken from Paris with his wife to "an unknown destination" by the Nazis. Dreyfus begged him to use the resources of the *Post* to try to find them, but Meyer had been strangely cold. "I was distressed to read your letter . . . about Leon and Suzanne. It was fearing this that I offered to bring them out. When they declined, I felt it was a mistake, because I could not imagine that they would have ultimately escaped. I was happy that such an event did not occur sooner." Dreyfus wrote again to say that he was sure Meyer was doing what he could; Eugene replied, "I cannot say that I am trying to do anything. I merely wanted the information [about them] for my records. I never heard of anybody in America being able to do anything for somebody in a concentration camp in Occupied France." Ten years later, Eugene told his son, Bill, who had been an army air surgeon in Europe, about "Dr. Leon Zadoc-Kahn, who was burned at Auschwitz, you may remember, with his wife during the war. He was the head of the Rothschild Hospital in Paris for a long time. . . . I was very fond of my cousin, Leon, and I lived with him at his apartment in Paris for six months." Characteristically, he said little else, though he hung Leon Zadoc-Kahn's portrait at Mount Kisco, above the mantel in the sitting room.

As the war rallied Americans to support the cause of the Jews, it overwhelmed many German Americans with guilt. Agnes felt a deep rift with her husband during those years, not because he was Jewish but because she was German, and he did not seem to think nazism a tragedy for Germany. When Hitler began eliminating his political opponents in the Blood Purge, depriving Jews of citizenship, dissolving labor unions, Meyer did not want to publish her views on the subject. It was a continuing source of tension between them that he barred her access to the pages of the newspaper, saying that her ideas were unsophisticated, although as a young woman she had been a journalist. (He continued to include Katharine in editorial conferences, however, encouraging her interest in the paper.) Eugene did take Agnes to Europe in 1937, when he and editorial page editor Felix Morley went to formulate the *Post*'s positions on the German threat; but as a matter of principle, as a Jew, he would not go with Agnes into Berlin; while the men visited France and Austria, she went alone. That was the beginning of her frustrating and lonely efforts to discover what had happened to the German soul.

Shortly after the Meyers' trip, Germany annexed Austria without an armed struggle, which Eugene saw as evidence that Hitler was accepted as a political leader in Europe. The *Post* ran a long analysis of the attraction of nazism which horrified and enraged Agnes. She addressed a lengthy letter to Morley (bypassing Eugene, as he had her) in which she accused him of "approval of Fascism as a program." Morley responded a few days later. "One of the most illuminating experiences of my trip with Mr. Meyer last Summer was when a Jewish banker friend of his, with whom we lunched in Vienna . . . said . . . that Hitler's idea of a synthesis between Nationalism and Socialism was 'a stroke of extraordinary genius,' " he equivocated. "The week before I had talked with an old Socialist friend . . . who told me that hundreds of thousands of former party members, as well as a large proportion of former German Communists, were now confirmed Nazis because of the unquestionably Socialistic aspects of the program. I am not (as you said) attempting to contradict the judgment of Thomas Mann," whom Agnes idolized, "that this is a spurious Socialism but . . . to the average run-of-the-mine Socialist worker that philosophy means that the State will find him work . . . and see that he shall not be exploited by an individual capitalist. The Nazi government certainly does all this. . . . I do not like this . . . I merely state . . . a fact. Infinite damage has been done by the . . . idea that the Nazi government is merely a dictatorship based on military police or Gestapo espionage. Those elements are there and they are used to terrorize the courageous minority of dissidents. But the real power of the movement lies in its enthusiastic endorsement by the . . . lower middle class—the same elements which would follow a Huey Long. . . ."

This sort of rationalism, Agnes believed, was precisely the way Americans acquiesced in the destruction of the German culture. Agnes, raised as a German, learning strict German virtues and speaking the rich German language, knew better than Morley. She had bitter arguments with Eugene, which Katharine witnessed. She began to drink; she was losing her country; Hitler was destroying the Germany she had known more completely than he was destroying the Jews. Eugene began locking up his liquor, she refused to buy her own, and they argued about that.

During this time Agnes found solace in Thomas Mann's novels; he was a compatriot whose writings explored the inner self in relation to changing values in Europe. Mann had been deprived of his German citizenship by the Nazi party in 1936 and was living in exile in Switzerland; Agnes prepared a long review of his allegorical *Joseph in Egypt*, which the *Post* printed, and the novelist began corresponding with her, writing in German. They met in Europe. She arranged for his family to enter the United States through Canada and to receive official immigrant status in May 1938. She rented a house in New York specifically so that he would come to talk, and she felt, each time he left, that two "god-seekers" had gone "their way together, for a little while." After he had settled in Princeton, with a teaching post, she wrote to him almost daily—importuning letters that demanded from him as much as she felt that she had given. Mann saw Agnes Meyer as a patron and friend, but she, to her family's embarrassment, thought of him as a spiritual lover. They had a number of meetings over a period of years.

A short time after his defection, Agnes went to Mann to persuade the writer that he should perform the politically heroic act of denouncing Hitler. She took Eugene with her, and he later recalled to Katharine that "it was a bit grim." As always, Agnes positioned herself at odds with Katia, Mann's brilliant wife, whom she did not like, although acknowledging that she was "necessary" for Mann's well-being. (Agnes had loaned "Mrs. Thomas Mann" a number of table linens, bed linens, bath towels, tea sets, and different linens for the "help," but in matters of the German mind and heart, she repeatedly demanded that *Mr.* Mann see her alone, in an intense encounter, though the emigration had left him nervous and frail.) Agnes reminded him of an essay he had once written, "Reflections of a Nonpolitical Man," which argued that an artist must participate in politics in order to preserve a creative society; nevertheless, she found, he was unwilling to display his family as a group of suffering German intellectuals. Agnes insisted; for a time he withdrew. "I adore him openly and he returns it diffidently," she wrote to Katharine after one of their meetings. Katharine had known Mann's daughters, Elizabeth and Erika, at Chicago and knew how he loved and admired them, as well as his wife. "I have the feeling," Agnes confided, "that I am one of the . . . very few women he has ever liked."

Neither wealth nor personal force could buy Mrs. Meyer the answers that she needed, even from the Nobel Prize–winning father of modern German letters. As Mann warmed to her attentions—in 1941 Agnes endowed a chair for him at the Library of Congress, where he became America's "Consultant in German Literature," at $4,800 per year; and she translated and reviewed his work—she saw him less as a "god-seeker" than as an unhappy old man. This understanding allowed her to get ever more personal; she gave him a velvet smoking jacket, the kind of gift a man would receive from his wife. She also began to pick quarrels. In February 1942, as she was preparing for a trip to his new home in Pacific Palisades, California, she complained about the intrusion of his family during her last visit, hoping they would be left more alone this time. Mann's answer was injured and petulant. "It does seem to me, dear friend, that you do an injustice to your first visit on this coast, and it saddens me that you have so inadequate a memory of it—I mean, remember it as having been so inadequate. We devoted two whole mornings to one another [Mann wrote between nine and noon every morning; Agnes was in fact the only person for whom he sacrificed his working time], were undisturbed and alone for hours both days, talked, had a reading and a walk on the beach, and then I believe you once gave us the pleasure of coming to lunch with me *en famille,* in the sphere in which my life is lived. But the idea that you saw me only *en famille* is an illusion of memory. . . . I would be delighted simply if it could be repeated just as it was. I grant, though, that is quite a responsibility to ask you to come, fearing as I would that you would again go away with the sense that it was a waste of time. . . . I do not overestimate the charm and importance of my company . . . and would understand only too well if you should not wish to see our good relationship *par distance* disturbed by my unpredictability as a human being. I am often tired and know that I can be deadly boring." Agnes's daughter Florence, who was married to the dark, brooding actor Oscar Homolka, was then living in Los Angeles. ". . . if you have so little time that Florence must go to San Francisco to meet you, then how can I presume to ask you to come all the way here on my account alone?"

The wisdom that she expected to find in him, the solemn interpretations of Nazi Germany, were not forthcoming. He was, as he said, "often tired" and worried about his children, who were fighting fascism more actively than he. Erika Mann went back into Germany to rescue her father's manuscript of *Joseph and His Brothers*; she produced *School for Barbar-*

ians, a report on the Nazi educational system; *The Other Germany*, on the German Resistance; and, with her brother Klaus, *Escape to Life*, the story of the German refugees. Yet even with his children's work, as with Agnes, Mann spoke only of literary matters, the effectiveness of political expression rather than politics itself. He was only an old man who had lost his country, but Agnes's disappointment in him turned to bitterness. She used his children to strike at him: why weren't his sons in the army, like her son and her son-in-law Phil? It was then that she had pushed him too far, and he let her know, in a ferocious letter in May 1943, exactly what he had come to understand about her: "I might say you had 'chosen' the moment when I was in the midst of conceiving a new book and therefore in a state of great, easily shattered nervous tension, to send me the insignificant blather of the lady from Smith College—not in order for me to see how malignant and hate-filled the writer is, but so that I could see what a good-for-nothing my son Klaus is," he accused. "I have suffered bitterly . . . from your having nothing but feelings of scorn and rejection for my children, for after all I love these children, by the same right that you love your children. . . . I can scarcely imagine a more horrible blow—to me personally—than that something should happen to your wonderful [sons] in the course of the war . . . [or] your [pregnant] daughters Katharine and Florence who are approaching their difficult hour."

Klaus was a courageous young man who not only wrote inflammatory books but worked with the European underground, for which he had spent three months in a concentration camp in France. Mann had even told Agnes that he feared Klaus would someday be "murdered in my place." Yet Agnes complained to him that Klaus was staying out of the American army "so that" American boys might die, even though, as Mann angrily pointed out to her, he "literally fought to be taken in," which Agnes had forgotten. "I reported this to you. You sent not a word of . . . congratulation."

He identified the source of her attack as a "profounder disappointment" of some sort, but guessed, wrongly, that it was a disappointment with himself as a man. "I have read aloud to you for hours from new work no one else has seen," he went on petulantly; "I have shown the most sincere admiration for your patriotic and social activities. But nothing was right, nothing enough. . . . You always wanted me different from the way I am. You did not have the humor, or the respect, or the discretion, to take me as I am. You wanted to educate, dominate, improve, redeem me. In vain I warned you . . . that this . . . was an attempt on an unsuitable object, that at the age of nearly seventy my life was too thoroughly formed." He did not realize that he had been for her the living symbol of a mythical, spiritual Germany, a wise father who could have helped her to understand, if not accept, her loss. Finally, when the war was over, she began, painfully, without Mann, to look for answers herself. "An older man, 52, with blond hair and blue eyes, aquiline nose, sloping forehead and tense eagle-like profile," Agnes wrote in the diary that she kept of her interviews with Nazis in the Allied prisons. " 'To think,' he gasped, 'that after all my friends . . . died joyously that [Hitler] . . . crept off and croaked like a rat in a corner. . . . Anyway, there's no place to go. You give yourself like that just once in your life and never never will we ever have such faith again.' "

Katharine had maintained a cheerful facade throughout the war, but the tensions between her parents, added to the strain of the war itself, had their effect. Their fighting made them objects of curiosity, even ridicule, in their small city, and ridicule was very distressing to Katharine. She made wry, offhand jokes to friends about the home battle front, but others thought she was perhaps too gay, her smile too forced. Her parties were sufficiently gracious and lavish, but the patriotism that had become the eternal theme of Washington parties did not resolve the problems at home. She waited for her husband's return and for normal life to resume.

Philip Graham came back in the fall of 1945 full of war stories and, as Pare Lorentz had warned, full of himself. He showed off his Legion medal; he played with his babies; he teased Katharine about having gotten fat. Katharine gratefully handed him the reins of their small family and spoke a little about things that had happened while he was away. She filled him in on gossip. She told him what had been bothering her, and he said something characteristically wise and flippant. She asked him what he was planning to do.

If one question is anathema to a soldier, it is how he will earn his way in civilian life. When Phil and Katharine had married, he was first a Supreme Court clerk; then a New Dealer; one of a small group of bright young men farsighted enough to lay the groundwork for war; then an intelligence officer fighting Fascists. Now he was none of these. Lorentz had predicted that he would be "unfit to live with for a while," and indeed he was. But the cause was not the happiness he had felt from the war, his pride in accomplishment; rather it was this sense of loss, the hero fading with the war's end. He had two children he barely knew. A lifetime stretched ahead of him with this rich woman (and all rich women were spoiled), and her father, seventy years old and anxious for an heir, was now pressing him to come to work at the *Post*. Katharine said she would do what he wanted, but when he said he wanted to go back to Florida and practice law (he was just "a poor boy from Florida"), perhaps run for Congress, she bit her lip nervously, and he knew he could not talk about it with her at all. He spent three days with his friends at Hockley, thrashing it out. It was late 1945, around Christmas, as Joe Rauh remembers, and "Phil was pacing around playing Hamlet. I didn't understand why. All I could see was that Meyer had offered him a job, a great opportunity. Twenty years later I knew why Phil was Hamlet."

THE PAPER

☆ **9** ☆

Philip L. Graham,
Publisher,
and His Wife, Kay

For the next seventeen years, Katharine's story was her husband's story, until his suicide took him from her and she succeeded to control of the *Washington Post*. Her story was his story, but he was used to carry on the Meyer family legacy. Phil became assistant to Eugene Meyer in January 1946; by June, Meyer had accepted President Truman's offer to become the first head of the World Bank and left Phil on his own as publisher and editor-in-chief of the *Post* at the age of thirty. This did not mean that Phil was rid of Meyer, whose gamble on an unproved young man had Meyer's friends waiting smugly for Phil to fail. Phil mastered the newspaper brilliantly, but then he had done so for the father. "The power that the father created for them was simply gorgeous," it was said, but it was the father's power. In an authentic tragedy (Phil as Hamlet) the victim brings about his own downfall. Phil was willing to carry on the Meyer legacy because he got what he wanted: he was soon, to borrow a phrase from one of Meyer's friends, "in control of forces larger than human beings" with that newspaper, for it had an impact uncannily beyond its journalistic merit. The danger was that "you can't have a normal family life on the basis of power." Opinion in town, however, was such that some people thought Phil might not be in control of the *Post* at all, that Meyer maintained his hold on it through Katharine. She insisted that this was not true. "He thinks I'm an idiot," she protested. "Honestly, I have no influence."

Katharine loved her husband and wanted to be a good wife. He had, she felt, stayed in Washington partly on her account, and a man of that caliber—so brilliant, so adamant about doing things his way—did not need competition from a wife. He needed support. Whatever Phil believed to be the proper role for a wife—he wanted her to continue writing and once said, "I couldn't stand coming home if you were waiting for me with a pie"—she had her own views, which were to do the opposite of what her own mother had done. A wife should be a wife, a mother should be a mother, unlike Agnes, whom she likened to "a kind of Viking." She told Phil that with the house and the children she did not have time to write, and that the columns were difficult for her. He said, "Your salary can pay the cook."

Her contribution was to ease him into the style of the rich. They definitely needed a more impressive house now that Phil was publishing the *Post*, if only to show that the *Post* was prosperous. She took him to see an eight-bedroom square brick structure on 31st and R streets, which was set a quarter of a block back from the narrow road, with a circular driveway, wide lawns, and columns on either side of the door. It was across the street from Oak Hill Cemetery; from the back one could look out over Georgetown. The house had belonged to William "Wild Bill" Donovan, the first director of the Office of Strategic Services, created in 1942. Donovan had built the OSS into a formidable tool "to procure and obtain political, economic, psychological, sociological, military, and other information which may bear upon the national interest." * His house was one of the most valuable in Washington.

Phil was drawing a salary of about $30,000, but it was not enough to buy the brick house. He told Katharine she was "crazy," as the story goes, and Katharine went to her father for the down payment. Phil was proud and didn't like it, but he *had* taken the *Post* and the Meyer style of life simply followed. Meyer put in his bid, and later in the summer of 1946 Katharine "woke up and found I had it and almost died." They decorated it in velvet and mahogany and hung modern French and old Oriental paintings.

Phil ran the *Post* the way he did everything: with complete concentration bordering on frenzy. Katharine woke up first, fed the children, and had his breakfast ready when he staggered down the stairs at about ten. "I get up hard," he liked to say. Katharine served him pancakes with syrup every morning in their dining room, which had a black and white marble floor. He drank three cups of coffee with cream and sugar. She drank coffee with him as he inspected that morning's *Post*. He took the *Post* upstairs and read it while he shaved and dressed. His clothes were conservative, as if to hold him in: wing-tip shoes, dark suits and ties, white shirts above which rose a long, deeply lined face that *Time* magazine later would call "Lincolnesque." He read the *Post* while Katharine drove them to work in their modest car, and one

---

* Donovan said this to Harold Smith, director of the budget under Truman, in a letter dated August 25, 1945. "While the intelligence community was in disarray" at the end of the war, writes William R. Corson in *Armies of Ignorance: The Rise of the American Intelligence Empire* (New York: Dial Press/James Wade, 1977), ". . . Harold Smith went about the task of studying the intelligence system and laying the groundwork for restructuring it in accordance with Truman's marching order, which said, 'This country wanted no Gestapo under any guise or for any reason.' " Donovan responded to Smith's inquiries "in sorrow more than in anger." OSS was disbanded on October 1 of that year, to be replaced by the Central Intelligence Agency, created as part of the National Security Act of 1947.

of his first acts upon reaching the office was to send reporters small handwritten notes complimenting their work.

Phil was a talented newspaperman. Sober or drunk, he could take apart and put together a page in a few minutes, a task that would take other men half an hour. He could place stories so that they had the proper emphasis, so that the reader's eye would fall on them in proper sequence and see their importance to the rest of the news breaking that day. From the first, people had a tendency to use the word *genius* when referring to Phil and his editing abilities—not only his friends but the editors that Meyer had put in place.

The issues, when Phil took over, were dictated by the close of the war: wage and price deregulation and an end to war-time rationing, veterans' benefits, labor unions that had grown within wartime factories, refugees and economic aid to Europe, the new Soviet threat and corresponding need for effective intelligence. The young publisher took predictable, liberal, politically sound positions, and Meyer felt that ". . . the best thing I have done . . . was to succeed in interesting him in making it his occupation." The old man went out of his way to assure people that Phil was completely in charge, but he did not transfer ownership to him. He and his wife remained sole owners and Phil their employee. The *Post* had been operating in the red ever since the Meyers had bought it, and they had poured in about $20 million of their own money. Phil had to account for what he spent and felt that to be a form of control. It caused tension between him and the Meyers. More than the great issues of the day, therefore (which in Washington were national issues), making the paper pay for itself was Phil's preoccupation. He instituted a gimmicky radio campaign over the *Post*'s station, WINX, which Meyer had bought in 1944, in an attempt to increase circulation. Better circulation would mean higher advertising rates. But, though it was a good idea, Meyer resented not having been consulted, even as a matter of courtesy.

Eugene was having his own troubles at the World Bank, where internal politicking was hurting its $7.5 billion loan program, a system of revolving credit for member nations. The World Bank had been created after the war as part of the United Nations, and its success would also mean the success of the great powers' attempt to have a council for regulating international disputes. If the bank failed in its initial stages, that responsibility would be Meyer's. As its first president, he designed a system for selling World Bank bonds on the securities market which would provide perpetual financing; but the New York banking houses, including his own former house, Lazard Frères, were reluctant to support the bank's efforts, which threatened their own role in international finance. The possibility that Meyer would have won their cooperation was thwarted by the infighting among the bank's board of directors, who were jealous of each other's influence and collectively wanted Meyer to be their puppet. Meyer was seventy-one years old then, at the point in life when he valued a confidential relationship more than a professional challenge. He spent time alone with Philip Graham talking about the problems of the bank (and Phil had a chance to say how the bank should operate, how it could help raise the standard of living in poor nations) but did little to try to solve them. "I could stay and fight these bastards . . . but I'm too old for that," he said in December 1946. He had loved publishing and wished aloud that he had had "sense enough to stick to it." Abruptly, with two weeks' notice to the bank, he resigned and went back to the *Post*, only six months after he had made Phil publisher.

Men with wealth, intelligence, and accomplishments do not retire easily. Meyer let Phil know that he would be available for counsel, "just the old man called chairman of the board," but Phil asked very little of him, and Meyer found himself sitting at his hand-carved desk with no decisions to make. When he did interject himself, Phil called him "an irascible old man" and said he would run the newspaper his way or return to the practice of law. Katharine, caught between her husband and her father, asked Phil to flatter him, make him feel important, for he had worked hard to build the paper and cared immensely about it.

Meyer, though unreconciled to old age, finally transferred ownership to Phil and Katharine, as he had promised, in the summer of 1948. The *Post* carried this story:

Eugene Meyer, Chairman of the Board of The Washington Post, announced yesterday completion of a plan to insure the continued operation of The Post as an independent newspaper dedicated to the public welfare.

Voting stock . . . has been transferred to Mr. and Mrs. Philip L. Graham, son-in-law and daughter of Mr. Meyer, and a committee of five has been named to approve any future changes of control.

Nonvoting stock continues to be held by Eugene Meyer and Agnes E. Meyer.

Members of the committee are:

1. Chester I. Barnard, President of the Rockefeller Foundation.
2. James B. Conant, President of Harvard University.
3. Colgate W. Darden, Jr., President of the University of Virginia.
4. Bolitha J. Laws, Chief Justice, District Court of the United States for the District of Columbia.
5. Mrs. Millicent C. McIntosh, Dean of Barnard College.

Mr. Meyer stated: "Mr. Graham has been associated with me in publishing . . . since . . . 1946. . . . Mrs. Graham has worked in various departments of the paper over the last 10 years. I am confident that under their control the paper will adhere to its principles of independence and public service.

"It is the joint concern of Mr. and Mrs. Graham and Mrs. Meyer and myself that The Washington Post shall always serve those principles. The committee has been established so that any control of The Post subsequent to that of Mr. and Mrs. Graham will also be determined by loyalty to the same ideals. It is our purpose that the control of The Post shall be treated as a public trust, and that it shall never be transferred to the highest bidder without regard to other considerations."

The Grahams' partnership was formalized on August 3, 1948, with Phil buying 70 percent of the voting stock from Agnes and Eugene, Katharine buying 30 percent. Phil could not pay for the stock on his own, so Meyer gave him $75,000, an outright gift, which Phil then paid back to Meyer in return for the stock. For the next few years, until the paper began to make money, the Graham family lived on Katharine's income from investments. The "committee of five" atrophied (it had been Phil's idea to model the *Post* after the *Times* of London, which had set up a similar committee in 1924, headed by the Lord Chief Justice of England), as the family has never sold control of the *Post*.

When her father retired, Katharine asked her old college friend Sidney Hyman to write the story of his life. Hyman, an energetic and committed young man, had been living in Washington since completing his master's degree in political science at the University of Chicago. In the few years he had been out of school, he had worked on the staffs of Senators Paul Douglas, J. William Fulbright, and Hubert Humphrey; had drafted speeches for Adlai Stevenson; and had done research for Secretary of State Dean Acheson—a career that covered a wide spectrum of issues, from the economic reforms of Douglas (who had been elected to the Senate after the war) to the farm-labor plank of Humphrey to Acheson's wariness of communism. Katharine and Phil had been seeing him socially, he got along well with Phil, he understood the greatness of the Meyer family, and Katharine thought he would be able to produce a book that would be a fitting tribute to her father. He accepted the assignment with a deep sense of responsibility and drew up a preliminary agreement with Meyer whereby he would have a draft ready for his approval in a year and a half.

Years earlier, Katharine's sister Elizabeth had wanted to write her father's biography, and Meyer had put her off gently by joking that he was not ready for the world to know "what a great guy I am." Now he and Hyman devoted themselves to each other to produce an official record of his life's work. Meyer put Hyman on his personal payroll, the account that Phil left open for him at the *Post*, and gave him access to the hundreds of boxes of his personal papers. Hyman traveled with him to New York, where they toured Wall Street, Meyer reminiscing distractedly: in this building I created Allied Chemical; over there we decided to finance Anaconda Copper. One day he told Hyman that if he had it to do again, he would be a psychiatrist, that "the mind is a more dangerous frontier than politics or finance." The book was to be—Meyer was adamant about this—an account of his professional life, not his private life. Yet in the course of his work, which lasted altogether thirteen years, Hyman fell victim to the writer's temptation of caring too much about his subject and being unable to treat the project as just a job.

Hyman was not married and spent a good deal of his free time with Katharine and Phil, going so far as to baby-sit for their children. (There were soon two more boys, William and Stephen.) He was included in many of their activities and received their confidences. He and Phil, especially, were united in their dislike of Katharine's mother. Hyman remembered that Katharine had cried when Agnes was too busy to attend her college graduation, and years later he would still talk about a scene he had witnessed while working on his book at Mount Kisco. Agnes was getting ready for a party, and her servant had not shown up to help her dress. The woman's son, or nephew, ran in shouting that she had died on the path between her cottage and the main house. Agnes reacted with annoyance—the woman's death was inconvenient. Eugene, Hyman noted, was "appalled at her insensitivity."

Nor was Agnes any too happy with Hyman. He seemed to work and work, taking the family's hospitality (after a while he had refused to accept any more money) yet never coming up with a satisfactory book. The task became agonizing for him. He showed parts of chapters to Katharine, who gave him "warm encouragement," which he believed to be "more an act of [her] characteristic kindness" than an expression of the book's merit. Phil took him aside one night and said that "your book has got to be impossible to write; this family needs a novel."

The years passed. In 1961, two years after Meyer died, Hyman (still working) wrote Agnes to explain that his job had been infinitely complicated by Meyer's dimming faculties, his natural secretiveness, and his conviction that the book was in fact a tombstone inscription. He said he deserved her harsh judgment, and Agnes, in turn, told her lawyer, whom she wanted to pay Hyman $50 to sign a release on the material, that "I really think he's a louse." Having reduced a talented young historian to humiliation (Hyman later said that he no longer had time for the book, as he had married "and started a family of my own"), she then handed the unfinished manuscript to *Post* reporter Merlo J. Pusey, who published *Eugene Meyer* with Knopf in 1974.

In 1948, the year Meyer turned over the *Post* to the Grahams and commissioned his biography, Washington was a very different place from what it had been during the war and before, when he had been an active publisher. It was a city no longer united in a cause, fighting fascism. The liberalism of the thirties had survived, but there was a new chilling force: the fear of Communist spies in our midst, which gave rise to the security-loyalty program and eventually to McCarthyism. Washington's industry was government, and an inner circle set the tone of its special society, discovering and often managing issues by consensus. The power of this inner circle was real and depended upon an inside knowledge of the workings of government, along with the means of influencing others. Katharine and Philip Graham, owners of the most exciting news vehicle in Washington, were at the center of this elite.

Philip Graham had taken over the *Post* at a time when it was gaining ground on the city's other newspapers. The *Daily News*, part of the Scripps-Howard chain, was editorially bland; the *Evening Star* concentrated on local news. And the *Times-Herald*, the *Post*'s stiffest competition, was floundering because its owner, Cissy Patterson, had died, two days after Meyer had transferred ownership of the *Post* to Katharine and Phil. Phil's first venture as owner, in fact, was to try to buy the *Times-Herald* from Patterson's heirs. Phil flew from Mount Kisco to Washington to offer $4.5 million for the paper, and it looked for a few days as if he would get it. If he did not, he told Katharine, he would "just die for a week." When he lost his bid to Colonel Robert McCormick of the *Chicago Tribune*, he telephoned Katharine with the news. She "wept as if the end were at hand," Pusey wrote. Phil, as he had predicted, fell into a week-long depression that did not end until he was convinced that the *Post* would eventually win its fight to dominate the Washington scene. Shortly thereafter, he persuaded CBS network radio to sell him 55 percent of its Washington outlet, WTOP, and the added influence from that helped to establish him as the city's most important publisher. Five years later he acquired the other 45 percent; and then Colonel McCormick sold him the *Times-Herald*, which gave the Grahams a monopoly on the morning news, the most critical news slot of the day.

When a company buys out a competitor, the transaction can be challenged under the antitrust laws, especially if the company's business is news and the market is Washington, D.C., where diverging views are an essential part of the political process. The *Post*'s takeover of the *Times-Herald* could have caused the Justice Department to consider bringing suit to block the combination. It was true that the *Times-Herald* had been losing money since Cissy Patterson's death had left it without a strong leader, and that cases involving "failing" companies are rarely brought. But in this case no questions were raised. The acquisition was approved within hours of the announcement, and Eugene Meyer (who had paid the $8.5 million for the *Times-Herald*—Phil did not have the money) told Sidney Hyman that "the real significance of this event is that it makes the paper safe for Donny." Katharine's first son was then eight years old; his mother, Pusey noted, "screamed in ecstasy."

Phil's emergence as publisher and heir had its effects within the Meyer family. Although none of Katharine's sisters, nor her brother, had wanted to be involved with the *Post* while the Meyers owned it, its growing stature (and the fact that it had needed so much of the Meyer fortune to keep it afloat) provoked Florence Homolka, Katharine's oldest sister, to a resentful outburst. She had not been close to her family for many years, and one of the few contacts they had had with her husband, actor Oscar Homolka, was when Eugene arranged for him to meet the Russian ambassador Maxim Litvinov and Madame Litvinov at Crescent Place when Homolka was preparing to play the part of the ambassador in the movie *Mission to Moscow* in 1942. The film, part of Hollywood's war effort, was based on former ambassador Joseph E. Davies's book, a nonfiction account of the attempt to keep America and the Soviet Union united against Hitler. "In order [for Homolka] to give a better interpretation of your personality," Meyer had written Litvinov, ". . . it would give Mrs. Meyer and myself great pleasure if you . . . could take luncheon with us at our home."

Florence and Oscar Homolka were divorced shortly afterward, and Florence, who had always been fat, started to gain more weight and began drinking heavily. She had established a reputation as a photographer—among her subjects were Charlie Chaplin, Thomas Mann, Aldous Huxley, and James Agee (her picture of Agee was used on the cover of his book *A Death in the Family*). Yet despite her success, she was deeply unhappy. She lived comfortably on the interest from a $3.3 million fund that Meyer had provided for her, dividing her time among Switzerland, Italy, and California, and each of her two sons had trust funds from Meyer; but she was convinced that she was being financially "punished" for having made an "unfortunate marriage." Each of her married sisters and brothers received several thousand dollars every Christmas (not to be spent, Meyer told them, but as "an increase in capital"); she did not. She continually tried to get her father and mother to pay her bills. Agnes might receive an invoice from a strange doctor and write Florence coldly to ask if anything was seriously wrong. Eugene once invited her to Washington for a week and was billed by the St. Regis Hotel for $581.83, a figure that did not include, as he irately informed her, charges for "telephones, restaurants, valets, and other things." He sent her a check for $1,000 and asked her to "take care of these matters in the future" herself.

A psychiatrist might have said that a rich woman's preoccupation with family money indicated a serious disturbance. But Florence's parents were merely offended. When Florence heard of the *Times-Herald* purchase, and that Meyer had expressly said that he wanted the newspaper eventually to go to Katharine's son Donny, she demanded a "fuller explanation" of Meyer's plans to provide for *her* sons. She had had to raise these boys without a father, she complained to him in a series of letters in June and July 1954, and she thought he had been "pleased with the result." Meyer pondered each letter for several days, then asked Phil, at whom much of her hostility was directed, to help him draft replies. On June 3 Phil wrote, and Meyer and his son Bill revised, an answer to Florence that said in part: "I know how hard the last years have been for you and . . . how faithful you have been in the job of bringing up two fine boys. . . . You wrote of my assurance that the boys had a future on the newspaper. But of course no one can give any youngsters any such assurance. What I was trying to say to you was that the family had a good newspaper, radio and television stations [in addition to WTOP radio, they had acquired WTOP-TV, and WMBR radio and television in Jacksonville, Florida], an important interest in a good chemical company [Allied]—not to mention an association with one of the best medical schools [Johns Hopkins] in America."

Meyer wrote another letter in July spelling out "the factual information that I think you lack. . . . The Grahams have purchased, at my wish, a certain amount of 'A' stock which gives Phil the managerial control over the paper. This he has to have. Incidentally, the income from ownership of this stock has been, to date, exactly nil. . . . The prime example of the results of fractionating management control is the Washington Star, which is reduced to a do nothing policy of 'not antagonizing people' [Phil changed this sentence to read "several examples of the results of fractionated management control may be cited among important papers in our country"]. . . . Nor do I expect Phil Graham to be more interested in passing control . . . to some member of his family than to preserve what he has worked . . . to maintain and improve, namely the character, the principles, and the aims of the paper. . . . I think that you . . . are insuring their future in the best way that you can, namely to bring them up as intelligent, decent, interested, and kindly people. . . ."

The self-consciousness of this family, which saw itself as a great American family, was part of what made its members want to contribute to all aspects of American life. "You can't," as Agnes repeatedly told them, "just sit around the house and be rich." They had taken this seriously: Bill became a physician, then a psychiatrist; Ruth was a nurse's aide at Bellevue Hospital in New York; and Elizabeth, with her husband, had founded Pare Lorentz Associates, a small company that did its part to promote peace by making United Nations films on world hunger. Perhaps her parents felt Florence (who died in 1962, at fifty-one, apparently from an overdose of drugs and alcohol) did not do her share: they could have thought that she wanted to be rich more than useful. Great families, though, who try to harness "forces larger than human beings" sometimes have to pay a price. Katharine Graham was certainly paying, not as her sister had, but in modest ways, "cleaning up after" her husband, she once commented, "lurking in the background," playing "idiot" (in both senses: the Greeks used *idiot* to mean the opposite of the public man), all so that Phil could run around Washington being brilliant, the beneficiary and keeper of the Meyer family's social conscience. Although he and Katharine owned the *Post* together, only Phil had the media power, the power to do good as he defined it. As he grew cocky, Katharine, who was not finding happiness as a housewife, responded by compulsively eating. And his drinking began in earnest.

Phil was an intellectual man who linked his actions with intellectual ideas. He was conversant with political theory, read widely and hungrily, and had a special fondness for the theories of the British political scientist and philosopher Sir Isaiah Berlin, by which he justified his view of the publisher's function. Berlin wrote extensively, the major body of his work devoted to refuting two popular and, he thought, dangerous views: determinism, whereby the individual is said to be controlled by history and therefore is impotent; and relativism, whereby ethical truths are said to depend upon groups or persons holding them, and therefore the individual is free of responsibility. Berlin believed that the forces of history may produce unpredictable events. Phil, improvising liberally, thought that if history does not mold men, then men can mold history. The notion was apropos for a newspaper publisher, and he felt comfortable in that role: feet on the desk, chain-smoking Parliaments, running the *Post* with little money but enormous charm, he sustained an awareness of politics on two levels. There was politics as it appeared to be, as filtered through his editors; and underlying that, politics as it really existed for him, as it was understood by the intelligence community. Politics as reported, then, with an eye toward government interests, formed a new category of thought called mediapolitics. Philip Graham, believing that the function of the press was more often than not to mobilize consent for a liberal government's policies, was one of the architects of a now widespread practice, the manipulation of journalists by the CIA.

The reason for his involvement with intelligence was anti-communism, an abiding concern of liberals after the war. Phil was convinced, as were some of the most outspoken champions of civil rights, that the Soviet Union was engaged in a campaign of worldwide conquest. Only if Americans defeated communism could men around the world enjoy freedom as it is known in the United States. This view was, for liberals, perfectly consistent with a belief in domestic reform. These schizophrenic politics were best articulated by a group formed in 1947 (the year that Truman created the CIA) known as Americans for Democratic Action, whose founders included two of Phil's closest friends, Ed Prichard and Joseph Rauh. Phil liked to retain the appearance of independence and his name was on none of the group's rosters, but he went to the founding meetings and often visited Rauh and Prichard in ADA's small cluttered office.

ADA was the outstanding liberal intellectual organization of the day, and many of its members were forces in their own right: Arthur Schlesinger, Jr., Jerry Voorhis, Will Rogers, Hubert Humphrey, Eleanor Roosevelt, Cornelia Bryce Pinchot, and Joseph P. Lash and James Wechsler, who had known Katharine Meyer in the thirties through the American Student Union. The union's progressive programs—civil rights, pacifism, support of labor—had suffered from charges that the union was controlled by Communists; and the leaders of the ADA knew from the beginning that they would have a similar problem. Therefore they set out to establish their anti-Communist credentials: "The democratic faith is obviously on the defensive through the world," said a confidential internal memo in 1947. " . . . Central to the problem of peace are the relationships between the United States and the USSR. These relationships cannot be solved by continuous surrender to Soviet political or territorial demands, since experience has taught us that the effect of appeasement is to encourage not the moderates in the country appeased, but those constantly insisting upon further aggressions." Another memo declared that the *primary purpose* of the ADA was to combat communism, a purpose not made public but one that hindered its effectiveness in every other arena during those years. ADA claimed credit for getting Truman to adopt his civil rights plank during the election of 1948 (after Eisenhower had declined ADA's offer to support him rather than Truman on the Democratic ticket), but in truth the plank *was* an extension of the reforms in housing, medical care, social security, and employment that Truman had introduced to Congress as early as 1946. After Truman's election the fear of foreign and domestic Communists continued to grow, and ADA was placed on the attorney general's list of subversive organizations. Then Francis Biddle, an ADA man who had been attorney general under Roosevelt, asked the House Un-American Activities Committee to remove ADA from the list, which HUAC did. For some years ADA spent most of its energies reaffirming its anticommunism. ADA was particularly concerned with a farther-left Democratic group called Progressive Citizens of America, formed to back Henry Wallace for president in 1948, whose members included playwright Lillian Hellman and Philip Graham's brother-in-law Oscar Homolka. Many former ASU followers also joined. When PCA members were called before the Senate Internal Security Committee and asked if they were Communists or knew Communists, ADA's position was that the inquiry was necessary but should be conducted circumspectly. Joseph Rauh defended Lillian Hellman in front of the committee, but few of the other members stuck their necks out, and at least one historian has concluded that because ADA, a "liberal" organization, acquiesced in rather than opposed the witch-hunting, it "bears a major responsibility for the Cold War and for the ugliness of McCarthyism." *

Thirty years ago Stalin was still alive. He had overrun Eastern Europe; he had promised to bring about Communist revolution worldwide. The appearance of the Communist threat was pervasive and dramatic, and it was the major important issue in politics. A politician who did not take a position against communism was called a Communist and became a pariah. It was of course largely a political game, in which congressmen chased down traitors, held sensational hearings, and in other ways made political capital, and only a few politicians benefited while the rest of the country suffered. Among them was a young Californian named Richard Nixon, who in 1946 had taken the congressional seat of ADA member Jerry Voorhis by accusing him of Communist leanings. Nixon quickly joined the House Un-American Activities Committee, where, in 1948, he promoted an accusation of communism against former State Department adviser Alger Hiss on charges brought by Whittaker Chambers.

---

* This quotation is from Richard J. Walton, *Henry Wallace, Harry Truman, and the Cold War* (New York: Viking, 1976). Walton discusses ADA's role in the politics of the late forties and early fifties in elaborate detail.

Nixon's handling of the case brought him to the Senate in 1950 and to the vice-presidency in 1952.

Hiss was a Harvard man, a former clerk to Supreme Court Justice Oliver Wendell Holmes, an exemplary product of the eastern liberal establishment. He had, like Phil Graham, been a New Dealer. President Roosevelt had appointed him staff attorney at the Yalta Conference in 1945, when Roosevelt, Churchill, and Stalin had negotiated the world's future after World War II—German war reparations, war crimes trials, and zones of occupation—negotiations which, Roosevelt's critics said, virtually handed the Soviets all of Eastern Europe. After Yalta, Hiss helped to draft the charter of the United Nations, in which Russia was given three votes, "a fool decision," the *Post* editorialized in 1948, which ". . . arose, as we delicately suggested, out of the plural personality of Mr. Roosevelt." When Hiss was accused, there was general alarm that he might have been the Soviets' instrument, highly placed to weaken our government. Philip Graham knew him slightly and knew his brother Donald a little better, and he defended him in print. "As things stand," said a *Post* editorial, "it is the committee [HUAC] which is subject to the most serious indictment of all." The defense of an accused Communist was always risky, but Phil had made the mandatory declaration of anticommunism a year earlier and felt he was on safe ground: "The world power which belongs to America," he had said elegantly, ". . . is anti-aggression, but on its other face it is pro-freedom. This is its saving grace. For nothing anti will survive in the struggle of ideas that makes the entire world a battlefield." Nobody was more anti-Communist than Philip Graham, or more in love with America's "ethical truth," the moral force of democracy. Philip Graham was a patriot, but when he stood up for Hiss, Congressman Nixon, who thought himself more anti-Communist than the liberal establishment, accused the *Post* of being Communist, a remark intended to hurt the newspaper and one for which he would eventually pay.

Liberal intellectuals believed that communism could be fought more subtly, more interestingly, and more effectively than by simply name calling. Their fascination with theory and tactics, with information, psychology, and political science, led them naturally to the field of intelligence. Hatred of Communists, they thought, might lead to suppression, but information about them could allow them to be manipulated; and it was the liberal intellectuals in Washington who worked in the newly formed Central Intelligence Agency to penetrate and disrupt communism in Europe. The agency's approach was threefold: espionage, counterintelligence, and covert operations, which included paramilitary, political, and psychological warfare. It penetrated Communist movements; and it aided youth, labor, intellectuals, components of the non-Communist left, on the theory that democratic socialists knew and had rejected communism and would cooperate freely with the CIA to defeat it. The CIA was known in Washington, therefore, as a left-leaning organization, which appalled conservatives; and J. Edgar Hoover, who was allied with HUAC in searching out domestic spies, denounced the CIA as Communist.

Central Intelligence was run by well-educated men from prominent families, people of a caliber to keep company with the Grahams, who had a kind of salon. The association was casual at first, views exchanged over drinks with Frank Wisner, Richard Helms, Desmond FitzGerald, Allen Dulles, fascinating and genteel men who encouraged the friendship to grow, until Phil, obscurely and obliquely, came to see that they were all doing much the same work.

Phil's experience with army intelligence gave him an affinity for the agency men. He understood their dedication, the uniqueness of their knowledge, and their resentment of

President Truman, who had not, when the agency was created in 1947, made it at all clear whether he would be willing to listen to their warnings of foreign Communist agitation. Phil had found men for the *Post* with intelligence backgrounds— Alfred Friendly and Russell Wiggins from the Army Intelligence School, Alan Barth from the Office of War Information, John Hayes from the Armed Forces Network of the OSS—and he believed in the rightness and sophistication of the intelligence world view. The agency men, though, thought of Phil as rather unsophisticated, a southern boy guiltily obsessed with civil rights and skilled in using the *Post* to campaign for the Negro; but not as skilled as he thought he was.

Washington was then a thoroughly segregated city. It had two separate school systems. Blacks could not eat in white restaurants. When segregation cases began reaching the Supreme Court in the early 1950s, the leading NAACP attorney was Thurgood Marshall, who, when he came to town to argue his cases, was obliged to stay in a slum hotel. The District of Columbia was governed by a congressional committee. It was a city whose population had no vote, where the black majority served the white minority, where even the simplest local matter had to be deliberated by Congress—a Congress dominated by southern committee chairmen who had seniority. It was a city where newspapermen could draw upon rich examples of hypocrisy in federal policy—one standard for the rest of the country, another for the place where the congressmen lived—and where the *Post*, by merely publishing accounts of racial confrontations in the District, could have a clear and direct effect upon the public conscience. That has always been the power of a newspaper. Yet when a *Post* reporter named Benjamin Bradlee came in with a story of riots caused when blacks tried to swim in public (white) swimming pools, Phil Graham decided not to run it but to manipulate the situation by threatening to print it. "We won't run the article tough and prominent," he told the secretary of the interior, who had charge of Washington's pools, "if you will agree to open those pools next year for everyone." Phil preferred to manage information rather than use it to inform the public, exchanging intrinsic press power for the illusion of independent political power, depriving the segregation issue of a public forum. The next year, when the pools were opened, Phil took some of the credit. But the skilled practitioner of intelligence would have printed the story to bring about the same results.

This sort of trading did not occur all the time—most of the news in a daily newspaper is necessarily straight news—but neither was it an isolated example. As early as 1947, three years before Ben Bradlee wrote the pool story, when Phil had controlled the *Post* for about a year, he had already found the first of his "higher purposes," the coverage of the presidential campaign of Henry Wallace, who opposed the anti-Communist foreign policy of President Truman. Wallace had impeccable New Deal credentials: he had been secretary of agriculture under Roosevelt, in which capacity he had developed a progressive and sweeping farm policy. Later he had been Roosevelt's vice-president, and then his secretary of commerce. When Roosevelt died, Wallace, who had remained at Commerce, was horrified that Truman used the atomic bomb to end the war with Japan, and their relationship deteriorated. As the president enunciated his policy of containing communism by "economic warfare," economic and military aid to underdeveloped countries that were "resisting attempted subjugation by outside pressures," Truman said, Wallace accused him of creating a blueprint for future war. With the support of the Progressive Citizens of America, the "Hollywood left," Wallace challenged Truman for the left-leaning Democratic vote for the presidency in 1948 (the Dixiecrats had already preempted the conservative Democratic vote). The anti-Communist liberals in Washington feared that Wallace would dismantle the apparatus—

economic aid offices, military outposts, Marshall Plan over-seers—by which America could monitor communism in Europe. The ADA, therefore, devoted dozens of speeches and newsletters to painting Wallace himself as a Communist, the quickest way to discredit any opponent, and Philip Graham, who in such matters followed the ADA line, printed an editorial "revealing" that "the Communist minority had the convention [where Wallace had been nominated by the Progressive party] in hand from beginning to end." He also said that Wallace as vice-president had insisted that America ship uranium and nuclear information to the Russians, when in truth those secret exchanges had been handled by Lend-Lease, the New Deal agency in which Phil had worked, although after Phil had joined the Army Air Force.

But to Phil the eccentric, disruptive Henry Wallace was a different man from the thin, nervous, aristocratic Alger Hiss. Phil quickly decided that he did not believe Hiss capable of passing documents to the Soviets. He tried to make light of Nixon's charges, accusing Nixon in turn of "excessive abuses" of Truman's security-loyalty program, which had put the fire under the Communist hysteria; and because he phys-ically resembled Hiss, being also tall and gaunt, he even joked with strangers that he was Hiss and would say, turning to a stout man on his left, "This is my brother Donald." As time went on, Phil developed so strong a dislike for Nixon's blatant, crude, publicity-oriented prosecution of Hiss—Nixon once took a cruise with reporters so that they could photo-graph him being rushed back to Congress in an army heli-copter when he got word of a breakthrough in the case—that when Nixon ran for vice-president in 1952, and the *Post* learned of illegal contributions to his campaign, Phil played the story on page one, and Nixon went on television with the humiliating Checkers speech. His cocker spaniel, Checkers, had also been a gift, Nixon tearfully told his viewers; should he also give away his dog?

Hiss was convicted of perjury in 1950, conditionally proving Nixon right, although that did not diminish the antagonism between him and the *Post*. "Alger Hiss had the misfortune of being tempted to betray his country," one of Phil's editors wrote, "in an era of widespread illusions about Communism . . . [but] that does not excuse him or minimize the enormity of the crime." Others of the liberal establishment continued to support Hiss, including Secretary of State Dean Acheson, who issued a statement saying, "I should like to make it clear . . . that whatever the outcome of any appeal which Mr. Hiss . . . may make . . . I do not intend to turn my back on Alger Hiss." But Phil, inexplicably, attacked Acheson, who, he declared, "has played right into the hands of the yammerers in our midst who are trying to rend our society with the Alger Hiss conviction as the instrument. . . . Judgment was obscured when Secretary Acheson decided to yield to a personal sentiment." His attitude shocked Agnes Meyer, who had repeatedly said that Communist hunting was little more than "gangsterism." More significantly for Phil, it angered and upset Felix Frankfurter, who had been watching his behavior as publisher with increasing alarm. "Please listen to me for a few minutes," Frankfurter wrote to him early in 1950. ". . . To worry [about] 'yammerers in our midst' . . . is to join the misinformed and the yammerers. I had supposed that the press enjoys its constitutional status because its duty is to enlighten and not to submit to darkness." Later letters told him that "you are not only publisher—that's only part of you. You are also a person, a man. And if as such, in your private judgment, you do not condemn the throwing of the Hiss stone at Dean Acheson, I should be much disappointed in you." And, "interfering with [your writers'] intellectual independence is one thing, but enlightening them through what happens to be the special understanding of the publisher is another thing. After all, you have had the benefit of a first-rate legal education and have shared for a year the experiences of a man who has had a good deal to do with [opposing] . . . the totalitarian scheme of things. . . . Why don't you give your editors an understanding of what all this means and what it implies in not talking about a case editorially or unfairly in the news column when men are called upon to stand trial." But Frankfurter pleaded with him in vain, for Phil's special understanding of the Hiss case came from his friends in Central Intelligence. Soon after Phil had declared Hiss to be innocent, someone from the agency showed him documents purporting to prove that Hiss in fact had transmitted information to the Soviets; without informing the public that the agency possessed such proof, which would have explained his confusing change of position, Phil began to rely on his friends for other insights, which led to a healthy working relationship between Philip Graham and the agency men.

The salon at the elegant Graham home was an informal affair, a Sunday brunch once or twice a month that ran into the cocktail hour. Guests would sit at small round tables on the wide screened veranda, where Katharine served from monogrammed silver platters ("A nice monogram makes such a difference," Agnes Meyer had taught her daughters). After the meal the men and women would separate, an enduring ritual at upper-class parties, and the women, who were sophisticated club women, talked travel and parties in the yard and watched the children playing football, while the men went to the living room, comfortably furnished with heavy, masculine pieces, hung with velvet draperies and Oriental art, to drink Scotch and talk politics. But though that was the accepted way of life for Washington wives, which was the life Katharine had chosen, she permitted herself to resent being excluded from the more interesting conversations. It did not matter if she entered the living room, for the men talked around her, making vague references to other countries and their plans to influence elections, encourage uprisings, defeat Communists. Katharine knew something was going on there. "I know they're talking English," she once complained to the other wives, "but I don't understand a thing they're saying. They're talking jargon."

They were all very aware of their superior knowledge, knowing that they knew more than the public; and knowing that they were liberals and patriots, the men felt it was their duty to maintain the democratic ideal abroad. In the months after Phil's successful settlement of a labor strike in 1949, and his purchase of more than half of WTOP, which gave him preeminence among the four Washington publishers, the salon was the scene of discussions on altering perceptions of foreign peoples who might be susceptible to communism. Work was already going on to that end, most of it attributable to the cheerful, portly, aggressive Frank Wisner, whose wife was Katharine's friend Polly.

Frank Wisner, like Phil Graham, had been born a southerner and had made his own way into the northeastern legal establishment. During the war he had been recruited into the OSS by William Donovan, whose house the Grahams had bought, and had been sent to the Balkans, where he conceived of and executed operations that became models for future psychological warfare. He had been excluded from postwar intelligence because of bureaucratic infighting, had been asked to return as deputy assistant secretary of state for occupied countries, an intelligence post, and by September 1948 he was named director of the Office of Policy Coordination, the covert operations arm of the CIA. (OPC and CIA were officially merged in 1952.) At OPC Wisner developed the vision that the war against communism would be fought not as another large war, but as a series of "guerrillalike skirmishes," a situation that he sought to control. Sometimes in cooperation with embassies or the Marshall Plan outposts, and sometimes not, Wisner had already begun wide-scale recruitment of foreign students and infiltration of labor unions. But he wanted something more, a way not only to subvert and disrupt, but to give foreign peoples a sense of America, to "alter their perceptions" against communism without violence; and thus Wisner, his deputy Richard Helms, and Philip Graham conceived of a formal program to recruit and use journalists, a haphazard practice until then; it was said to have had the code name Operation MOCKINGBIRD.

MOCKINGBIRD was the CIA's response to a propaganda body called the International Organization of Journalists, which had been founded in Copenhagen in 1946 and which, Wisner had learned, had been taken over by Communists. The group received money from Moscow and controlled reporters on every major newspaper in Europe, disseminating stories that promoted the Communist cause. "They had stolen the great words," a CIA man named Tom Braden later wrote. (Braden, an executive assistant to Allen Dulles in those years, now writes a newspaper column.) Young people reading such stories, Braden complained, grew up to "assume that . . . 'Peace' and 'Freedom' and 'Justice' must also [mean] Communism."

By the early 1950s, Wisner had implemented his plan and "owned" respected members of the *New York Times, Newsweek,* CBS, and other communications vehicles, plus stringers, four to six hundred in all. Each one was a separate "operation," requiring a code name, a field supervisor, and a field office, at an annual cost of tens or hundreds of thousands of dollars. Whether the journalists thought of themselves as helpers of the agency or merely as patriots, agreeing to run stories that would benefit their country; or even if they did not know where their information was going, or that information they received was "planted" with them, the agency considered them to be operatives.

Philip Graham's name has been conspicuously absent from recent debates on the question of the CIA and the press, except for a brief reference to the fact that "it was widely known that Phil Graham was somebody you could get help from. Frank Wisner dealt with him." * Of course Wisner did not want to insult Phil by suggesting that he lend his own reporters to MOCKINGBIRD, so he "dealt with" him in such a way that he believed he was not compromising himself. Over a period of months, at the Graham salon and other meeting places, Wisner apparently picked his brains on which journalists were for sale and at what price ("You could get a journalist cheaper than a good call girl," said one agency man, "for a couple hundred dollars a month"), on how to handle them, where to place them, and what sorts of stories to produce. Phil recommended target reporters for jobs with other newspapers, especially those with overseas bureaus, and Wisner, knowing Phil's frustration at being unable to afford foreign correspondents for the *Post*, reciprocated by paying for *Post* reporters' trips, which was not the same, Phil believed, as the CIA "owning" them, and which future investigators could not say was proof of a relationship. Reporters whose stories appeared in the United States played up the Russian threat, which was said to be growing daily, and urged President Eisenhower to develop air power, including intercontinental ballistic missiles, which, because of mounting public pressure (and pressure from what Eisenhower called the "military-industrial complex"), he finally agreed to do. But MOCKINGBIRD propaganda disseminated overseas did not have such predictable results. In Eastern Europe, where the CIA was always trying to "twist the Russian bear's tail" by encouraging revolts in the satellite countries, the Hungarian uprising of 1956 was crushed with Soviet tanks, and sixty thousand people were killed, demonstrating Isaiah Berlin's theory that converging forces may create unpredictable events, that men cannot control results. Hungary was the start of Wisner's disillusion with covert operations, a personal

---

* This quotation appears in an article entitled "The CIA and the Media" by Carl Bernstein (*Rolling Stone*, October 20, 1977), the best piece to date on the subject.

crisis helped along by his drinking, his thwarted drive for power and lost sense of mission, that resulted in 1964 in his suicide, a year after Phil's suicide.

The Graham salons were also, at times, purely social events. Katharine wrote her mother about one of these in the early fifties. The dinner had been given for John Stembler, a college friend of Phil's with whom he still kept in touch, and his wife, Kate, who were in town from Atlanta. Katharine noted to Agnes that the occasion gave her an opportunity to repay sixteen obligations, so she hadn't minded the large group. The party included quite an assortment of people, from both journalism and government: Crosby Boyd; Philip Perlman, the U.S. solicitor general; Georgia Neese Clark, the U.S. treasurer, who the next day sent Lally and Donny dollar bills that she had signed; the Drew Pearsons; the Frank Wisners; G. Frederick Reinhardt, from the Office of Eastern European Affairs at the State Deartment; and his wife. Also present were Benjamin Bradlee, a young reporter at the *Post* whom Phil thought highly of, and his wife, Jean. Jean was a cousin of Senator Leverett Saltonstall, the former governor of Massachusetts, who had been appointed to the Senate in 1944 to fill the vacancy created when Henry Cabot Lodge, Jr., joined the army. He was one of a very small and secret group of congressmen and senators who met informally to oversee the CIA, a group that included Richard Russell, Harry Byrd, and Lyndon Johnson, an opportunistic young senator from Texas whom Phil Graham was bothering about civil rights.

It was not common for the Grahams to entertain young reporters, but Ben Bradlee was of aristocratic northeastern stock. His father, Frederick Josiah Bradlee, whom everybody called "B," a banker, had married his third cousin, who was a Crowninshield, also a banking family; and they lived in Beverly, north of Boston, neighbors to the Lodges, the Saltonstalls, the Taylors who owned the *Boston Globe*, and Gates White McGarrah, president in the 1930s of the Bank for International Settlements, organized to collect and dispense German war reparations, a bank that has been called "the most ambitious experiment in world finance ever undertaken." McGarrah was also on the board of the Astor Foundation, which controlled *Newsweek* magazine until Philip Graham bought it in 1961. His grandson was a boy named Richard McGarrah Helms, who was Ben Bradlee's friend from earliest childhood.

Ben Bradlee, like his father, affected rebellion against his class, which he did by imitating his father's dirty language. He married Jean Saltonstall and after the war was able to invest $10,000 of his money in a new newspaper called the *New Hampshire Sunday News*, where he worked until the paper was purchased by William Loeb, whom he did not like. He then rode the train down the eastern corridor, as he has recounted, intending to get off and look for a job in Baltimore, but staying on until Washington because it was raining. Family connections, bankers or politicians who knew Eugene Meyer, seem to have helped him get onto the *Post*. He was assigned the police beat, which he had worked up in New Hampshire, and stuck with it for three years, when he told Phil that he wanted more excitement and was thinking of quitting. Phil talked to a few people about Bradlee, and he was hired as an assistant press attaché in the American embassy in Paris in 1951. A year later he was on the staff of the Office of U.S. Information and Educational Exchange, the embassy's special propaganda arm.

Bradlee's work for USIE, which is now the USIA, was in something called the Regional Publication Center, or the Regional Service Center. It produced films, magazines, research, speeches, and news items for use by the embassies, the Marshall Plan offices, and the CIA throughout Europe. It controlled Voice of America. It was not the CIA—it was mandated by the Smith-Mundt Act of 1948 to disseminate pro-American "cultural information" worldwide—and Bradlee had an honest State Department appointment. State Department officials, however, say that the Paris Regional Center (another of its names) during those years produced CIA material upon request, and that Ben Bradlee did so.

The Paris Center was controlled from Washington by a man named Edward Ware Barrett, an assistant secretary of state for public affairs and a seventeen-year veteran of *Newsweek*. Barrett had been appointed when the center opened in 1950, and when it closed three years later, Ben Bradlee started working for *Newsweek* in Paris. His most notable feat as a foreign correspondent was to obtain an interview with the FLN, the Algerian guerrillas who were then in revolution against the French government, an interview that had earmarks of an intelligence operation—clandestine meeting places, contact men, danger, and glamour—and which caused the French to expel him from the country in 1957. By then he had a new wife, Antoinette Pinchot, an American artist who lived on an island in the Seine with four children, a product of a fine old Pennsylvania family, the cause of his divorce from Jean Saltonstall. Bradlee began working at *Newsweek* in Washington, and in 1961, the year he became bureau chief, he is said to have heard from his friend Richard Helms, who heard it from his grandfather, that *Newsweek* would be put up for sale. Bradlee contacted Phil Graham, who by then had been diagnosed a manic depressive and was in one of his manic states. Phil gave Bradlee a handwritten check for $1 million to convey to McGarrah as a down payment.

☆ **10** ☆

The Man or the Empire: Katharine Loses Phil

Power and achievement overwhelmed this intelligent and high-strung young man. The complicated, influential men with whom he dealt, the rush of events, the inevitable ramifications of every action, every word, all taking place within a rigid, confined social framework that was never to be violated, the snobbishness and cattiness of the men and the women, the judgments, the advantages that they took for granted, the unending comments on his usefulness to the family—"Kate sure had good sense to marry someone who could run the *Post*"— made Phil more nervous, more driven, the more success he had. Accomplishment was something that the Meyers merely expected, whereas lack of it was usually the fault of bad judgment, the equivalent of bad taste.

Katharine had grace, spoke fluent French, and exercised great patience and good humor in handling Phil, reminding him that he could afford to dress more elegantly, that certain things—the obsequiousness of employees, for example—just went with the territory. The ease with which she accepted what was her due made him feel, when his confidence was shaky,

143

that he was out of place. In public, Kay was his fall guy, his stooge, the butt of jokes about her intelligence and appearance. And because her husband treated her offhandedly, so did his men at the *Post*; their attitude would be the seed of later problems.

There was another element to the dynamic. The *Post*, the object of tension and envy in the family, could have been hers, and they both knew it. Had Katharine married a doctor, a scientist, a man with no ambitions toward the newspaper, she would have continued to learn the operation, as she had been doing when she met Phil; and when her father was ready to retire, after she had had her children, she would have succeeded him. The one hundred editorials that she wrote when her father was publisher were rehearsals for future policy decisions. She thought so, and the rest of the family thought so. Then when Phil, obviously brighter, more aggressive, a better choice, came along, Katharine simply stepped aside and let him have what he wanted, which was to have everything at once, his way, or to go back to Florida. Meyer retired early to satisfy Phil, and Katharine accepted less than one-third of the stock, which Phil demanded so that the Meyers could never overrule him. But all of this was conditional upon his fulfilling the promise to infuse the *Post* with his energy and brilliance, and as the years wore on and some of his judgments missed the mark, as his faculties deteriorated, his hostility increased; his wife interceded more and more in his business, which impressed him again with the fact that it was the Meyer family's newspaper and convinced him that he was being used.

The trouble began in 1952, when Phil walked sadly into the newsroom one morning, his head hanging, and said he did not feel well enough to run the paper for a while. He was going to stay home for a few weeks. He said the executives could handle whatever problems might arise. Then he went home and went to bed, humiliated, exhausted. Katharine spent the day with him, telling him not to worry, that nobody thought less of him; everybody needs a rest. He was convinced that people were laughing, delighting in his failure. He stayed away from the paper for a quarter of a year, spending most of his time in a long white dressing gown, in which he greeted his visitors. He read a book about Africa. He thought. He played with the new baby, Stephen, his fourth child, who had been born that year. At times he seemed lost and lonely, dependent, complaining, and fearful, and nothing that Katharine could do allayed his feeling of emptiness. Other times he acted well. Katharine told friends that it was only overwork. Her parents insisted that they be informed if anything was really wrong with Phil. Katharine, a bad liar, maintained that there was not; but she asked her brother, Bill, a psychiatrist at Johns Hopkins University Hospital, to have a casual talk with Phil, and Bill referred him to another psychiatrist for formal diagnosis. Then he spent time familiarizing his sister with manic-depressive psychosis. It was considered the most difficult of all mental disorders to work with, incurable, an illness that psychiatrists did not like to treat because manic depressives were frequently able to manipulate their doctors. The "peculiar frankness and intenseness, [the] lack of complexity and subtlety" * that were so characteristic of Phil, for which his friends and family loved him, were in psychiatric terms typical of the manic depressive; and once the diagnosis was made, neither Phil nor Katharine could be sure which aspects of the personality were really Phil and which were manifestations of the illness.

He pulled himself out of the depression (the psychiatric "tendency toward health") and returned to work, and once again he ran the *Post* beautifully; but the breakdown had shown him how easily everything he had worked for could be lost. He read books on manic depression and learned that his

* The psychiatric phrasing in this chapter is taken from *Psychoanalysis and Psychotherapy*, selected papers of Frieda Fromm-Reichmann (Chicago: University of Chicago Press, 1959). She was a pioneer in the study of manic depression.

wittiness, talkativeness, his social aggression were "stereo-typed social interactions," not a "talent for . . . aliveness or freedom in expression" but substitutes for it. The Meyers readily gave him another chance, and his political associations did not seem to suffer from his incapacity. But from that time until the end of his life he was haunted by the fear that in everything he did, every political involvement, every judgment, he was somehow a fraud.

Psychotics suffer an "uncanny, frightening, gruesome" loneliness, caused, psychiatrists think, by childhood isolation (the child experiencing an intense, vivid inner life) and aggravated by "the taboos with regard to touching . . . among people of . . . upper social strata." Loneliness is not necessarily a physical state; it can be an inability to trust the very people upon whom one is dependent, members of the family, especially women if one is a man. The greater the dependence, the greater the distrust, and the greater the feeling of fraudulence, the fear that someday he will be found out. Phil was painfully aware of what can happen to those who fall out of favor; Florence Meyer and Ed Prichard preyed on his mind.

This was not a question of morality so much as the rules of the game. Power has its own nature. The user no longer has an interest in old friends, and when he loses power, the powerful no longer have an interest in him. This was what frightened Phil the most—what power does to the powerful. He was still reeling from what had happened to James Forrestal, the secretary of the navy who became the first secretary of defense in 1947. Forrestal had been not only a powerful man but one of wisdom and dignity. Publishers trusted him. Phil did him favors. In 1948 Phil had invited sixteen other publishers to his home, including Arthur Sulzberger of the *New York Times,* so that Forrestal could talk with them about the atomic bomb. Russia, Forrestal said, was threatening to block the Berlin airlift. Would they support his using the atomic bomb against Russia? They talked for a while about possible effects, and Forrestal's persuasive abilities were such that the publishers all said that they would *expect* him to use the bomb. Yet the following year, Forrestal exhibited symptoms of manic depression and his friends deserted him. He was forced to resign, was put in the psychiatric ward of a military hospital, on the sixteenth floor, and received few expressions of concern and fewer visitors. At three o'clock one morning he committed suicide by walking out an unguarded window.

In spite of these ghosts, the Grahams overcame Phil's illness this time. Phil was again a devoted father, "playful," Katharine commented, "nutty." His favorite child was his daughter, Elizabeth, whom he called Lally. He warned her solemnly, when she was approaching adolescence, that "sex is a part, just a part, of life." The older women were of course more of a problem. Agnes had a standing arrangement with Phil to publish all her articles, for which she was to be compensated only expenses, yet he would not read her submissions. "I am sending [this] to you," she said in a note to Phil's assistant, "because I don't want him to put it in the bottom drawer and forget about it." He also was wary of Katharine, who had learned something of the *Post*'s operations while he had been ill, in addition to taking care of him, and now was rather too free with her advice. He nudged her aside, jealously, saying that what she understood to be politics was not the way politics worked at all. Her competence unnerved him. She had begun to work with her mother's campaign to establish a department of health, education, and welfare, which in 1953 was given cabinet status by President Eisenhower. The first HEW secretary was a female newspaper publisher, Oveta Culp Hobby of the *Houston Post*.

Obvious good causes were fine for his wife, but Phil, so he told himself, operated on a level other than the obvious. For him, politics was not campaigns, but relationships, agreements, tacit understandings, *quid pro quo*. His most clearly political relationships during those years, the ones that corrupted his publishership and contributed to his destruction more directly than others, were those he had with Senator Lyndon B. Johnson of the Armed Services Committee, the majority leader, one of five who watched over the CIA; and with Senator John F. Kennedy of Foreign Relations. Both pragmatic men, they were genuine friends to Phil, as far as it is possible for men in politics to be friends, using him (to tell their versions of stories) and letting him use them (the stories were frequently exclusive), but without malice. In using him they brought him to new heights of self-importance, teased him with power that he felt was more real than his own, the power not for talk but for action. Being the sick man that he was, this kind of attention satisfied a need even while it damaged him.

Phil's association with Johnson began when Congress drafted the Civil Rights Act of 1956, the first such package since Reconstruction. Phil approached Johnson to ask for his help. Johnson refused, resenting not so much Negro progress as the influence of "ADA liberalism" in Texas politics. Phil argued with him, cajoled him in a southern accent, notified him that he could be the leader of a new modern South and that the *Post* would, if the opportunity should arise, support him for president. Johnson eventually received credit for carrying the act through Congress, but there is some question of who enlisted whom: Phil agreed to adopt a more moderate civil rights line, declining, at Johnson's suggestion, to publish the inflammatory articles written by Agnes Meyer, and insisted on printing editorials outlining the difficulties that Johnson had, as a farsighted southerner, in doing what was right without alienating his constituents. Believing that he had swayed an intractable man, Phil would not accept reports that Johnson had "gutted" the act, that it could have passed without him in a stronger form. Instead he used this victory as an excuse to delude himself that he could become a permanent part of the policy-making apparatus, that politicians, up to the president, would naturally include him in their discussions, solicit his advice. He was suddenly more than a publisher, he was a mastermind.

Later in 1957, after the passage of the Civil Rights Act, Phil designed a plan by which President Eisenhower could, Phil believed, force the integration of the schools in Little Rock, Arkansas, where Governor Orval Faubus was making a stand for the Old South. Faubus had declared that he would defy an integration order by the Supreme Court, and it was the president's responsibility to enforce the ruling with, if necessary, the National Guard. Phil felt that he was an interested party to this problem, a southerner with a conscience. He stayed up for two or three nights and days, writing instructions for the president, notes, legal bases for action, all on a long yellow pad, a habit retained from his legal training, going without food, becoming distraught and agitated. He presented his document, finally, to the president, who, not surprisingly, did not read it. The humiliation and rejection that Phil felt, coupled with exhaustion and the shock of his misjudgment, caused the manic depression to appear again, five years after the first major attack. But this time it did not cure itself with bed rest. It stayed with him, hovering near the surface, coming out at increasingly shorter intervals, making him at times seem gay and unpredictable, at other times sad and fragile. Manic depression is not simply a series of mood swings, with the victim going from elation to gloom. The manic depressive's basic psychotic pattern is depressive. He becomes mad, wild, irrational, excessively friendly—manic—to try to escape an unbearable feeling of loneliness, which is brought about by a defeat or a loss. With the mania or without it, the depression remains.

Again Katharine hid his illness. He was rumored to be an alcoholic, which he was, but the drinking obscured the far more serious problem, and rumors therefore were better than truth. He remained brilliant, still able to put together *Post* pages with attention to "style, placement, and timing" of stories; but the loose, rebellious manner became more obvious. He commited adultery in the company of John Kennedy, a neighbor in Georgetown, often sharing women with him. (Thus was established a political bond.) The tension between promiscuity and marriage which delights the common play-boy, however, added to Phil's feeling of fraudulency. He was hurting his wife, he was disillusioning their teenage daughter, Lally, and providing no example for his sons. He was casting doubt on Eugene Meyer's judgment in giving him the *Post*. He was, in accordance with the manic-depressive script, bring-ing about his own downfall.

In 1959 Eugene Meyer was dying, and Agnes asked Phil to make the funeral arrangements. Several days later she wrote to the Reverend Duncan Howlett, the minister of the All Souls Unitarian Church, that Meyer's lung cancer had progressed to a stage that required him to remain in bed, tended by nurses around the clock. She thought he had weak-ened so much that the end was near. Phil was preparing to leave for Paris in a few days, to join Katharine and the chil-dren, and Agnes did not want him to go without discussing what the family would do for the funeral, in case Eugene died before the Grahams returned from abroad. "After all, Eugene is a public figure and there are so many friends and admirers . . . that their feeling for him must be considered. . . . At present . . . he is somewhat better. . . . That is why I urged the Graham family to carry out their plans, made long ago, to give their four children a chance to see something of Europe. If necessary, they can return in a few hours."

Phil went to Paris. It was July; he always liked to take his vacations in the spring or summer. The family was living in a suite in an elegant old hotel. They spent their time tour-ing and shopping. Katharine was at ease there with her perfect French; she ordered the food in restaurants, talked with cab drivers. Phil, not having been taught the language, could not exercise his ability to charm. He was anonymous, just a man, a husband and father. The tedium of a long series of family meals; his anxiety about Meyer, whom he loved better than his own father; Katharine's forced gaiety during the final stages of the cancer, all added to Phil's sense of alienation. One morning he and Katharine went to the Paris office of *Newsweek,* which Ben Bradlee, now a neighbor and friend of John Kennedy's, had suggested that they do. *Newsweek,* with its connections to intelligence, was an important source of stories about the politics of Europe, and Phil thought he might be able to work out an exchange. While the Grahams were speaking to the bureau chief, they were interrupted by a messenger: Robin Webb, the alluring, dark-eyed daughter of an Australian diplomat, thrilled to be in the presence of the powerful Philip Graham. He had an intense and immediate reaction to her. With her sensual gifts and her lack of interest in the constraints of his position, she helped Phil escape the desolation of the vacation in Paris. He allowed himself to love her, wanting not just an affair but another marriage.

Eugene died on July 17, at eighty-three, after going into shock from choking on orange juice; the Grahams returned for the funeral. "Eugene is so magnificent a patient," Agnes had written to the Reverend Mr. Howlett, "and so philosophical that it is an exalting experience to be with him. I said to Adlai Stevenson who came to see him two weeks ago, 'I am not to be pitied, I am to be envied.' . . . One more thing: We should like passages read from the Old Testament —some of the Songs of Solomon, Proverbs, or Psalms—that are full of faith in the beauty and goodness of life. . . . He never had any official connection with the Jewish religion as neither one of us . . . [has] any feeling for orthodoxy; as far as Eugene is concerned I am reminded of something John Dewey said when accused of 'Godlessness': 'I am as good a Christian as any of them.' "

The Meyer family's concern for what the public need and need not learn about Eugene Meyer, "what history should record," resulted in a compromise Unitarian service, a bloodless, horrible event, at which Chief Justice Earl Warren gave the eulogy and a list of Meyer's achievements was read. Afterward, the family argued bitterly whether to honor Eugene's last request, to be buried in Israel—a result of senility, Katharine felt. In his old age he had turned increasingly toward his Jewish heritage, taking trips to Israel, advising Israeli bankers. He confided his desire to be buried there to Felix Frankfurter, who told some of his former law clerks and may have told Phil. The request was an embarrassment, as Eugene, in his more lucid days, would have understood. He had always been sensitive to the problem. When Agnes was awarded an honorary membership in the Washington chapter of Hadassah, the Women's Zionist Organization of America, in 1949, for being "a distinguished citizen of the United States of America and great humanitarian," Eugene had sent each of his children a note about the award that was almost apologetic in tone. His daughter Kate was the most adamantly opposed to the last wish, and Eugene was cremated and placed in the Meyer mausoleum in Kensico Cemetery near Mount Kisco, which he had built in the twenties when such things were the fashion among Wall Street bankers. He had planned the structure with his brother Walter and sister Rosalie, looking over blueprints, commissioning a stained-glass window, discussing the placement of urns and plaques. Both of his parents had been placed there, as had his brother Edgar, who had been killed on the *Titanic*.

Philip Graham, witnessing the burial rites of this odd family to which he more oddly belonged, was overcome by a wrenching sense of loss. Isolation. He lived with an anxiety and guilt that he could not understand. The depression that set in became a deep well, an almost physical "deterioration of personality" that he was incapable of fighting. In a perverted attempt to defend his dead father-in-law, he alternately claimed that he was "more of a Zionist than Eugene Meyer" and described his assimilationist family as "a bunch of kikes." His sexual powers, depleted from the years of alcohol, became of serious concern, as they do with manic depressives, and he invited Robin Webb to live in Washington in a large house that he bought for her on wooded, secluded Foxhall Road. Then he bought her a farm. Katharine, whom he now saw as the villain, demanded that he begin psychiatric treatment.

In 1959, as at present, Washington had an active and cohesive psychiatric community, dominated by the experimental work at three area institutions: Johns Hopkins University Hospital in Baltimore, Chestnut Lodge sanitarium in Rockville, Maryland, and the small, prestigious Washington School of Psychiatry. Many of the doctors who form the core of this community are on the faculties of two or all three of the institutions; they are the writers, theorists, lecturers, those whose patients are the most interesting and the most famous. Katharine's brother, Bill, at Hopkins, specialized in psychosomatic illness but was in the mainstream of Washington psychiatry through the Eugene and Agnes E. Meyer Foundation, which he had persuaded his parents to establish in 1944 to finance projects in mental health and law. He was also (as was his sister Elizabeth Lorentz) a large contributor to the Washington School, where in 1959 the chairman of the faculty was Dr. Leslie Farber, "the poet-philosopher of the current human predicament," an advocate of the integrity of the will in the psychoanalytic method and the author of such essays as "my wife the naked movie star" and "oh death where is thy sting-a-ling-ling?" * Farber was more than a psychiatrist. He was a social success, having induced Martin

---

* "The poet-philosopher . . ." appeared on the book jacket of Farber's *lying, despair, jealousy, envy, sex, suicide, drugs, and the good life* (New York: Basic Books, 1976). "my wife the naked movie star" was published in *Harper's* in 1969, and "oh death . . ." in *Commentary* in 1977.

Buber, philosopher and Zionist, to come from Israel to Washington in 1957, when he was seventy-nine, to lecture on the "philosophical anthropology of psychology," something of a coup for the Washington School. Buber's words inspired Farber, who took on the difficult case of his colleague's brother-in-law, the guilty, tormented Philip Graham, probably in 1959 or 1960, after which Bill Meyer became chairman of the Washington School's board of trustees, Farber remaining as chairman of the faculty. If the publisher of the *Washington Post* would endure the shame of psychiatric treatment, he would do so with a man of essentially the same social position.

Much of the time the children were at school, Lally at Madeira, the boys at St. Albans. Their father had always been there for them when they came home, but as months went by, and normalcy became more elusive, the cruel gossip reached them through other children. They would walk in and see Mother crying. Most often Daddy would be away. Friends felt compelled to choose sides in this exciting event, the breakdown of a marriage, and talked among themselves about whose dinner parties to attend—Katharine's, which she gave alone, fighting back tears; or Phil's, which he gave expansively with Robin; a difficult choice, for Phil was violating social norms, but Katharine seemed the obvious loser in a city preoccupied with winners. Her friends said she maintained a good appearance. One or two suggested divorce. Unaware of the diagnosis or the tragic life script, they assumed that she cared what they thought. Few of them understood that the parties were for her own distraction and the tears were for him. She worried about him whenever he was out of her sight. He might damage himself. Robin did not know he was sick. When he came home it was to explain rationally, with piercing eyes and a sweet, sad smile, that he did not want to destroy what they had built together, that he was going to get well. Katharine repeatedly took him back. She saved her affection for the children, who were feeling the strain, Don becoming moralistic, Lally nervous and anxious. Katharine told them that they were not to think badly of their father, that he was ill but was a wonderful man, that no matter what people said, they were always to respect and love him.

The dialogue with Agnes was of another sort. Living alone with several servants in Crescent Place, which had taken on the character of her own mausoleum, Agnes sat for hours, her feet on an ottoman to permit circulation of blood, downing martinis (the cause of the bad circulation) and trying to write an autobiography, *Life as Chance and Destiny,* a chronicle of the fifty years she had shared with Eugene Meyer.* In the winter one of the servants was attacked in the yard and so she encased the mansion in a high brick wall, a symbol of her new life as an aged recluse. Visitors came and went, but she was most interested in her daughter and her grandchildren. She saw that Katharine was not in the best of health, overweight, gray-haired, continually tired—a weariness that developed into tuberculosis in 1961. Agnes knew enough to blame Phil, whom she saw through mercilessly, and considered an ingrate, like her daughter Florence. After Phil left Katharine's house and moved in with Robin, about the time Katharine went into the hospital for tests, Agnes accepted the explanation of his "illness" (which she came to believe) for the sake of his children. "I think your letters are terrific and I think your idea of sending him a copy of the letter he wrote you is superb," Agnes wrote to Lally. "Let's just keep fighting, girl, and we are bound to win." But to Katharine, to whom she took cold madrilene soup, cold chicken, and wine jelly ("Hospital food gets boring so quickly"), she said that the *Washingon Post* should be "ours." Katharine had a mother who had always told her the truth. Now, with an irresponsible man

---

* Agnes Ernst Meyer wrote her first autobiography, *Out of These Roots: The Autobiography of an American Woman,* in 1953 (Boston: Little, Brown and Company). She wrote one book on art and two on politics and translated two by Thomas Mann.

in control of the Meyer family's power, Agnes told her what she wanted to hear.

Kennedy was president, a phenomenon for which Agnes felt she was partly responsible. "If it interests you," she had written to Katharine in August 1960, just after the Kennedy-Nixon television debates, "I found out that the labor unions, although they do not like Nixon, are indifferent to Kennedy. So Eleanor Roosevelt, when she sees him Sunday, is going to ask him to devote a day to visiting the factories in New York City to captivate the women. I got this idea from one of the labor leaders and passed it on to her." In this matter she competed with Phil Graham, who had written a long memorandum telling of his role in helping Kennedy to be elected, by putting him together with his good friend Lyndon Johnson. Phil had circulated this memo among the reporters at the *Post*, which enabled Phil to make history because it later found its way into the history books; it was included in T. H. White's *The Making of the President 1964.** Phil credited himself, in his memo, with putting together the only combination that could have beaten Nixon, implying that only he could have done it—an idea that Kennedy, who knew how to play the press, did not dispute. Instead he allowed Phil to think that he could work with him to create national policy. This dangerous illusion was fed by the Grahams' inclusion in Kennedy's "Hickory Hill seminars," informal weekend meetings at Robert Kennedy's Hickory Hill estate that were patterned after the Grahams' own salons of the fifties. Katharine sat once again with the wives—Margaret McNamara, Virginia Rusk—and heard the men discussing the fantastic, and saw the fantastic coming true. In the anti-Communist fever that Kennedy brought back to foreign policy Phil believed himself to be the president's accomplice (as Kennedy was his regarding Robin): invading

* New York: Atheneum, 1965.

Cuba, facing down Khrushchev in Berlin and Vienna, putting a man on the moon before the Russians did, committing advisers to Vietnam (a plan that Phil particularly urged on him). The *Post,* one of the vehicles for the Camelot myth, supported Kennedy in all his knightly ventures, more uncritically than it had ever supported Lyndon Johnson, who after accepting the vice-presidency with the rationale that "power is where power goes" was not included at Hickory Hill. Observing all this, Agnes once said to Katharine with understated sarcasm, "Has the *Post* fallen for Kennedy?" and Katharine shrugged. Manic depressives adopt the views of the men they admire at the moment; they lose their independence of thought. Phil fantasized that he had made Kennedy, the evidence was right there in the White House, and now the president of the United States was his friend, and he, Phil Graham, was one of the powers behind the president. Of course, he didn't need therapy anymore.

The reality was of course very different. Apart from theoretical discussions which the publisher regularly translated into pro-Kennedy editorials and features, such as the spread he printed on Kennedy's opinions of Khrushchev (all negative), there was little presidential interest in him. Something as simple as giving a job to one of Phil's old law school friends, a well-known and excellent lawyer, which was the most standard kind of political payola, was beyond Kennedy's debt to him. Phil unconsciously knew this and countered it, as manic depressives do, by telling the president that this job was going to be Phil's way of doing something for *him*; Phil's friend was going to take care of Kennedy's brother. He stayed up all night drafting a long letter, then called his friend to the *Post* to discuss it.

"Phil was unshaven and looked terrible," the friend remembers. "Maybe his hair was combed and maybe it wasn't. He looked as if he had slept in his clothes. He had a long yellow pad. He said, 'I want to read this to you. This is something I'm going to be giving to Jack Kennedy.' He flips through it. It was something like this: 'Mr. ——— has been recommended to you for assistant attorney general. You can depend on him. He will look after Bobby. Bobby will need all the help and protection . . . he'll keep Bobby out of trouble . . .' It was all Bobby. Phil says, 'I'm saying all these things about you. Can I say this? If I do will you promise me to do it?' 'Yes, of course.' 'What do you know about Bobby? Everything you've read about Bobby is wrong. Bobby is frightened. Attorney general overwhelms him. Bobby need assurance. Bobby is a sensitive, compassionate, warm, loving human being. You've seen how nasty he was dealing with Hubert Humphrey. It wasn't the real Bobby. If you want to do something for your country you'll go over there and put his interests and protecting him above everything else.' "

With Phil's importuning, the friend was put on at the Department of Justice, where he worked as an assistant attorney general for several weeks without being officially hired and without meeting Bobby. "One day Bobby sent for me and conducted a reluctant interview. 'I understand you want to be assistant attorney general.' 'Yes, sir.' 'What law school did you go to?' 'Harvard.' " The friend was then in his forties and had argued landmark cases before the Supreme Court. " 'What were your grades?' " A week later Bobby sent for him again and asked nervously, " 'What are your long-range ambitions?' 'Only to serve you and President Kennedy.' 'Does it have to be in the Department of Justice?' " Bobby fired Phil Graham's old friend and replaced him with the ambitious young Nicholas Katzenbach, who later, after Phil's death, became attorney general and then vice-president of IBM Corporation, and who subsequently was invited by Katharine Graham to join the board of directors of the *Washington Post*.

Compounding this insult, which in political society showed a loss of status, was Kennedy's not admitting Phil into the two most significant intelligence operations of his presidency, those called MONGOOSE and Special Group CI. MONGOOSE was the plan, laid out in NSAM (National Security Action Memorandum) 100, "to use all available assets . . . to help Cuba overthrow the Communist regime"; it gave rise to the Bay of Pigs invasion and the eight or so separate attempts to assassinate Castro. Special Group CI (counterinsurgency), established the year after MONGOOSE by NSAM 124, was assigned the task of designing a war, so to speak, in reaction to the failure of MONGOOSE. The group, which included CIA director John McCone, Attorney General Robert Kennedy, and national security adviser McGeorge Bundy, devised Kennedy's "counterinsurgency doctrine," a legitimization of Frank Wisner's early "strategic hamlet" concept, and it was Kennedy's way into the guerrilla war of Southeast Asia.* Because it included McCone, it was a joint presidential and CIA operation; because it included the newsman Edward R. Murrow, who was invited to sit in as an observer and was soon made a voting member, it was an operation of mediapolitics. Murrow, who had been vice-president of CBS until 1961 and was then director of the USIA, was therefore not only an architect of the Vietnam war (and Phil wasn't), but was instrumental in mobilizing consent for it, through the USIA and through CBS. That network, in addition to promoting the cause in its news broadcasts, held government contracts to provide war communications—"Photoscan" electro-optical systems for war reconnaissance.† Murrow was where Phil

---

* For a discussion of NSAM 100 and 124, see Corson, *Armies of Ignorance*, pp. 398–99.

† CBS manufactured Photoscan under its CBS Laboratories division, which existed from 1955 until 1975. Photoscan, according to CBS's annual report for 1960, "is unique in that it worked equally well with cameras that record photographic, radar, or infrared intelligence." Another CBS Labs product was VIDIAC, a Visual Information Display and Control generator that was included in a major defense communications system built by Thompson Ramo Wooldridge. Both products were used in the Vietnam war. In 1975, with the end of the war, CBS Labs was reorganized into CBS Technologies, which, the company boasts, accepts no outside contracts but does only re-

Graham had been, during MOCKINGBIRD, and now wanted to be again: on the inside.

The jealousy that he suffered over Murrow and the alienation from Kennedy were, however, only the consequences of his increasing cynicism about the nature of power. He had begun to talk, after his second breakdown, about the CIA's manipulation of journalists. He said it disturbed him. He said it to the CIA. His enchantment with journalism, it seemed, was fading. "Newspapers are the rough drafts of history," he now thought; mediapolitics did not become history until the moral judgments were in. As he became more desperate, unable to control the forces that controlled him, one of the manic depressive's greatest fears, he turned against the newsmen and politicians whose code was mutual trust and, strangely, silence. Their ethic led them to keep Phil's insanity "out of the papers," as he had kept stories "out of the papers" for his friends; but now the word was that Phil Graham could not be trusted, and his friends began to see very little of him.

In the final stages, Phil's deterioration was rapid. The newspaper was run completely by the executives, and Phil would lie on the couch in his office for hours on end, drinking, crying, threatening suicide, calling his half brothers in Florida and reminiscing about their childhood in the swamps. An assistant recorded his mutterings on scraps of paper. He was preoccupied with Katharine, whom he hoped to badger into divorcing him with the demented strategy "I must torture Kay." He abused her in public. His attorney for the divorce

---

search and development for CBS. The CBS Labs' Professional Products Department was sold to Thompson Ramo Wooldridge, and its military operations were sold to a Boston company called EPSCO, which with the war's end could get no military contracts and went out of business after a year. (CBS was not the only network involved in the Vietnam war. NBC is owned by RCA, which did, and does, military contract work through its RCA Laboratories in Princeton. ABC's only involvement in the war was reporting on it.)

was Edward Bennett Williams; it was to be a battle for control of the *Post* empire, and Katharine was to be cut out.

Agnes Meyer "broke off relations" with Phil during this time. She sternly told her acquaintances that he was not to be considered her son-in-law anymore. The split seems to have come after a violent argument about the space program. "You must remember that it all began when President Kennedy had lost prestige over the Bay of Pigs incident. The inside ring then got their bright heads together and decided there had to be some sensational program to take people's minds off the debacle in Cuba, so Kennedy announced—I forget his exact words—that America would put a man on the moon."

Phil was then the chairman of COMSAT, the government-owned Communications Satellite Corporation, which was the single honor that Kennedy had offered him, an innocuous position on the periphery of the space program, where he had also put Lyndon Johnson, as chairman of the Aeronautics and Space Council.

Phil resented Agnes's contemptuous remark. Whatever the "inside ring" may have thought of COMSAT, even if it was a diversion from real politics, Phil was determined to make it work. He was going to launch a communications satellite that would, in addition to its commercial functions, help the United States penetrate the Iron Curtain with propaganda, and in the process he would become an international communications baron, as he had become a national baron with the purchase of *Newsweek*. Using all of his powers of persuasion in this last effort, he succeeded in hiring a satellite expert away from the State Department to become his full-time COMSAT adviser. He spent days interviewing prospective staff members, researchers, planners, scientists. He held meetings of the board of directors.

For all his will, though, he was unable to sustain a rational facade. He called the State Department to say that propaganda in Europe was his responsibility now, that it should call its own men home. He punched those who disagreed with him at meetings, shouting, throwing books and water glasses. Kennedy realized that he had made a serious error in judgment. Fearing that Phil would start to talk about the internal workings of COMSAT, he asked Clark Clifford, former intelligence adviser to President Truman, the future head of the National Intelligence Advisory Board, and Kennedy's personal lawyer, to report Phil's activities to him. Clifford could oblige with no trouble because he was already involved with the Grahams' problems as Katharine Graham's attorney and Agnes Meyer's adviser.

If Katharine could have done something, anything, to help Phil, other than continue to love him, which she did, she did not know what it was. "Desperately hungry for reconciliation," Leslie Farber once wrote of the manic depressive, "he becomes increasingly estranged from those loved ones who might conceivably offer him some relief, were it not being demanded of them. . . . Even if the loved one manages not to fall into despair himself, he may still feel himself charged with the responsibility to love, so that in a self-conscious way he attempts to will what cannot be willed. . . ." * If the loved one, that is, the family member, the wife, gives up hope or stops caring, the patient usually loses his remaining hope as well. Katharine must certainly have understood this, but she also, with great sadness and pain, accepted that he would never get better; she had asked Clifford to represent her in divorce. Katharine wanted the settlement to assign control of the *Washington Post*, and all of the *Post* companies,† exclusively to her.

* Farber, "despair and the life of suicide," in *lying, despair, jealousy . . .* , p. 78.

† The empire that Phil had built up from her father's bankrupt newspaper would grow, after his death, to include not only the *Post, Newsweek*, and WTOP-TV, but Newsweek Books, the *Trenton Times* and *Sunday Times-*

The case never reached the courts, but was negotiated between the lawyers, Agnes pushing and Katharine holding back from filing divorce papers, which would have meant publicly accusing Phil of being insane. But the threat was always there. Agnes believed that if Phil tried to ride out the storm and wait another two years until he could get a divorce on the basis of separation, as Agnes thought he would, then Katharine would have to go to court and prove that he was unfit, mentally, physically, and morally. Agnes felt that Phil would not readily relinquish control because he had no position at all unless he was publisher of the *Post*, but Katharine thought that he would; she knew that he dreaded an open fight even more than she because he obviously could not win it.

A man with a debilitating mental illness is in danger of suicide if the things that make him what he is are lost. If he is very rich, he is able to buy the best medical help, but he frequently uses his position and money to avoid the effects of the therapy.

In early 1963, while the divorce proceedings were in process, Phil flew to Phoenix on a Gulfstream I, a ten-passenger executive jet that the *Post* leased from a charter service, and he put up, with Robin Webb, in a modest residence motel. When he had been there for several weeks, he called Katharine to ask that she send Lally out to see him, which Katharine flatly refused to do. Phoenix was soon the scene of a newspapermen's convention, to which Phil had not been invited. He got wind of it, appeared in the banquet room during a speech, grabbed the microphone, and drunkenly announced to the crowd, many of whom knew him, that he was going to tell

---

Advisor, Robinson Terminal Warehouse Corporation (newsprint warehousing), the Washington Post Writers Group (syndication), WJXT-TV (Jacksonville, Florida, a CBS affiliate), WPLG-TV (Miami, ABC), WFSB-TV (Hartford, CBS), Bowater Mersey Paper Company Ltd. (Nova Scotia, newsprint manufacturing), *International Herald-Tribune* (Paris), and the *Los Angeles Times/Washington Post* News Service.

them exactly who in Washington was sleeping with whom, beginning with President Kennedy. His favorite, screamed Phil, was now Mary Meyer, who had been married to CIA official Cord Meyer and was the sister of Ben Bradlee's wife, Tony. Mary lived in Ben Bradlee's carriage house, where she had her art studio, and Kennedy visited her there. Bradlee, Phil claimed, kept Kennedy's love letters from her, and from others, in a drawer. As Phil raged, one of the newsmen called Kennedy, who immediately called Katharine, wanting to know if, as a friend, there was anything he could do to bring Phil under control. The call came as Katharine was meeting with the *Post* executives in her home, planning to bring Phil back forcibly and commit him to a psychiatric hospital. She declined the president's offer; Kennedy had done enough. Phil's assistant James Truitt was neither so angry at Kennedy nor so proud. He took the phone and asked Kennedy to send Phil's doctor, Leslie Farber, to Phoenix on a military jet. Phil was brought back to the motel, where he was injected with a heavy sedative, and he was then taken to the airport in an ambulance.

The Gulfstream which had taken Phil to Phoenix in the early spring now carried Katharine Graham to the Phoenix airport. On board with her were John Sweeterman, who had the title of publisher, and Frederick Beebe, the *Post's* attorney and chairman of the board of the parent Washington Post Company. Katharine had little to say to the two men during the long flight. She was worried and sat biting her lip. She was also deliberate and calm.

The ambulance was waiting at the airport. Phil was carried out of it and placed in the Gulfstream jet. He was dressed in pajamas that were spotted with blood from a deep cut his nails had made in the face of one of his captors. After he had stopped struggling, when the sedative had taken effect, he had been bound in a straitjacket. On the flight back to Washington he lay quietly. He and Katharine did not talk. Robin

164

Webb went off separately. When Phil regained consciousness, he begged to be allowed to go to George Washington University Hospital, to which Eugene Meyer had donated nearly $1 million. Katharine obtained a court order committing him to Chestnut Lodge.

Chestnut Lodge lies on eight gently rolling acres in Rockville, a town in Maryland about fifteen miles outside Washington, and looks like a small college campus. There is a colonialstye main building that was once an old hotel, four apartment-dormitories that house altogether eighty patients, two suites of doctors' offices, a recreation area, which gives the sanitarium a clubby atmosphere, student nurses' residence, and several lovely stone houses which the most dedicated doctors inhabit. There are oak trees, dirt pathways, asphalt roads, fields for team sports, and openings to a residential street in Rockville that are not barred. Most of the patients are young, almost youths, with a chance to get well and begin their lives again. Phil Graham was one of the oldest patients there; he had already had his chance at life and had lost it.

Chestnut Lodge is one of the most expensive psychiatric hospitals in the country: it cost more than $1,500 per month in 1963, when Phil was there; $4,860 per month today. It is also one of the finest. It was the first hospital that did *not* use electric shock or lobotomy in the treatment of psychoses, those disorders that Sigmund Freud, who treated neuroses, thought to be "inaccesible as yet to psychoanalytic method." Dr. Frieda Fromm-Reichmann, a student of Freud's, lived and worked at Chestnut Lodge for twenty-two years after her emigration from Nazi Germany. Fromm-Reichmann made psychosis "accessible to psychoanalytic method" by using classical psychoanalysis, which addresses the intellect, with an added sensitivity to emotional reaction. She herself was "highly sensitive," wrote a colleague, "—otherwise she could not have accompanied her patients so fully into the depths of despair, into the horror of loneliness, into the frantic impulses of destructive rage." She recorded her work painstakingly: her efforts to dissolve the "patient's fear of his own unbearable malevolence," to alleviate "intense anxieties and guilt feelings," to "collaborate" with the patient to "reconstruct" the "disintegrated personality," to "form a bridge between him and those sectors of reality from which he had withdrawn" * —and when she died in 1957, the literature she had created on schizophrenia and manic depression continued to guide the work at Chestnut Lodge.

Phil entered the sanitarium only six years after her death, his family expecting that he would receive sophisticated and sympathetic care. His case, however, was complicated by his ability to play people off against each other, making it difficult for his two doctors, John Cameron (on the staff of Chestnut Lodge) and Leslie Farber, to provide him with consistent treatment. Farber, though he was not on the Chestnut staff, was a distinguished member of the faculty at the Washington School of Psychiatry and was therefore not to be lightly brushed off. He was, at his insistence, allowed to share responsibility with Cameron, presumably with Katharine's consent. The case of Philip Graham is now legendary in psychiatric circles.

John Cameron worked to build a tenuous "transference" with Phil, a relationship in which Phil would trust him enough to begin to act out his guilt and fears. Thus could the doctor begin to treat them, although, because Phil was already badly "deteriorated," with only limited chance of success. The initial stages of therapy concerned Phil's inability to adjust to institutional life—going through channels, respecting symbols of power that he considered inauthentic or primitive, obeying ward rules and medical orders, enduring a monotonous daily routine, fitting in with the other patients, whose society he called the "sewing circle." This acting-out did indeed tell

---

* Editorial note by Dr. Edith Weigert in Fromm-Reichmann, *Psychoanalysis and Psychotherapy*, p. vii.

Cameron what he wanted to know about Phil: his need always to be outside, or at the top of, every hierarchy; but it made Cameron, who was keeping him down, the enemy. Phil expended a great deal of energy charming the nurses, lending money to the staff aides, making them love him, trying to bribe them for weekend passes. Alternately, he stayed in bed for days and spoke to no one. Cameron told Katharine to encourage visitors, but most of his old friends felt too sorry for him to make the trip; they would not know how to act or what to say. One of the few who did visit him was Robert McNamara, the secretary of defense, whose kindness Katharine remembered and who later was given editorial support when he was criticized for his role in the Vietnam war. McNamara sat on the edge of Phil's bed and just gossiped, told him jokes, treated him as if he were normal. His attention "restored fire to Phil's eye," * one of McNamara's biographers recorded, and made his last days a little happier. It eased the immediate danger of suicide, which with self-destructive patients it is the doctor's first and most important duty to prevent.

Leslie Farber was a more eclectic thinker than Cameron and saw suicide in its philosophic dimension. The suicidal person, it seems from Farber's writings, is guilty of egotism. "The absurdity and pathos of the life of suicide," Farber reasons, "stem from the despairer's will to achieve—through suicide—his status as a moral human being. . . . Even the extent of the despairer's suffering must be witnessed and authenticated by suicide. Repeatedly, he announces to himself that his state is unbearable. But, should he be challenged on this score [by the therapist]—that is, how is he to know what is and what is not bearable for himself, in other words, what gives him this godlike certainty?—his answer, to himself at least, is that it must be unbearable, otherwise he would not be thinking of

* Henry L. Trewhitt, *McNamara* (New York: Harper & Row, 1971).

suicide. In solitude this answer appears unassailable to the despairer. In fact, it may happen that the act of suicide seems to have become necessary to demonstrate how unendurable his pain is, in which case he commits suicide in order to prove it unendurable. Here, the despairer takes his own life to prove that he is not responsible for taking his own life. By definition, what is unendurable cannot be endured; therefore his suicide is not a matter of choice but an externally determined response to a situation that has deprived him of choice. The flaw in this construct, of course, is that his definition of his condition as unendurable is very much a matter of choice, and, thus, obviously, so is his suicide." * Farber says that suicide is "moral grotesquerie." Nowhere in his literature, however, is there a consideration of why a person comes to feel, rightly or wrongly, that his life is unendurable to him, or how, other than cynically, the therapist should respond in order to save the "despairer's" life.

Bill Meyer lamented to Katharine that being unpredictable to himself was an intolerable idea to Phil; but that did not excuse the possibility of poor medical judgment. Bill concluded that the suicide had been a tragedy—in the literal sense of the word, he said. Agnes told friends that "for Phil it was the last straw to be locked up with a lot of lunatics [and] he took the brave way out."

Death preoccupied Phil all that spring. Three times, with permission to leave Chestnut, he visited Edward Bennett Williams to rewrite his will, each time reducing Katharine's share of his estate. On the second visit he demanded that Williams burn the first will. On the third, he had him burn the second. These wills rescinded and superseded a carefully thought-out document of long standing, one that provided trust funds for his children and gave the bulk of his estate to his wife. After he died, during probate, Katharine's lawyer challenged the legal-

* Farber, "despair and the life of suicide," in *lying, despair, jealousy . . .* , pp. 79–81.

ity of the last will. The probate proceeding enabled Katharine to take control of the *Post* with no significant legal problems, although with the discredited will not on the public record, it is not known whom Phil might have designated in her place. Manic depressives frequently plan their deaths on the anniversary of a significant event; Saturday, August 3, 1963, was the fifteenth anniversary of the formation of the Washington Post Company, the umbrella corporation for the *Post* and other properties, in which Katharine and Philip Graham were sole partners. On the morning of August 3, Phil telephoned Katharine from Chestnut Lodge and said that he was feeling much better. He asked if he could spend the weekend with her on their farm. Katharine called Joe Rauh and told him happily, "Phil is better! He's coming home! Why don't you come over and see him on Tuesday?" On Monday he would spend the day with the children. She picked him up at Chestnut Lodge that morning and they drove to a small Virginia town called Warrenton, in Fauquier County, forty-two miles southwest of Washington, in the Virginia hunt country. The farm, Glen Welby, was that of a gentleman and weekend hunter, equipped with television and telephones, books and paintings, shotguns for hunting deer and rifles for quail-shooting parties, horses, servants, a large, well-stocked kitchen and bar. Katharine and Phil spent some time together, and then Katharine took a nap. Phil went downstairs and sat on the edge of the bathtub and shot himself in the head.

Fame and obscurity, the future and the past. "Katharine has been so really brave," Bill Meyer wrote to Agnes, who at the time of Phil's death was cruising on the Black Sea, "so thoughtful and considerate of others (and there were *many* others) that I can't really describe it to you. She and all the children—Lally & Donny especially—were just first-rate in every respect. They have set an example of courage that you will hear about." On Monday, August 5, Katharine went before the board of directors of the *Post* and "spoke briefly

& to the point," Bill wrote, "in respect to her intention of carrying on 'as is' & in the spirit & principle of her father & husband. She did a superb job,—just wonderful and it was very reassuring to everyone. . . . Of course all the Wash. Post are behind Kay." After she left the meeting, Bill told the men that the Meyer family fortune was in back of Katharine's publishership. Later in the day, Alfred Friendly and Russell Wiggins, in a gratuitous gesture, let the sole owner of the *Washington Post* know that they really did want her to be their boss.

After a showy public funeral, Katharine met her mother on the yacht on the Aegean Sea. They visited Rumania, Turkey, Greece, Bulgaria, and Russia and met the leader of Russia, "I mean Mr. K.," said Agnes, "who was at his dacha on the Black Sea." Katharine interviewed political leaders. She interviewed Khrushchev. She found, only days after Phil's death, that she was still a natural journalist, as he had been.

But who had he been? A man whose family exactly duplicated the conditions necessary to produce manic-depressive psychosis: a family of outcasts, living outside the social fabric (in the swamps), thinking of themselves as tightly knit but without emotion, functioning as an economic unit; the father unwilling to recognize the brilliance and sensitivity of his oldest child, whom he used as an economic asset (taking him out of college to drive trucks); the mother looking to the oldest child to attain the recognition that the father had not, and then dying while the child was still young. The Meyer family had loved Phil, but his script, it now seems, had been written in advance.

☆ **11** ☆

Katharine's Wars

Katharine became a very different newspaper publisher from
Phil. Acutely aware of her less engaging personality, her less
dazzling intellect, she cultivated a management style that was
the opposite of his: logical rather than intuitive, methodical
rather than sporadic and inspired, technical rather than general, and more rigid, more principled, more politically naive.
In this manner she guided the *Post* through the most turbulent
dozen years in recent American history—supporting the Vietnam war; neither liking nor understanding the radical sixties;
crying when Lyndon Johnson refused to run for reelection;
disliking Richard Nixon and publishing stories about him
that brought about his downfall; creating her own fame. Because of Watergate, Katharine Graham is known as a "great"
publisher, one who has mastered the contradiction between
corporate interests and public service.

The shock of widowhood was diminished by her husband's
long illness, which had allowed her to prepare for life without
him, but she still felt what all widows feel: numb, lonely, and
confused. When the numbness faded, there was sadness, pain,
anger, and guilt; she had the paper only because her husband
was dead.

According to many psychiatrists, a widow grieves for up to two years, during which time she sees few people, does little, and thinks about the futility of life. This mourning period is a necessary and healthy part of the recovery process; by allowing herself to experience the enormous pain of a loved one's death, the widow learns to accept death and becomes able to love again. Katharine has never gotten over Phil. She escaped some of the feelings of the mourning period by frantic activity, dedicating herself to the *Post* and to her children; now every summer, near the anniversary of his death, she becomes depressed. She still has tears in her eyes when she talks about him; and although men like her, she has remained uninvolved, as if she were still married to him. "When Phil died," she once said, "I had to choose between another husband or running the newspaper and remaining a monk." Before leaving for her Aegean Sea cruise, Katharine buried Phil in Oak Hill Cemetery, a small, wooded graveyard directly across the street from her Georgetown house. He was just inside the gate, near the fence, at a site she could see from her bedroom window. It was marked only with a two-foot-high rectangular stone of gray granite, engraved simply:

PHILIP L. GRAHAM
1915–1963

These same words still appear daily on the *Washington Post* masthead, under "Eugene Meyer, 1875–1959."

All that first autumn, while starting to relearn the *Post*'s operation, she was subjected to the probate proceeding, an unpleasant affair in the best of circumstances, and complicated in this case by the wills that Phil had drawn with Edward Bennett Williams. The register of wills quickly ruled that these later wills revoked the well-drawn will that Phil had made in 1957; since they had been destroyed, Phil had effectively died intestate, leaving his wife and children to fight each other for pieces of his estate. Most important, to Katharine, he had left 7,889 shares of class-A *Washington Post* stock, which did not now go automatically to her. Under the 1957 will, Katharine had been guaranteed 100 percent of this stock; in his two later wills, Phil had reduced her share of the stock and then reduced it again. The final will would have left her enough stock to bring her own holdings up to 55 percent, a controlling interest in the *Post* but not an absolute one. The absence of any will, however, meant that the *Post* stock would be distributed according to the terms of the 1948 trust agreement that had created the Washington Post Company: all of Phil's shares would go to his children. Katharine's interests would therefore best be served if the court accepted his 1957 will as his real will, while the children's interests would technically be served if the court did not accept it. A hearing on the matter, however, would have had to include a discussion, on the public record, of Phil's mental condition, which Katharine wanted to avoid. "Under the circumstances," wrote the register of wills in his recommendation to the judge, Joseph McGarraghy, "and particularly considering the fact that a contest over the 1957 will would place the mother and the children in the embarrassing situation of entering into a contest with each other, which all parties desire to prevent, it is proposed to enter into a compromise agreement."

In the compromise with her children's lawyer, James F. Reilly, who had been appointed by the court to be their guardian for the duration of the action, Katharine traded her children her own interest in Phil's trust, over $1 million, for all of the 7,889 shares of *Washington Post* stock. Their trusts were increased from $.5 million to $1.5 million, and they could receive the income immediately instead of waiting until Katharine's death, although, the court noted, "all of the minors are independently wealthy from other sources." Katharine, who did not need money, was awarded, in addition to the stock, a token marital inheritance of $500, which she took in the form of three paintings. She would have bargained for *Post* stock no matter what its value, but as it happened, the shares were worth $382 apiece, or a total of more than $3 million. They also represented a new life, fame, greatness, power.

Power is the ability to command men and resources, greatness the ability to use them wisely. Both have become negotiable concepts; people attribute these characteristics to one another, for achievements of varying degrees. In politics they mean the capacity for independent leadership; in business, the creation of an efficient corporate machine. A publisher has corporate concerns and public concerns and is conscious as well of "the essential oneness" * of the corporate interests and the strategic interests of the state.

At the University of Chicago, Katharine saw politics as a radical, theoretical, critical, analytical process that works against the government; students wanted power to keep the government's power in check. During her marriage she adopted the views of many Washington wives: if a politician is your friend, his actions and motives are usually honorable; if he is not, they are suspect. The rule was to be social, familiar, charming, accepting, deferential, feminine, and to leave the harsh realities of politics to the men.

The women's world was at once inane and brutal, but it permitted a kind of innocence. Katharine once went to a party at the exclusive F Street Club, where she wore a new gray dress. A friend came up to her and said that the dress was very pretty but would Katharine please wear her yellow dress the following Friday night at the friend's dinner for the Robert Lovetts. Lovett was a former secretary of state, former secretary of defense, Wall Street banker, the man who

* Bernard Baruch.

had advised President Kennedy to hire Robert McNamara and Dean Rusk; and he liked yellow.

Another time Katharine gave a small family dinner that included columnists Walter Lippmann and Joseph Alsop, who had an argument. It had been vaguely about Western Europe, Katharine recalled, and fur flew all over the place. On yet another occasion she and Phil had one hundred people to cocktails, among whom were most of the members of the Atomic Energy Commission. One of them was a funny little man who went around pinching all the women; but he was *the* expert on isotopes, and he was, Katharine felt, entitled. The subject of isotopes had recently been taken up in a series of *Post* editorials, the controversy being that atomic energy commissioner Lewis Strauss had made public his dissent against an AEC plan to ship radioactive materials to Europe. Sentiment was against Lewis, who had violated protocol; Katharine joined others in believing that he should have kept his dissent a secret. Felix Frankfurter also spoke to the problem at one of the "seminar-luncheons" that Katharine hosted at the *Post*. Frankfurter took that opportunity to label Strauss's action a "pretentious disclosure," after which the controversy grew more intense, and the isotope men, in the interest of truth, became hot new party guests.

For twenty-three years Katharine had been a society woman with an ordinary intellect, not a promising candidate, in the view of the *Post* editors, for the game of mediapolitics. But she had the strength to do what most women or men would not have done: to learn a new way of thinking at the age of forty-six. That strength came from her family. So strong was the force of the family, as Katharine once told her mother and father, that she and her sisters and brothers had all passed through at least one phase of rejection until they were able to live with the fact that the family was sometimes accepted, sometimes rejected, depending upon their parents' activities at the time. That seemed to Katharine, in hindsight, to be a better way to grow up than most and meant that the family was a source of comfort to all of them.

Having known radical theory and conformist social ritual, Katharine now had to learn to understand and manage power. Her first lesson was with the men who ran the newspaper, an old-boy group who had worked without direction from the onset of Phil's illness and showed an immediate incapacity to take her authority seriously. The mysterious ways that men, particularly newsmen, cement their friendships, helped along by Scotch, cigarettes, and girlie pictures coming in over the wire, produced a vision that allowed them to mistake femininity and shyness for weakness. She was a female animal, "a shaky little doe on wobbly legs coming in out of the forest." She was a child, "a new girl in school," a silly "girl reporter," who apologized that she did not want to bother them with her questions, whereupon they told her "good, don't."

They had many secrets and met after hours in wood-paneled restaurants to discuss what she should and should not be told. There were special arrangements with officials that gave the *Post* its advantage in predicting and interpreting events to the public: inside information in exchange for sympathetic treatment of the government's position. If Katharine were aware of these complexities, the editors fretted, her enthusiasm for the government's cause might lead her to make the trades too cheaply; or, alternatively, she might invoke the ideal of journalistic independence and demand that the collaborations stop. "It was on this business that he had come to talk," wrote President Eisenhower's national security adviser Robert Cutler about *Post* columnist Joseph Alsop. "He spoke of 'confidants' in the press whom former Presidents had used to create a favorable background and of the benefit derived from that relationship. Such a person, trusted by a President, could provide an anonymous channel to help shape public opinion. I listened attentively. In 'our' case, he went on, there could be a much closer relation of confidence. His family's tradition was Republican. He and I had known each other during his college days and had shared good times. . . . Naturally, he did not contemplate that I would reveal anything of a secret nature. But by periodically outlining background material I could provide enough orientation to make his column an authoritative, but of course anonymous, spokesman for the President without the world being aware of the source of the background. While there was no mention of 'exclusive,' I sensed that Joe anticipated such a sensible arrangement." *

Alsop was one of the men at the *Post*, when Katharine started there, who took for granted that such "arrangements" serve all interests: officials have a forum for their views, newsmen have their sources, and readers have their opinions shaped. Alsop had been a minor columnist until World War II, when he joined the navy. He was sent to India, where he became part of a semiofficial, semimilitary outfit called the American Volunteer Group, or the Flying Tigers, run by a retired general named Claire Lee Chennault. General Chennault organized air defenses for Chiang Kai-shek in 1941; in 1942 he was returned to active military service and competed with General Joseph Stilwell for primacy of command of American forces in China. Alsop appeared on General Chennault's personal staff, as speechwriter, letter writer, and public relations aide, in 1943.

The Flying Tigers was in part an intelligence operation, opposed to Stilwell's even-handed treatment of the Nationalist and Communist armies, and Alsop was its propaganda arm. He supported Chennault "fanatically." He was "literate, excitable, and persuasive with just enough superficial acquaintance with the situation to be opinionated and to appear knowledgeable." Alsop wanted President Roosevelt to replace

* Robert Cutler, *No Time for Rest* (Boston: Atlantic–Little, Brown, 1965), pp. 317–18.

Stilwell with Chennault. He wrote repeatedly to Harry Hopkins, Roosevelt's special assistant, promoting Chennault's cause, asserting that Stilwell's command was "a national tragedy . . . a national scandal . . . grossly dishonoring to President, Army, and country," * and helping to bring about Stilwell's removal from command in 1944. Later, in 1951, Alsop testified against Stilwell in front of the Senate Internal Security Committee, blaming him for the fact that Mao's Red Army had defeated Chiang Kai-shek in 1949.

Alsop's link to intelligence made his journalistic career secure. After the war his columns became more informed, opinionated, anti-Communist, doomsaying, and were understood to reflect official voices. He went on fact-finding trips for the newly formed CIA, which had absorbed the Flying Tigers, making him a very early Mockingbird. He has said, in defense of his activities, which he does not deny, that "the notion that a newspaperman doesn't have a duty to his country is perfect balls." Phil Graham brought him to the *Post* in 1958.

The theories of intelligence and propaganda (two aspects of the same activity: information handling for political ends) that were developed in the twenties and thirties were tested and refined during World War II and coincidentally molded the men who put the theories into practice. Some of these men were the editors that Philip Graham had hired to run the *Post*, men who, like Alsop, understood the role of information in promoting the national interest. James Russell Wiggins, the executive editor, had been an instructor at the Army Air Force Intelligence School, training officers, including Phil himself, in cable interception, code-breaking, enemy disinformation, a background that sensitized him not to the journalist's absolute duty to publish, but to the dilemma, as he entitled his book, of *Freedom or Secrecy*.† Chalmers Roberts, the na-

---

* Barbara Tuchman, *Stilwell and the American Experience in China* (New York: Macmillan, 1971), pp. 339, 358.
† New York: Oxford University Press, 1964.

tional affairs editor, had been a communications specialist in the Pentagon, part of the "brotherhood of communications intelligence specialists," in the jargon, where he intercepted and deciphered Japanese cables, one of the most sensitive jobs of the war. Membership in the "brotherhood" endowed Roberts with a permanent trust; he knew, and as a newsman never revealed, the details of Truman's decision to drop the atomic bomb on Hiroshima; he was the expert on diplomatic affairs at the *Post* precisely because he knew what not to tell the public.

The Office of War Information was one of two early agencies specifically built upon the new information theories. The other was the Economic Cooperation Administration, created after the war by the Smith-Mundt Act of 1948 to promote "worldwide cultural information." The names Smith and Mundt stand with that of Nixon in sponsorship of laws in the late forties that were the darkest side of our postwar Cold Warriorism. To fight Communists within the United States, this team pursued passage of laws that required fingerprinting and registration of aliens (the Smith Act); tried to outlaw sedition (the Mundt-Nixon Bill); and established both an attorney general's list and internment camps for subversives (the McCarran Act, pushed through jointly by McCarran, Mundt, and Nixon and incorporating the provisions of the failed sedition bill). The laws had a degree of popular support, for Nixon had known then how to use the press. Conceived by these minds, the "worldwide cultural information" that was to be perpetrated first on Europe, from Marshall Plan headquarters in Paris, involved agents posing as journalists who planted inflammatory stories in European newspapers; they posed as labor union men and incited "Communist" riots. The purpose of such activities was to create additional, "deeper" support for the Marshall Plan by provoking anti-Communist backlash. ECA, which administered Smith-Mundt funds, also used Paris embassy personnel as if they were ECA staff, including Benjamin Bradlee and E. Howard Hunt, the latter a CIA agent who was in turn using the embassy as cover. Presiding over these Byzantine affairs, as director of overseas information for the ECA, was Alfred Friendly, a newsman, whom Katharine Graham later encountered as the managing editor of the *Post*.

The wartime privilege that the *Post* editors had in helping to shape national security policy became a taste, a habit, and a world view. They were an informational elite who moved naturally into defining national security issues throughout the Cold War (and later for most of the Vietnam war), always by the same three measures: American cultural dominance, American military dominance, communism as a threat to the American way of life. They were sincere in saying that the news process is free, equally sincere in believing that national security items must be managed. The absence of sustained intellectual inquiry disqualifies these contradictory views as a dialectic; one is a myth, the other a prejudice supported by the same assumption that guided their war work, that information is a tool for the elite in manipulating the masses.

The information theories developed in stages, modifying and then perverting the original reason for a free American press: that an enlightened citizenry is a political necessity in a democracy; that information is a citizen's power. In 1925 this basic tenet was attacked by a political scientist named Walter Lippmann, later a *Post* columnist, who wrote a book called *The Phantom Public* in which he "demolished whatever illusion existed that 'the public' could be regarded as a . . . collectivity equipped to decide the affairs of state." * His argument, extended over the years in other books, was circular. In 1925 he said that "average men" exhaust their energies earning a living and do not need to be told about

* New York: Harcourt, Brace, 1925. The comment is by another political scientist, V. O. Key.

public matters. In 1955, in *The Public Philosophy*, he lamented that "average men" could not learn enough "by glancing at newspapers" and insisted that decisions ought to be left to those with "experience and seasoned judgment." The "duality of function" between elite and masses is quite natural, he added, having "a certain resemblance to that of the two sexes. In the act of reproduction each sex has an unalterable function. If this function is confused with the function of the other sex, the result is sterility and disorder." * Lippmann worried too that disorder would result if "average men" were free to speak, think, and criticize, a contention that he hoped would prove that the "average man" does not care about politics, but which in fact proved the opposite.

Lippmann's seminal writings set the intellectual framework for other theorists, who were then able to "tackle empirically the real issue—what kinds of publics exist for what sort of messages?"—a line of thinking that accepted Lippmann's ideas as truth. The argument was first taken up by Harold Lasswell, also a political scientist, who wrote a book curiously entitled *Psychopathology and Politics* † in which he reaffirmed that superior information is the elite's power and admonished them to exercise it with "prowess." They were, Lasswell told them, to use "communication in the achievement of preventive politics," a condition whereby the elite accept the "burden" of social administration and save the public from issues that "would be detrimental to [its] interest." The elite save the public by withholding information from it. Additionally, Lasswell said that one of the tasks of the communications specialist is "surveillance of the environment" to find the preconceptions of the audience so that "messages" can be slanted appropriately.

Lasswell's work stimulated research on audiences, out of which grew the field of motivation research, the basis for both

* Boston: Little, Brown, 1955, p. 31.
† Chicago: University of Chicago Press, 1930.

propaganda and advertising. The "father of Madison Avenue" was a sociologist, Bernard Berelson, who designed a method for "content analysis" of informational messages that allowed communicators to achieve more specific and predictable results. His colleague Paul Lazarsfeld, a German émigré, conducted studies for the government in the 1930s on the psychological responses of radio audiences, a continuation of the motivation research he had contributed to German social science which was later turned to the benefit of Adolf Hitler. These American studies were most immediately of commercial interest, to help advertisers sell to consumers, but they, like the German, soon became the foundation for wartime propaganda agencies, the Armed Forces Radio Network and the Office of War Information, and after the war ECA's Voice of America and the CIA's Radio Free Europe and Radio Liberty.

Gearing messages to different audiences and putting out information to evoke certain psychological responses are techniques that are not easily unlearned. The role that the *Post* men had played in creating consent for government policies was one that they continued to play at the *Post,* with class consciousness but without self-consciousness. They were so completely the products of the information theories that they could see the world no differently, let alone explain their system of thinking to Katharine Graham. Alfred Friendly from ECA, Chalmers Roberts from the Pentagon, Russell Wiggins from the Intelligence School at Harrisburg, understanding themselves to be the elite, ran a newspaper that had a startling coincidence of interest with the government, a situation augmented by their ownership of nonvoting *Post* stock, which Phil had offered to eighteen executives in 1952 in place of a pension plan. The stock encouraged them to think of the *Post* as their company. Their dedication, despite the low salaries, had enabled Phil to build the *Post* into the money-making corporation that it was when he died; but it also put

Katharine in the position of confronting a group of near-millionaires with the claim that the *Post* was hers, not theirs, while they jealously guarded their prerogatives as owner-managers.

The *Post* was in many ways like other "companies," as Walter Lippmann called the news organizations, fighting deadlines, living uneasily with unions, suffering with "technical conditions [that] do not favor genuine and productive debate." But the *Post* was also unique among news companies in that its managers, living and working in Washington, thought of themselves simultaneously as journalists, businessmen, and patriots, a state of mind that made them singularly able to expand the company while promoting the national interest. Their individual relations with intelligence had in fact been the reason that the Post Company had grown as fast as it did after the war; their secrets were its corporate secrets, beginning with MOCKINGBIRD. Philip Graham's commitment to intelligence gave his friends Frank Wisner and Allen Dulles an interest in helping to make the *Washington Post* the dominant news vehicle in Washington, which they did by assisting with its two most crucial acquisitions, the *Times-Herald* and WTOP. The *Post* men most essential to these transactions, other than Phil, were Wayne Coy, the *Post* executive who had been Phil's former New Deal boss, and John S. Hayes, who replaced Coy in 1947 when Coy was appointed chairman of the Federal Communications Commission.

It worked like this. Hayes had been commander of the Armed Forces Radio Network ETO (European Theater of Operations) and in that capacity had made intelligence connections all over Europe. He came to the *Post*, after turning the network to the service of the Marshall Plan, with the title of vice-president for radio and television. In Washington he became friendly with Frank Wisner, father of MOCKINGBIRD, and with Allen Dulles, an OSS man who became the second director of the new CIA in 1953. The relationship with Dulles was particularly important because of Dulles's ties to Wall Street, from which intelligence, industry, and government all draw their leaders, the men who form this country's ruling clique. Between 1937 and 1943, when he joined the OSS, Dulles had been a director of the Schroeder Bank, which, in Germany, had misjudged the oneness of corporate and national interests to the extent of helping to finance Hitler, because he promised to stabilize the German economy. From his membership in the tiny merchant banking community, which includes at any time only about a hundred active partners distributed among the Morgan, Lazard, Rothschild, Hambros, and Baring houses, Dulles knew and respected former Lazard associate Eugene Meyer. From his corporate law work at Sullivan and Cromwell, the preeminent foreign policy law firm in America, Dulles was close to Post Company attorney Frederick S. Beebe at Cravath, Swaine, and Moore, another foreign policy firm. A quiet, thoughtful man, Beebe had been recruited out of Yale, 1938, by Cravath senior partner Roswell Gilpatric, later the assistant secretary of defense under Robert McNamara during the Vietnam war. At Cravath, Beebe had been assigned to handle estate planning and other legal affairs for the Meyer family and eventually became their chief corporate as well as personal counsel, representing their interests in every significant transaction over three decades, including the legally complex, monopolistic acquisition of the *Times-Herald* in 1954.

The merger was critical for Katharine's family, confirming their power and influence in Washington and making the paper financially "safe enough for [her son] Donny." It was also critical to Hayes, Phil Graham, Beebe, Wisner, and Dulles, men who had a political interest in her family's newspaper, because the *Times-Herald* maintained a bank of dossiers that it routinely made available to the FBI, the CIA's rival in domestic Cold War intelligence. When Colonel McCormick decided to sell his nearly bankrupt Washington

The Meyers' Mount Kisco estate in Westchester County, New York.

Picnic at the Mount Kisco estate, 1912—
left to right: J. B. Kerfoot, Agnes Meyer,
Mrs. Alfred Stieglitz, Alfred Stieglitz,
Paul Haviland, Abraham Walkowitz,
Katharine Rhoades, John Marin.
Archives of American Art, Smithsonian
Institution, Abraham Walkowitz Papers.

A sketch by Agnes Ernst Meyer in
Alfred Stieglitz's *291* magazine
(published between March 1915 and
February 1916). Notes to the printer
are in Stieglitz's handwriting.

Eugene Meyer, 1937.
Wide World Photos.

Agnes Meyer, 1945.
Wide World Photos.

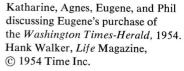

Katharine, Agnes, Eugene, and Phil discussing Eugene's purchase of the *Washington Times-Herald,* 1954. Hank Walker, *Life* Magazine, © 1954 Time Inc.

Phil and Katharine on board the liner *United States,* sailing to Europe in 1956. United Press Photo.

Phil Graham testifying on December 11, 1956, before a special Senate committee investigating lobbying and political influence. Wide World Photos.

Elizabeth Graham and Yann Weymouth
leaving the U.S. Navy Chapel
in Washington after their wedding
on November 28, 1964.
Wide World Photos.

Donny and his bride,
Mary Wissler, at the
Bond Chapel at the
University of Chicago
on their wedding day in
1967. Wide World Photos.

Katharine at Truman Capote's
Masked Ball in her honor at the
Grand Ballroom of the Plaza Hotel
in New York City, November 29, 1966.
Associated Press Photos.

Katharine and Ben Bradlee
outside the U.S. District Court
in Washington, D.C.,
after the ruling that the *Post*
could publish further Pentagon
Papers. Wide World Photos.

Katharine with Bob Woodward (right) and Carl Bernstein at the *Post* in 1973.
Magnum Photos © 1973 Mark Godfrey.

Katharine with grandchildren Pamela
(with glasses) and Katharine Weymouth at a
broadcasting meeting at the RCA building
in New York City. Wide World Photos.

Richard Ober, arriving to testify
before the Rockefeller Commission on
alleged domestic spying by
the CIA (1975). Wide World Photos.

newspaper, he asked Eugene Meyer the price of $8.5 million for it, about three times its worth. John Hayes went to Chicago in March 1954 to make the initial payment in cash.

The merger drove up the value of the *Post* stock and made the executives richer. It also increased the CIA's access to information, news sources, and cooperative newsmen, to the benefit of MOCKINGBIRD, which Frank Wisner had been expanding throughout the Cold War. As early as 1948 he had become fascinated with the possibilities of broadcasting in addition to his program for print journalists and had conceived of two "private" broadcasting companies, Radio Free Europe and Radio Liberty, that would monitor ("surveill") information transmittals from within Communist countries in Europe. The information that the stations would pick up would serve two purposes: to enhance Wisner's intelligence network, and to form the basis of programs that would be broadcast to "the captive peoples of Europe." He promoted his idea by organizing "citizens' committees" in New York and Washington, which placed advertisements in newspapers asking for donations to pay for the stations' programming. Wisner's dream was realized in 1949 when Wayne Coy, in his capacity as FCC chairman, attended the World Administrative Radio Conference in Paris, where he negotiated to set up relay stations for Free Europe and Liberty in Germany and Portugal. While in Paris, Coy lived at the elegant Hotel Continental, temporary home of many Americans working for the Marshall Plan; and he and Phil Graham carried on an interesting correspondence. "I am glad to hear that you are getting the Post," Phil wrote in July of that year, "and I shall pass this information along to our efficient ———— [the CIA agent who delivered the *Post* to Coy daily]. Your suggestion about destruction of the files when parties are found loyal is probably theoretically all right, but practically I think perpetuation of the files, for some time at least, is one of the evils inherent in a world where Communist conspiracy exists." In 1950 Radio Free Europe and

Radio Liberty established headquarters in Munich and began broadcasting to Poland, Czechoslovakia, Hungary, Rumania, and Bulgaria. In 1976 the board of directors of the two stations appointed as its chairman former Post Company vice-president for radio and television John S. Hayes.

Hayes had been able to contribute to Post Company broadcasting largely because of his wartime acquaintance with Colonel William S. Paley, the founder and chairman of the board of CBS. Paley was a businessman who believed that the commercial media, as well as the military, must develop "all manner of propaganda" to help in the war effort; Hayes was the director of a radio network that was the military extension of Paley's commercial network. When Hayes came to the *Post*, which then owned only one local radio station, he looked to Paley, who owned a Washington outlet, as the company's entrée into national broadcasting.

Paley's own friendship with Allen Dulles is now known to have been one of the most influential and significant in the communications industry; he provided cover for CIA agents, supplied out takes of news film, debriefed reporters, and in many ways set the standard for future cooperation between the CIA and the major broadcast companies. But in 1948, despite the mutual intelligence connections, when Hayes and Graham asked to buy WTOP-CBS radio, Paley refused to sell. Within a year, though, an arrangement was worked out, Dulles having spoken of Graham and Hayes to Paley, and 55 percent of the WTOP stock was transferred to the Post Company. Wayne Coy at the FCC approved the license reassignment, and CBS and the *Post* began sharing their Washington news staffs (reporters then worked interchangeably for print and broadcast). In 1950 Phil bought a small Washington television station, license approved by Wayne Coy, and changed its call letters to WTOP-TV; it became a CBS affiliate. That year he and Hayes hired a news analyst who for two years after the war had been chief correspondent for United Press International in Moscow, a man who had experience with American intelligence and was also endowed with a good television presence; the man's name was Walter Cronkite. He soon worked his way onto the network staff.

Paley sold the remaining WTOP stock to Phil in 1953, a year before Wayne Coy died, giving the *Post* complete control over the CBS radio and television outlets in Washington. The *Post* men continued to see Paley and Cronkite every. Christmas at a dinner given by Allen Dulles at a private club quixotically named the Alibi. The club is in an old, dark red brick townhouse in the middle of downtown Washington, the only house on a block of office buildings. It bears a simple brass plaque and brass doorknob; membership is limited to men in or close to intelligence and is by invitation only.

There was no need for Katharine, who admitted that she came by the paper "through matrimony and patrimony" rather than merit, to understand either the philosophy or the particular arrangements that characterized the *Washington Post* in 1963. She needed simply not to sell the paper, not to ask questions, so that the executives could continue their control. President Kennedy had warned the American Newspaper Publishers Association on April 27, 1961, one week after the failure of his Bay of Pigs invasion, reports of which Katharine had watched on television with her mother at Crescent Place, that "in time of war, the government and the press have customarily joined in an effort, based largely on self-discipline, to prevent unauthorized disclosures to the enemy. In times of clear and present danger, the courts have held that even the privileged rights of the First Amendment must yield to the public's need for national security.

"Today no war has been declared—and however fierce the struggle may be, it may never be declared in the traditional fashion. Our way of life is under attack. Those who make themselves our enemy are advancing around the globe. The survival of our friends is in danger. And yet no war has been declared, no borders have been crossed by marching troops, no missiles have been fired.

"If the press is waiting for a declaration of war before it imposes the self-discipline of combat conditons, then I can only say that no war has ever imposed a greater threat to our security. If you are awaiting a find of 'clear and present danger,' then I can only say that the danger has never been more clear and its presence has never been more imminent. . . ."

This philosophy had remained in force through all of Kennedy's crises, effective not because it intimidated the newsmen but because it made the flattering suggestion to passive men that they could have an active role in helping the president to do his difficult job. Kennedy exploited that desire during the Berlin crisis, when he took the Grahams with him to the Berlin Wall, where they all cried; and during the Cuban missile crisis, when Kennedy asked Phil, while Katharine's mother raged against the secrecy of the "inner ring," not to publish the fact of American troop movements before he presented his ultimatum to Khrushchev. After Phil's death he exploited it further, by using the resources of Katharine's newspaper for a strictly political task. Without asking Katharine, Kennedy appointed John Hayes, still the *Post*'s vice-president for radio and television, to a secret CIA task force that was to explore methods of beaming American propaganda broadcasts to Communist China. The other members of the team were Richard Salant, president of CBS News; Zbigniew Brzezinski, a professor at Columbia University who had been on the agency payroll for several years; Cord Meyer of the CIA; McGeorge Bundy, special assistant to the president for national security; Leonard Marks, director of the USIA; Bill Moyers, later special assistant to the president and now a CBS correspondent; and Paul Henze,* the CIA chief of station in Ethiopia who had established secret communications capabilities there and who now works on African problems for Brzezinski in the Carter White House. Hayes's concern for Katharine's authority was such that he did not tell her, or ask her, but he did clear his participation in the project, which was activated in late 1964, with Frederick Beebe,† who had given up law at Phil's request to become chairman of the board of the Post Company in 1961, two years after Meyer, who had been chairman, had died. Beebe did not tell Katharine either; although she was only three years his junior, she was like a daughter to him.

Katharine's struggle to control her newspaper was defined, and complicated, by this array of issues: conceited and patronizing men; politics, money, power; the manipulative nature of intelligence, editorial opinion, and news; her naiveté and her ordinary intellect; her guilt that Phil's death had been her opportunity to learn and grow. Her struggle was simplified by an intuitive feeling for business, from her father, and ambition, from her mother; her class consciousness; her belief in the careful and benevolent uses of information; her pride; and her determination, twenty-three years after she had made her marriage, to get hold of what was hers.

Journalism during the Kennedy years was not what it had been at the San Francisco dockyards in 1939, and the difference was not merely one of perception. Katharine's crisp, articulate narratives about union organizing among seamen

---

* Bernstein, "The CIA and the Media."

† Beebe became the effectual guardian of the Meyer-Graham empire after Eugene Meyer's death, sitting on the board of directors not only of the Post Company but also of every outside company in which the family was involved: Allied Chemical, Bowater Mersey newsprint manufacturers; Tricontinental investment corporation; Sengra, the Graham brothers' development corporation in Miami, named for their father, Ernest Graham, who had become wealthy from his dairy farm and real estate and had, in his forties, gone into politics and been elected state senator; Southeast Banking Corporation, the holding company for Sengra property north of Miami.

had been journalism in the old sense, good writing on a worthy subject. President Roosevelt had been an idealist, and journalism during Katharine's youth had reflected that. National journalism under Kennedy, though, seemed to be a series of arguments disguised as news: points in question, matters of contention, major developments, all supporting Kennedy's main theme: America's intentions toward the "enemy," Kennedy's personal courage against the Communist "danger." His ruthless glamour—a word that once meant "the association of erudition with occult practices"—was his political device, toward his friends as well as toward the public, and particularly toward journalists through whom he spoke to the public. His preeminent journalist friend was Benjamin Bradlee, on Katharine's payroll as Washington bureau chief of *Newsweek*, who produced stories and covers at Kennedy's casual hints but rarely printed what Kennedy did not want him to print (when he once did, Kennedy ostracized him for three months, and Bradlee learned his lesson). Bradlee later wrote a manual for the political use of journalists, *Conversations with Kennedy.**

Bradlee's work and the work that John Hayes performed for the CIA were mediapolitics at its extreme, the conversion of political secrets into corporate secrets, to the corporation's detriment. This practice, the old intelligence principle translated, contained the seeds of political blackmail: once the newsman or his organization has been compromised, the politician can threaten to expose his (its) lack of independence unless he (it) cooperates further. Many Mockingbirds have been faced with this choice. After Katharine took over the company, the implicit threat to her employees was that she could be informed about them, and the knowledge would hurt her. She did not learn of Hayes's involvement with the CIA

* New York: W. W. Norton, 1975.

until Carl Bernstein, the co-author of the *Post*'s shattering Watergate stories, wrote about Hayes in another magazine in 1977. She has never learned everything there is to know about Bradlee's role in getting the Watergate story.

Less dramatic, more pervasive than threats, was a body of etiquette that dignified most government-news relationships during the Kennedy years, allowing for routine cooperation even on, or especially on, sensitive subjects. This etiquette, to which all media in Washington subscribed to some degree, was further codified, and made a formal part of the news process, by *Post* managing editor Alfred Friendly in 1958.

"We do not make the circumstances under which some information is available," Friendly wrote in a staff memo that was quickly embraced throughout the industry. "They exist. We have to live with them. It is the purpose of this memorandum to make it more convenient to live with them and to minimize the possibilities of misunderstanding between the newspapers and our colleagues and our sources. . . . Off the record" means that a reporter "may not use [the information] in anything he writes, even without attribution to the source, however guarded. A violation of a confidence of this kind is considered, and properly, a cardinal newspaper sin. . . . For background only" refers to a variety of forms of attribution other than by name. "In such cases," Friendly instructed, "the reporter may not, of course, identify the source and may not hint at, imply or suggest his identity. In some cases, the source may insist that no attribution be given even to [his] agency. . . ." Friendly advised reporters to accept precise wording of attribution as the source specifies it. "In all circumstances, and whatever the conventions stated or implied, remember that a cheap [scoop], won by cutting a corner, by a technicality, or by violating the spirit if not the letter of the understanding of the news sources . . . is empty, usually worthless, and is followed by penalties and regrets far heavier and longer enduring than any momentary gains that are obtained." *

"Off the record" is commonly understood, by journalists who abide by it and by those few who don't, as a politician's way of saying, "I will now tell you why you should let me deceive the public," the only reason that a politician would in fact make such a request. Like "background," and to extend the absurdity, "deep background," all essential tools of media-politics, it assures the politician that if he confides in a news-man, he will get the better part of the exchange.† It is asking a journalist, whose job is to report, *not* to report, on the prom-ise that he will get another piece of information at another time that he will be permitted to report. Or it is asking him to report something different from what he knows.

No matter how Friendly reached the decision that stories obtained outside the boundaries of his system were "empty, usually worthless," such stories were scarcely seen during the glamorous Kennedy years. For example, the *Post* editors pro-moted official opinion about the Cuban threat before the Bay of Pigs invasion from the moment Kennedy took office, but did not report their prior knowledge of the invasion itself. They minimized critical news coverage the following year for the Cuban missile crisis; and in December 1962 the military issued a set of instructions entitled "Ground Rules for Discus-sion with the Press, Interviews, Press Conferences and Press Briefings," modeled after Friendly's rules, which the army used

---

* Alfred Friendly, "Attribution of News," in *Reporting the News*, ed. Louis Lyons (Cambridge, Mass.: Belknap Press of Harvard University, 1965).
† Leon V. Sigal, in *Reporters and Officials* (Lexington, Mass.: Lexington Books, 1973), has estimated that 70 to 80 percent of the *Washington Post*'s national news is taken from press releases, press conferences, planned events, and background briefings, all official forms of information. Nine-tenths of one percent comes from the reporters' own analysis, and 2 to 3 percent comes from leaks, the sources for which legitimately require protection be-cause they expose wrongdoing at their own risk. The public figure who regu-larly manipulates the news deserves no such protection.

in handling the journalists who were beginning to arrive in South Vietnam.

All these inhibiting guidelines helped to produce the harmless Vietnam reportage that made the Pentagon Papers, released in 1971, so shocking. They created a climate in which Katharine Graham, by publishing them, suddenly achieved national prominence, despite the fact that her newspaper had provided neither criticism nor serious analysis of the war throughout the 1960s.

Against this difficult and intriguing backdrop, Katharine Graham, a society woman newly widowed, tried to make a place for herself in the company that her family loved, had built, that she now owned but did not control. The *Post* was the Meyer family's identity, and without it, as Agnes had once remarked about Phil, she, the children, and the grandchildren would have "no position at all."

Now the custodian of the family's fortunes, she was to some extent still immobilized by widowhood and still longed for the protection of the husband who had abused her, for the wisdom of the childish man who had elevated himself at her expense. Phil, the poor boy from Florida, had cut away at her self-esteem throughout their marriage. His themes had been in the two areas where she felt most vulnerable, her intellect and her heritage: "I think to some extent you suffer from not being brought up by more cultured parents," Phil had told Donny and Lally in 1960, when they were both near college age. "Also you suffer from living in a secular home in a secular era." The latter referred to Katharine's lack of Jewishness, and therefore to her Jewishness. There had been discussions of her weight, her thin gray hair; Lally had been told to try to be "better" than her mother. Yet the widow mourned her dead husband. "There is no recovery really from grief," Katharine told a friend, "—even the void left by having to take care of someone who isn't well. . . ." She knew enough to suspect the attentions of other men (there were many, whom she called "vultures") as designs upon the family business; she decided early into her life alone not to marry again. "There is no recovery really from grief . . . but after some time passes, you become someone else." *

A long-buried personality began to find its way to the surface. A feminine head of the family who disliked masculine women (defining as masculine any attitude in a woman that was not of a piece with "Wear the yellow one for me Friday night"), she was also genuinely assertive, temperamental, hard-minded. It had been she, for instance, who did not allow the children to smoke (the youngest boy, Stephen, rebelliously became a heavy smoker) and who insisted, along with Agnes, that they take their schoolwork seriously, an opportunity for their father to tell them not to become "greasy-grinds," that mother and "grandma [are] full of baloney." Yet she paradoxically allowed Lally to travel alone in Europe with a boyfriend the summer of her father's death and invited both of them to stay for a week on the yacht in the Aegean, where she had gone with Agnes. Perhaps she too would have liked at this time to have had a love affair.

Katharine had within her a capacity for action, anger, spontaneity, boldness. As a product of wealth, she knew to pay experts to bring out her desirable characteristics: speech from a dramatics professor, resulting in a low, sluggish, throaty finishing-school voice; hair styling from Kenneth; straight, narrow dresses from Halston. Femininity, but effective femininity. There were also hints of her visiting a psychiatrist. The executives were not to know; they *must* not know.

Sometime after Katharine began her efforts to appear to be coolly at ease, a good appearance being half the battle (although closely bitten nails gave her away), a friend remarked

* Chalmers Roberts, *The Washington Post: The First 100 Years* (New York: Houghton Mifflin, 1977).

that she was once again as she had been at the University of Chicago, which was to say happy. And she was; it was the surprised happiness of a woman overreaching herself and finding that the impossible was within her scope after all.

She was of course a different woman now. Student radicalism was half a lifetime ago. She was now frankly interested in money, power, position. Each new issue among Washington society was grist for the mill, none a matter worthy of great passion. Unlike her mother, who was always something of an outcast precisely because of her endless political passions—poverty, civil rights, peace, public education, Israel, Adlai Stevenson—Katharine's fight was for herself. That is how she ran her newspaper business. Money, power, and position became her corporate tools, and issues were the corporate raw materials, to be reported, edited, printed, folded, delivered, consumed, thrown away. Her preference for management, where judgments are impersonal and can be mathematically correct, enabled her to build the *Post* into an important newspaper while she remained relatively ignorant of the complexity of political issues. She did not compete intellectually with her editors, but did arrange and attend seminar lunches to which reporters came to talk with the people in the news they wanted to meet. Sophisticated management techniques would come with time; at the beginning, Katharine achieved control of the company by following her father's three basic rules: "Know everything there is to know, work harder than anybody else, and be absolutely honest."

In family businesses management problems can become personal battles. Executive maneuverings are perceived as intrigues and betrayals. Union agitation appears as an attack on the owners. "[Managing editor William] Haggard, threatened by the improvements in efficiency . . . began to buck and finally resigned," Agnes had confided to Katharine, away at Vassar, in 1935. "As Dad accepted his resignation on the spot he tried to start an insurrection and got twelve people to hand in their resignations with him. . . . It was rather upsetting to everybody but Dad who cannot be threatened. . . . From some rumours that we have, it looks like a very deep plot about which I cannot write you." Katharine's thirty-year association of employee activity with distress for her family and her quite reasonable mistrust of the executives caused her to turn for help, when she became publisher, to men she knew were absolutely loyal to the Meyer-Graham cause. That meant absolutely loyal to her.

Soon after taking over, Katharine made a trusting and desperate offer to James Reston, the *New York Times* columnist, whose relationship with the family was such that Phil had named him in his will as guardian of the Graham children should he and Katharine both die and had left him and his wife $100,000. Reston had lived and worked in Washington since 1941 and was, like Katharine's own editors, deeply on the inside. But he was also in the awkward position, when Katharine approached him, of being out of favor with his superiors in New York for having fallen victim to his own connections. New York felt that to be one of the hazards of the Washington beat. Reston was too "impressed by pleas that printing certain stories might go against the national interest . . . [and] allowed his news judgment to be influenced by his patriotism," * an oblique reference to his advice prior to the Bay of Pigs invasion that the *Times* should not print a story about the plans on the grounds of national security. "Jack Kennedy was in no mood" to call it off, the well-informed Reston had said.

The *Times* consequently ran a vague story about an invasion that was vaguely being planned, not mentioning that the target country was Cuba. When Kennedy later told the *Times* that a strong story might have prevented the invasion, that they should have run one, Reston began to notice

* *New York Times* editor Turner Catledge as quoted by Sigal, *Reporters and Officials*, p. 82.

his exclusion from high editorial and management conferences. Katharine then told him what he could have if he came to her newspaper: stock, editorial authority, a column, a large amount of money. She would make him rich. She needed him. In his masculine imagination, she was too eager, needed him too much. Reston took nearly a year to decide that bad treatment at the *Times* was preferable to being honored at the *Post*, so great was the difference in prestige of the two papers. Reston continued to advise her, while telling other prominent Washington men, all of whom very much wanted to know, that Katharine was looking for someone who would be more than just another employee. Every man who has worked successfully with her has been to some extent in love with her— once she learned to use her vulnerability to her advantage.

Katharine wanted to find a man who would be simultaneously her confidant and corporate lieutenant and would teach her to run a multimillion-dollar company without thinking that it was his company. She needed someone to control both labor unions and executives for her but not himself usurp her power, someone who would sustain her emotionally during this difficult time yet never come too close. She looked for a man who would be better than a husband, and her search became a critical part of her life alone, the life of a woman running a complicated, profitable, politically sensitive, and strike-prone business.

It was this continual danger of strikes that soon reduced Reston's refusal to insignificance. Her most immediate problems, she found, were labor problems, for which Reston's political acumen would have been useless. In December 1964 the American Newspaper Guild, to which she had belonged in San Francisco, threatened to strike and after having rejected an offer that Katharine considered to be fair, with the aid of federal mediators forced the inexperienced publisher to grant contracts under which *Washington Post* reporters would be paid $200 per week, the highest reporters' salaries in the country. This humiliating defeat was the beginning of Katharine's legendary anti-unionism and brought her to depend upon a man in her employ named Jack Patterson, who had built a career fighting newspaper unions. He was an unlikely working-class ally, but he was there for her when she needed him—not her mythical perfect man, but a strong and good man who had also suffered, and whose own fight was as personal as hers.

Patterson had been at the *Post* for eleven years by the time Katharine became publisher. He was not of the East, not "one of the boys," a man much too hardworking to have time for the social life in Washington and too unpolished to have been included. He had worked as intimately with Philip Graham to build the *Post* as had any of Phil's sophisticated editors, and so, because it was a family business, the Pattersons and the Grahams knew each other well.

As a young man he had dreamed of becoming a doctor and had supported his family by working nights as a distributor for the *Seattle Star*, sitting at an outpost and parceling out newspapers to small delivery trucks, while studying science during the day. He was repeatedly denied admittance to medical school; he channeled his energy and frustration into his newspaper job, determined to break into the upper ranks of management. The *Star*, like its chief competitor, the *Seattle Post-Intelligencer*, employed truckers for distribution who were members of the Teamsters Union, which Patterson, who did not want to be labor yet was forced to work among labor, hated for its corruption, inefficiency, and violence. He became the *Star*'s circulation manager, distributing newspapers from a desk inside the printing plant instead of in the field. He tried to improve the distribution system, clashed with the union, and felt its muscle. Over the next fifteen years, as publishers competed among themselves for greater shares of the urban and suburban market and home delivery became an increasingly important way to control the market, Patterson followed better jobs around the West: home delivery manager of the *San Francisco Chronicle,* circulation director of the *Los Angeles Mirror,* promotion director and assistant to the publisher of the *San Antonio Light.* Whenever he tried to implement smoother, more profitable distribution systems, the Teamsters opposed him, made his work difficult. But his reputation as a union fighter spread. Philip Graham heard about him in 1952 and offered him a job at the *Washington Post,* where the Teamsters had never taken hold.

For all his efforts, Patterson and his family still had precious little, and Graham could give them little more. They came to Washington without savings and moved into a cramped apartment. Patterson started at the financially shaky newspaper as assistant circulation director, with a salary insufficient to support a wife and children and "a block of shares of worthless stock." He found a young publisher who had unlimited access to his father-in-law's fortune, who was running the paper at a deficit, and who had identified union wage demands as a major cause. The publisher said that he wanted to control his workers but he seemed constitutionally unable to do so; he sometimes provoked confrontations with them, but more often he drank and joked and signed overly generous contracts, a symptom of his obsession with being universally loved. "The weekend was quiet except for the threatened strike Sunday night which didn't come off," Katharine wrote to her mother in 1950. Phil had become excited by developments at the *Miami Herald,* where automation had produced the dual effects of saving money and cutting into union strength. Katharine told her mother that Phil felt the threatened strike might materialize later in the week, but that the union knew about his enthusiasm for what the Miami newspaper had done and therefore might not risk a strike at all.

While Phil ran the *Post* on his wife's father's money, which made the problem of the union's growing power less urgent to him than it was to her, Jack Patterson was fighting her family's fight, at great personal hardship. His method for eliminating the union from newspaper delivery was to contract for services with independent small truckers who took pride in working for themselves. The tactic angered the Teamsters deeply. Patterson physically fought with Teamster organizers who stepped onto the *Post*'s premises; he endured bomb threats, menacing telephone calls, men in trucks parked for hours outside his apartment building; he was jumped by thugs and would come home with knife slashes across his face. While Phil dabbled in politics, Katharine visited the families of employees. She visited Patterson's home, saw how poorly he and his wife and children were living, and out of her personal funds repaid the Pattersons for some of the danger by helping them to buy their own small house.

Phil's death enabled Patterson to return the kindness. Mrs. Philip L. Graham, as the widow called herself, needed a man, Patterson thought, who would spend long hours simply talking with her. She needed to be encouraged to be strong, she needed to know that men were attracted to her (as her husband, in his last years, had not been). As she emerged from her netherworld, confronted first with editors who acted like management and then with writers who banded together against her like labor, she needed to be told how to achieve control. The confused company records that she found upon Phil's death, the fragmented authority, the easygoing labor policy, his having given the unions a "stake in the *Washington Post*" through profit-sharing because he lacked the money for a pension plan—these practices, all of which grew in some way out of Phil's character, suddenly seemed to Katharine, who knew something about business, to have been rather amateurish. They left her in the position of keeping alive an idealized memory of her dead husband (he was still her husband) while asking Patterson, who began to stay late with her at the office, to help her to reverse the damage Phil had done.

Patterson saw that the shy (aloof) and nervous (brittle) woman was resented merely for replacing the outgoing, casual Philip Graham. But being ill at ease as a publisher, as she was as a widow, she also provoked other sentiments: either she was pitied because she was probably not going to be able to do his work, or she was a bitch because in spite of the tragedy, she could. The ability of that common English word to convey an escalating series of derogatory notices about a woman—assertive, therefore domineering, therefore spiteful, thus sexually frustrated, thus driven to success (if she is a successful bitch) by her psychological problems—makes it a persuasive deterrent to feminine action. In spite of this, Katharine developed an ability to control the corporation, to master its men and resources, and to "work them" efficiently. She made the *Post* economically dominant in the Washington news market, which directly and distinctly contributed to her political power. Economic dominance within the capital city enabled Katharine Graham to become a publisher-hostess (unavoidably a politician) who is known for her grace, confidence, and gentility, although her hard business methods cannot be separated from her public, polite journalist's life—they are its foundation and its means.

Patterson's advice was her preliminary training for power. His techniques, developed over a lifetime of personal struggle, were pragmatic to the point of being almost cruel. Do not care about being loved, he told her after the guild action the year after Phil's death; that had been Phil's mistake. Care only about respect. It is better to be feared than to be taunted. Do not ask for loyalty, demand it; make the workers know that they are working for you. Use rewards and punishments to divide the union men against one another. Take union officers into your confidence, give them responsibility, a taste of the privileges that come with management. Ask them to understand your problems during contract negotiations. If they remain militantly pro-union, tell the men that their leaders are not bargaining in good faith, which will create dissension between the leaders and their men. Make plans to automate, as the unions have asked you to do, thinking that new equipment will make their work easier; but instead of retraining them, as they expect, bring in nonunion workers to run the new machines. Turn the guild victory into your act of goodwill; acknowledge that the guild's wage demands were an effort to achieve dignity, professional status, and announce that the *Washington Post* is the first newspaper in the country to pay reporters professional-level salaries. Professional men do not have much interest in unions; they like to think they are working for themselves, or for you; they compete against rather than ally themselves with their colleagues.

In her effort to become an exemplary manager, Katharine departed radically from the ideas of the family in whose name she was running the newspaper. If she avoided Phil's foolish excesses, she also betrayed her mother's commitment to social justice and her father's Jewish philanthropic tradition. His rules—to know, to work, to be honest—had been the rules of wisdom, not coercion. Eugene Meyer too had had management problems, but he had treated the unions as if they were part of the publishing process and in 1951 had been made an honorary member of the pressmen's union. A decade and a half later, his ambitious daughter would be able to say, with little difficulty and in marked contrast to her earlier views, that "unions interfere with freedom of the press" and that "unions come between management and its employees."

Her anti-union imperative also dictated her relations with a series of business executives, whom she would hire with great fanfare, pay salaries of $100,000 a year or more, assign entire areas of the corporation to manage, and abruptly fire if they failed to control the unions to her satisfaction. This ritual eventually took in former Secretary of the Navy Paul Ignatius, her executive vice-president for labor negotiations, whom she hired in 1969 at the suggestion of Robert McNamara (Ignatius was to bring military cost-accounting methods to the *Post*) and fired in 1971 because he spent weekends at his farm instead of learning the labor operation intimately by "riding the trucks."

The upheavals, sacrifices, and bloodbathing that took place during Katharine's first five years produced a pretax corporate profit that was double in 1969 what it had been in 1963. Some of that profit came from money saved by stringent labor policies; a good deal more came from advertising. Readers had been increasingly drawn to the paper by the editorial flash of Ben Bradlee and his brilliant roster of reporters, costly though they were. By 1969 the *Post* was attracting more than half the advertising revenue available in the Washington market, more than the *Star* and the *Daily News* combined.* This ability to attract advertising was Patterson's triumph, not only because it made the *Post* economically the strongest of any Washington paper, and made him, once the owner of "a block of shares of worthless stock," a wealthy man, but also because it made Katharine Graham happy. The same could not be said for Patterson's wife, who had lived for years with him at the underside of the *Post*'s corporate world and disliked the social milieu to which her hardworking, rough-edged husband now aspired. Increasingly concerned with his "social interactions," as executives came and departed and he gained influence within the company, he took his wife to Katharine's parties, where she was uncomfortable enough to say to Katharine that she wished her husband would not spend so much time with her; Katharine laughed modestly; she never got involved with her employees. After Mrs. Patterson threatened to leave Washington with-

---

* The *Washington Daily News*, financially the weakest of the three papers, folded on July 12, 1972, selling nearly all its assets to the *Washington Evening Star*. In its last years it had been plagued by strikes, and Katharine had offered some of the strikers jobs at the *Post*.

out Jack, and after she had left, having bought a house on an island in Canada with some of their money and another house in Florida, Patterson was promoted to corporate vice-president in 1974, following a traumatic Newspaper Guild strike, and to senior vice-president in 1979, three years after a violent pressmen's strike. Whenever possible he visits his wife, whom he has not divorced, at one or the other of her houses; he continues to advise Katharine, whose needs and rewards are greater than those of other women and who still, although she has become the nation's top female business executive, the chairman of the board of a Fortune 500 corporation, relies upon his fundamental strength.

There were limits, however, from the beginning, to what Patterson could do. The purpose of a corporation is to make money and distribute its products, and for this Patterson would have been valuable anywhere. But the "higher," more prestigious activities of this particular corporation—the use of information, political influence, pursuit of "the public welfare" —were in the hands of men whose secrets Patterson did not know. The ethic of the news industry was that he ought not to know them, that publishers should have goals for society that are separate from the inelegant necessity of using somebody like Patterson to solve its distribution and personnel problems. Publishers want to make money but want to speak only about their contributions to the social order.

In spite of the editors' lack of appropriate respect for their publisher, Katharine was one of them. As a member of a newspaper family, she believed in the power of information. She believed that information should be used responsibly, for the public interest, and at first she believed that those who controlled information in Washington, the people with whom she socialized, the men who had worked for Phil but did not want to work for her, were capable of judging what the public interest was.

Katharine wanted to be a publisher with worldly concerns,

confident, respected. Her presumed lack of ability that was Washington's hottest piece of gossip, fueled by the lamentations of her editors in their private men's clubs and by James Reston's opinion as to what she *really* wanted, caused her great anguish. These men neither sheltered her from the routine pressures she began to feel as a publisher—complaints about accuracy, bias, trust, betrayal—nor prepared her for approaches that would be made toward her, the attempts by politicians to "get to her," to flatter or threaten her, during major political events.

The first of these was the Republican National Convention held in San Francisco in July 1964, where Barry Goldwater was nominated to run for president against Lyndon Johnson. Katharine attended with her daughter, while her editors went on their own, and she was shocked to witness Republican antipathy toward the entire eastern ("liberal") press. Former President Eisenhower delivered a twenty-minute speech attacking "sensation-seeking columnists and commentators" that drew cheers from the audience, and Richard Nixon, who two years earlier had lost his bid for the governorship of California and was consequently looking for a national issue, echoed Eisenhower. Among the various ideas expressed emerged Goldwater's conviction that the press was Communist because the reporters' union was Communist (as were all unions): "If this country of ours ever falls," warned Goldwater, "go back to the day [in 1933 when *New York Post* columnist Heywood] Broun founded the American Newspaper Guild."

From the Republican experience with the pro-Kennedy press, in particular with Phil Graham's *Post* inside Washington and his national magazine *Newsweek*, came a media theory that served the Republicans well over the next decade, particularly in 1968 and 1972 as a campaign issue for Richard Nixon. From the Democratic experience with the *Post* came the assumption of Katharine's unqualified support. After the Democratic convention the following month in Atlantic City, to which Lally again accompanied her and where she had been among friends, Lyndon Johnson treated her so solicitously that she became one of his strongest supporters for the remaining years of his presidency.

She was supposed to leave with Lally on a chartered Martin, a fifty-passenger twin-engine plane, and was waiting with her at the airport when Johnson arrived by helicopter to board Air Force One. He saw Katharine, insisted that she accompany him to Texas, and sent Secret Service agents to find her bags while Lally returned home. On board the presidential aircraft, Katharine congratulated Johnson on his nomination and his selection of Humphrey as running mate. Johnson said that when he dumped the "cabinet" (his euphemism for Bobby Kennedy), he had to be sure to get the right man with widespread support. In the end, said Johnson, the Kennedys and other vital people were all pushing him to have Humphrey, which was exactly as he wished it to happen.

After the amenities, Katharine became uncomfortably aware, also as Johnson wished it to happen, that this friendly trip was going to have its price. He started to talk about Phil; Phil had always thought he (Johnson) was better than other people did; he owed his nomination to Phil. Then he assessed Phil's reporters: he had not at first trusted Ben Bradlee, then of *Newsweek*, but was very impressed with the accuracy of his report of an interview with him and now did trust him.

At the Johnson ranch the president escorted Katharine through picnics, waterskiing, a visit to his aged aunt, all with a conspicuous absence of pressure. At the end of her few days in his home, Katharine asked for a minute alone with him. He took her into his bedroom; she sat on a chair while he lay down on the bed. Anxious to explain herself to Johnson, who was, after all, the president, Katharine talked of her feeling that Johnson had separated her in his mind from Phil, that in general they agreed, that as much as she had admired President Kennedy, Phil had gotten along with him better than she had. She told Johnson that she respected the legislation he had gotten passed. She was for him, and she wanted to make sure he knew it. She said that her mother wanted to contribute to his campaign and wondered if there was any particular direction in which he would like it to go. Johnson answered smoothly. He appreciated her help and had in the past; they should see each other more often; he understood that she had to run an independent newspaper. He thanked her, hugged and kissed her, and she left.

Their relationship was soon to be strained by the Vietnam war. Aware as Johnson was of the difficulties that this "pretty, clear-eyed, soft and endearing" woman was having in controlling her corporation, he nevertheless insisted on her accounting *personally* for every story of which he disapproved, for the actions of every reporter he did not "trust." His petulant demands forced her to confront her editors sooner than she might otherwise have—to achieve control for a "great" purpose. Johnson of course defined the purpose, the war, and since Katharine was a woman, he explained it to her in terms she would understand: the war was tearing at him, the war was keeping him from his family, the war was causing him mental anguish. She supported him faithfully, yet because she could not save him, the embittered man later told her sadistically that "if Phil were running the paper it would have been a different presidency for me."

MEDIAPOLITICS

☆ 12 ☆

Katharine the Great

As Katharine looked back, remembering her youth, her marriage, the world war, the growth of the newspaper that had preoccupied her family for most of her lifetime, and the political authority that the paper had given them, she tried to distinguish between herself and the Meyer family imperative: to be of service, to be an exemplary American woman. An unhappy wife who has become a widow in her forties, whose husband has been a victim of "forces larger than human beings," is only too conscious that power does not make for a "normal family." Yet the power of the newspaper was all that she and her mother, as well as their men, had ever wanted, all that her children had ever known.

At the time of the suicide, Lally was a sophomore at Radcliffe and Donny a freshman at Harvard, and the two younger sons, Bill and Stephen, were at St. Albans, a prestigious boys' school run by Washington's wealthiest Episcopal church. Agnes was suffering from a variety of ailments, including alcoholism, gout, an acute sense of isolation. The autobiography remained unfinished, because of the alcoholism, which did not prevent her, in all her magnificent spirit, from rejecting overtures from publishers as late as 1970, the last year of her life. Anthony Schulte at Knopf learned that she would not want to work on so intimate a project with somebody she did not know and trust; Byron Dobell at *McCall's* was told that they could get on perfectly, but that she did not like their list of publications. No, she did not need a publisher; the book became an obsessional, confessional chronicling of the life of one good German woman, and finally an attempt to vindicate the Germany she loved.

Katharine called her mother every few days and had lunch with her on Saturdays. She was developing her own compulsive working routine: tennis at 7:00 A.M., shower and change clothes at the office, walk the corridors with a notebook, present lists of questions to Jack Patterson at night, and study business texts until early morning. She was flying to New York once a week to learn the *Newsweek* operation, staying overnight at her apartment at United Nations Plaza. She was combining visits to her children in Cambridge with speeches in Boston and in other ways forcing herself to appear in public.

Agnes one night saw Katharine on David Susskind's television program and thought that she was a little nervous, but on the whole looked more distinguished than any of the men, and that her features came across more clearly on the screen. She noticed that her voice was good and that the points she made were original, but she worried that her daughter worked too hard in preparing for such ordeals.

Agnes felt slighted if Katharine failed to communicate the most trivial item of gossip, like the time that Katharine did not bother to tell her about the party at the home of Chief Justice Earl Warren because it was, Katharine thought, quite routine. Agnes resented and envied Katharine. She also proudly told friends that Katharine had never looked happier or more beautiful; or alternately that she had never seemed more tired, that Katharine, who had had tuberculosis in 1961, might have inherited a weakness of the lungs from her father. Agnes smoked heavily but did not like to see

Katharine smoke; she was sorry but knowing when Katharine had to swallow a tube so that her lungs could be X-rayed in 1968.

And she was, even with the occasional praise, eternally critical of Katharine's intellect. Lally had an ancient Chinese horse's head, which Katharine had dismissed as a copy, and Agnes informed Lally that her mother did not understand that copying was an honorable tradition in Chinese art and not the dishonest one that it is in ours. If Kay had been more familiar with Chinese customs and traditions she would have understood this, Agnes told Lally; furthermore, if Katharine were sure of herself she would not care what anybody thought.

Yet Agnes was a comfort to her, and to the children, for whom she was a better grandmother than she had been a mother. She was forever scolding, advising, sending them money, though Agnes would add, in an accompanying note, that she knew they were already well provided for. She took a liking to Mary Wissler, with whom Don had worked on the Harvard *Crimson* and whom he had married in 1967, and offered her eight antique chairs and a couch covered with lovely Chinese red leather, as well as a thirty-foot table which she said Mary could cut down to size for eight people. When Don enlisted for Vietnam, Agnes sent him boxes of candied fruits ordered from a San Francisco tea shop; when he worked as a policeman during Washington's antiwar rioting, she told him that the family was afraid for him.

Bill, she thought, was a sweet, considerate boy for helping Phil's brother to renovate the farm that Phil had bought for Robin. She informed Stephen, the youngest, whom Don believed had not yet found himself, that she was glad that he had gotten into the school of his choice, namely Harvard— not, honesty forced her to add, that she was so crazy about Harvard. Steve was interested in theater, so Agnes warned him about the vulgarization of sex on the American stage. Because he was, in his mother's estimation, a wild kid, she also told him sternly that they were all against the Vietnam war, but that he must be careful not to get mixed up with the very left wing, who lacked good sense.

Agnes could be overbearing, and there were times that Katharine had to compensate her children for the old woman's insensitivity. In the fall of 1964, shortly after her father died, Lally became engaged to a young man named Yann Weymouth, a promising architecture student at MIT who bore an uncanny resemblance to Phil. Agnes did not like the fact that the boy was Catholic. This seemed to worry Lally, so Yann finally wrote to Agnes that although he was Catholic, he hoped that he was not aggressive about it. He did not find it heretical to say that he abhorred the Inquisition, he informed her, just as he would not deny his U.S. citizenship because of the murder of Medgar Evers. To blunt the sting of the matriarch's disapproval, Katharine made her only daughter an elegant Catholic wedding and sent the couple to their married student life with the loving gift of six dozen disposable frying pans. Lally went on to become a feature writer at the *Boston Globe*, where, at Katharine's suggestion, she interviewed Joseph Alsop. Then Yann was offered a job at the influential architectural firm of I. M. Pei & Partners and the Weymouths moved to New York City. They were eventually featured in *Vogue* magazine for their work with "the colored situation," as Agnes called it. "Young, attractive, involved . . . the Weymouths are lookers—both tall, handsome, spirited, with dark hair and brown eyes. They belong to the new young breed that thinks the way to tackle ghetto problems is to wade in and help—working with people in the neighbourhood, on the block-and-storefront level. Both have been deeply involved with the program to improve conditions in Brooklyn's problem-wracked Bedford-Stuyvesant section. Yann . . . designed and executed the first 'superblock' in Bed-Stuy, actually a three-block area of renovated homes with an interior park. Lally has worked in Bed-Stuy on two different projects: helping to set up a community TV program of local news and interviews, on a tiny budget; and helping to organize a triumphal rock concert. . . . They live in a white-white, sun-flooded modern apartment. . . ." *

The Weymouths had two daughters and named the first one Katharine. She was truly her grandmother's namesake, independent, orderly, industrious, quietly aloof, and Katharine adored her. The younger child was named for a British friend of Katharine's, Lady Pamela Berry. Katharine was particularly concerned for both of them at a young age when their parents were divorced.

Katharine shared her children's lives but did not want to burden them with her own problems. Her mother existed more and more in the past. Katharine went on long trips once or twice a year when work left her frustrated and depressed. In January and February 1965, immediately after her expensive wage settlement with the Newspaper Guild, she toured four weeks in Cambodia, Vietnam (where she shopped for blue and white china), Tokyo (Vietnam, she said later, naturally came up immediately), New Delhi (Indira Gandhi, she thought, behaved like a snake), Cairo, and Beirut.

Later in the year, in July, when tensions in the *Post* newsroom reached new heights with her hiring of the ambitious Benjamin Bradlee, she took another month in London (having to defend Vietnam, as usual, she complained), Paris, Greece (Mrs. Niarchos was charming, had a marvelous figure, and wore not an ounce of makeup), Yugoslavia (after Tito had sent word through his embassy that he would see her), and Moscow (where she defended *Newsweek*'s coverage of Vietnam and had her hair washed in the American embassy by a Russian hairdresser whom the diplomats' wives thought to be "quite mad").

In London she had a call from her second son, Bill, who

* *Vogue*, June 1970, p. 96.

had arrived with his group and a French boy they had picked up. They were staying in a fleabag hotel, and Katharine took him with her to dinner at the home of Ambassador David K. Bruce. They talked until midnight; Katharine gave him advice and money, then he left in a taxi, Katharine feeling that she had lost him again. She found him later at the American Hospital in Paris with pneumonia, after one of the boys had called the Paris *Newsweek* office to ask if he was insured. She left him in the care of Avis Bohlen, the wife of Chip Bohlen, the U.S. ambassador to France.

In Yugoslavia, as planned, she met up with Truman Capote, her neighbor at United Nations Plaza, a confidant to and observer of wealthy women, and together they went to Greece to see Lally and Yann, who were vacationing there with Margaret Mead and Barbara Ward. The brains, Agnes said competitively of them; both had the gift of gab but neither had done any original work in years, in her opinion. She and Barbara Ward had been particularly close to Adlai Stevenson, who had died suddenly just a few days before Katharine and Capote, looking happy, arrived in Greece. Katharine had just seen Stevenson in London, she reported to her mother, and had had a long talk with him the night before he died. He had told Katharine that much as he admired her, he wanted her to know that she was not the brain that her mother was. Katharine duly reported this and assured Agnes that he had been planning to visit her when he went home.

The serious attention of foreign leaders, to which she was unaccustomed, the social and personal side of politics, to which she was, helped Katharine to put her problems at the paper in better perspective; but by the following June, having gone unrespected by her own men for yet another year, she was once again feeling so "low," as Capote was able to observe, that he told her, "I'm going to give you the nicest party, darling, you ever went to." The third anniversary of her husband's death would be in August, and she was still committed to being a woman without a man, "a monk," as she put it, listing herself in the telephone book as Mrs. Philip L. Graham when she could easily not have had a public listing; not having lovers—no one would ever be able to marry her for the *Post*—but "masculine friends," one of the most trusted of whom seemed to be Capote, a homosexual.

Capote had just finished *In Cold Blood*, which after five years' work "had really washed me out," when he decided to give her a party; perhaps he was already collecting material for the book that he still has not finished, a brutal, explicit study of Society (*high* society) that he would title *Answered Prayers*. Katharine Graham and her children may or may not have been particular subjects for this book, but Capote cultivated them as he did other society families, seeing Lally in New York and visiting Katharine in Washington, flattering them, sharing their concerns, studying them even as they studied themselves.*

Capote decided that Katharine's party would be a live version of the horse-race scene in *My Fair Lady*, which had been created by Cecil Beaton, with beautiful, stylized people moving to music, outfitted in black and white. Capote sent out orange-and-yellow invitations to five hundred "real friends" whom he spent "oh, so many hours" selecting; they had to dress in black and white and be "either very rich, very talented, or very beautiful, and of course preferably all three." He rented the ballroom of the Plaza Hotel for Monday, November 28; engaged the all-white Peter Duchin Orchestra and the all-black Soul Brothers, who would alternate on the

---

* Capote was not the only one of Katharine's friends who closely observed the family. The contrast between Lally and Donny was extraordinary, Lady Pamela Berry once noted. Lally was straight out of Scott Fitzgerald (her nickname for Lally was Gatsby), while Donny was just the opposite—intensely modest, frugal, prudent. Pamela confessed to Katharine that she used to worry about Donny until she realized that this was typical of him.

stand; planned decorations; asked a dozen closest friends to give dinner parties before the ball and provided them with guest lists. A real-life Cecil Beaton movie: to remove it all again from reality and indulge his sense of drama, Capote told everyone to wear a mask.

Katharine was uneasy about her role as guest of honor at Capote's Black and White Masked Ball, as it came to be called, and began worrying. She would have to order a gown —what kind of gown?—make appointments for nails, make-up, hair; serve as hostess, in a city that dwarfed her home city, to sophisticated and glamorous people who would be asking each other in whispers, "Who is Katharine Graham?" She had lunch with the *Post*'s New York bureau chief. What should I wear? she asked him nervously; who will be there, will they like me, how should I act? The bureau chief was a good-looking dark-haired man at least fifteen years younger than Katharine. He was embarrassed and touched and re-assured her with the propriety due a boss, without responding to her, he hoped, "as a man to a woman." She supposed she would have to wear a low-cut dress, she said; you would look equally elegant in a high neck, he said. What sort of fancy thing should I do with my hair? she said; wear it smooth and simple, he said. What should I talk about? she said; just ask them about themselves, he said. Thank you for all your help, she said; just call me if you need me, he said.

On the fateful night Katharine went to dinner with Capote and then at 10:00 P.M. received guests with him at the Plaza in a custom Balmain creation that was conspicuous for its modesty. Other women wore dresses without sleeves, without backs, with bodices that exposed or emphasized their breasts; hers covered her like a tunic, one solid sheet of white from her chin to the floor, with long, full sleeves that ended just above the wrists. Both neck and sleeves were set off, for an Egyptian effect, with rows of black ornaments. Once introduced, she became quite incidental to the evening. *Life* magazine,* which did a seven-page spread on the "gala fete," mentioned her as the guest of honor, but concentrated, to her relief, on the "jarring juxtaposition" of the others: Marianne Moore and Henry Geldzahler, Frank Sinatra and Alice Roosevelt Longworth, Janet Flanner and Andy Warhol, Henry Ford and Norman Mailer, McGeorge Bundy and Douglas Fairbanks, Princess Pignatelli and Alvin Dewey, the detective from Garden City, Kansas, whom Capote portrayed as the hero of *In Cold Blood.* Alvin and Marie Dewey bought plain dime-store masks; others spent up to $600 on masks with sequins, jewels, feathers. There was one picture of Katharine dancing with Capote, towering above him, and the comment that she owned *Newsweek,* but "on the Fame-O-Meter," *Life* concluded, "nobody ranked higher than Frank and Mia, whose arrival caused by all odds the biggest scrimmage among the photographers lining the stairwells below the ballroom." Still, "one and all, they were denizens of Truman Capote's frugging, waltzing, glamourous, nervous, pedigreed, productive and fantastically eclectic whole world."

Although Capote was remembered for the Masked Ball, and Katharine wasn't, his introducing her in such a manner on that damp November night brought her, for the first time, attention in magazines and newspapers. There was immediately a profile in *Vogue,*† written by Arthur Schlesinger, Jr., who had known Phil, with a stilted black-and-white portrait of her (to continue the theme) by Cecil Beaton, who felt that he could in a small way take credit for her new fame. "Attractive, gentle without necessarily yielding, soft without mental flab," Schlesinger wrote, "knowledgeable without aggressiveness, a woman with a woman's smart mind, a mother of four—that is Katharine Graham. . . ." In the tradition of his writings on the Kennedys, he then said, wishfully, "She runs a sizable empire and is the acknowledged boss. . . . To

* December 6, 1966.   † January 1, 1967.

219

do that with grace (as Kennedy would have), she listens long and makes reasonably quick decisions. [With] her stamina and her brains and her good looks . . . [she] manages the intricacies of her life partly because she takes two steps at a time. She likes it that way." In fact, she had a tendency to burst into tears at odd moments, thinking about Phil, and would tell friends, "I liked it better before."

A year later there was another article, this one impressively in *Esquire*,* written by William F. Buckley, Jr. The sarcastic Buckley called his essay "The Politics of the Capote Ball," the politics being, in his view, the matter of who was included and who left out. He had liked the party and felt that to sustain its mood he would have to discredit the one effort that had been made to put the party and the Vietnam war into a cohesive piece of writing. Buckley attacks: "Let's dispose of [this] problem once and for all. . . . There was a . . . columnist, Mr. Pete Hamill, who reviewed the affair most awfully sociologically, from his desk at the New York *Post* (from where else?)." Buckley quotes Hamill: " 'And Truman was just marvelous! He was the first to arrive, along with Mrs. Kay Graham, who was the guest of honor. You see, *she* threw *him* a party in Washington, and he did get on the cover of *Newsweek*, and she *does* own *Newsweek*. . . . Truman is a little fat fellow, you know, and he was so nice and round and sweet and polite that, God, you just wanted to *hug* him . . . (*The helicopter landed in a scrubby open field six miles north of Bong Son. It was very quiet . . . when the machine gun started hammering from the tree line. You could hear the phwup-phwup of a mortar and the snapping of small arms fire and then when it was quiet again, you realized that the young man next to you was dead. His right eye was torn from his skull*).' " Buckley comments: "The implicit point . . . is that one shouldn't enjoy oneself publicly

* December 1967.

while there is a war on, and of course such advice would be easier to accept [if] Mr. Hamill [did not so] enjoy weaving . . . Vietnam through his editorial loom. But it is true," Buckley admitted, before moving on to his main subject, "that certain functionaries intimately involved in the Vietnam war deemed it inappropriate to frug-with-Kay at Truman's blast, indeed that was just the reason why Secretary McNamara did not come; at least, that is the reason he gave . . . for regretfully, declining his kind invitation."

Katharine wanted to be part of her time. If she was publishing the *Post* for any single contemporary purpose (keeping the paper in the family and proving that she could be a publisher being not purposes but motivations), if one editorial theme would characterize the *Post* for most of her first decade there, it was support of the Vietnam war. The month that she had toured South Vietnam, February 1965, was the month during which Johnson began regular bombing of North Vietnamese military installations. He asked her to go —a "*Newsweek* trip"—as he had gone to Vietnam for Kennedy. He arranged for her to see the diplomats, the generals, to have a field tour; he debriefed her when she returned.

It was still, then, a relatively "private war," * an elite war, created by men whom she knew to be good men; far away, painless, reasonable, and fashionable, a strategically brilliant response to the exotic political forces of Asia. Katharine visited the Delta, where she saw a village that had been adapted to the pacification program, and learned that the national police were instrumental in detecting Viet Cong within the hamlets, where they "kidnap young men of 15 or 16." The police, she was told, posted billboards "telling the people what to do in case of Viet Cong attack" and watched

---

* This term was first used in Ralph Stavins, Richard J. Barnet, and Marcus G. Raskin, *Washington Plans an Aggressive War* (New York: Random House, 1971).

the hamlet dwellers themselves for signs of Viet Cong allegiance. A police official showed her a graph of the population and a wall chart with the names of families with Viet Cong relatives. They discussed their system of psychological interviews with her and spoke at length about the Viet Cong infrastructure. They said that as a result of the pacification program, the villagers who did not speak to them a year before now freely reported guerrilla squads.

She was taken by helicopter back to Saigon that evening, in time to go to the U.S. embassy, where McGeorge Bundy, a special assistant to President Johnson for national security affairs, was being given a stag party. The next day she met the acting premier and had dinner with columnists Stuart Alsop and Rowland Evans and, later, drinks with them at the Caravelle bar, from where she could see flares dropping in the streets.

Notable in Katharine's views were the muddled theories of the war makers themselves, that the Viet Cong were simultaneously aiding the villagers and terrorizing them; that "pacification" (hauling them before internal security police) made the people less discourteous, therefore more loyal; that they were both their own enemy and the victims of an encroaching army from the north; that anticommunism as a comprehensive ideology was the appropriate way to understand all of this, although by that formulation the Communists are always gaining and the future for America is always bleak.

Her trip, and consultation with the president, made Vietnam the single issue in which the *Post* men recognized Katharine's editorial authority; it was the only one about which she felt strongly enough to ask each of her editors pointedly what he thought. Several days after her return, the newspaper's unsigned editorial said that the violence of the war "disclose[s] with dreadful clarity that Vietnam is not an isolated battlefield but a part of a long war which the Communist world seems determined to continue until every vestige of

Western power and influence has been driven from Asia."
A month later the paper suggested mildly that "President
Johnson forgo the use of all gas and napalm in this war
theater," but that was a temporary lapse, remedied within
four days—"there is considerable . . . pious hypocrisy in
some of the moans of outrage over the use of nontoxic [*sic*]
gases." After that the paper's editorials remained, until Richard Nixon was elected, exemplary pieces of obfuscation,
reflections of the calls that Katharine received from Johnson
and from Robert McNamara, of the editors' privileged contacts with Pentagon officials, their readings of secret cables.

Throughout the decade no questions were raised about
the bombing, although Johnson's decision to bomb had been
based upon the "fact," thought up in an adviser's office, that
Ho Chi Minh was not really a guerrilla fighter "with nothing
to lose," but had an "industrial complex" (a few factories)
to protect. Ho would therefore surrender, this theory went,
if only he were bombed enough.

On the matter of the war, Katharine and her editors had
no differences, although the blame for supporting it has gone
to them; no one could take a woman seriously as a hawk.
But she had come back from Asia in 1965 knowing that
Vietnam was an issue that could mature the paper (every
journalist needs his war) and understanding also that war is
a young man's business and it could be her weapon against
those editors close to retirement age, as most of them were.
Alfred Friendly, the managing editor, in particular, had been
sluggish, as well as condescending, taking two months' vacation per year, one of them for "contemplation"—not a good
editor for wartime; and though he was a friend, a father figure
to her children, she returned from Vietnam having decided
to replace him with a younger man.

By April, a year and seven months before the Capote
party, she became interested in Benjamin Bradlee, whom
Kennedy had made famous, the chief of her *Newsweek*

Washington bureau. Bradlee's father, she vaguely remembered, had been president of the Cosmos Chemical Corporation and had done business with her father, founder of Allied. Bradlee claimed, during their interview, to have no politics, no opinion on the war, but he did say that he would hire no "son-of-a-bitch reporter" who was not a patriot. He had recently refused a promotion to New York—Washington was his turf, his inside track—and now he wanted desperately to regain his momentum within the corporation. Katharine asked him what he wanted, alluding to Friendly's job, and since that day is now seen as the beginning of the fortuitous Graham-Bradlee partnership, his remark has been preserved by chroniclers of the occasion: "I'd give my left one for it."

Katharine put him in as assistant managing editor and he immediately started agitating for Friendly's retirement. "Don't be in such a hurry," Friendly told him nervously. Katharine, for her part, was not sure that she would keep him. "I hardly knew him"—she was conscious mainly that he had said around town that there was nothing wrong with Phil that a good divorce wouldn't cure—"and didn't like him at all."

Ben Bradlee was considered by some members of the Washington press to be insensitive and ruthless, professionally and socially. He was indiscreet about having been on intimate terms with Kennedy, one aspect of which was that his sister-in-law Mary Pinchot Meyer, who had lived in Bradlee's renovated garage, had been Kennedy's lover. Mary Meyer had been murdered in October 1964. She was killed near her house, or by the C & O Canal in Georgetown, shot or stabbed—the location, even the manner of her death, varies with each account. Immediately after she died, James Angleton, the CIA's chief of counterintelligence, searched her apartment for a diary she had kept about Kennedy and took it to CIA headquarters, supposedly to burn it, although because of his training he never destroyed any document. A year later, when Bradlee went to the *Post*, the slaying was still unsolved (it has never been solved); Bradlee was uncharacteristically silent about it.

Nineteen fifty-six. Ben Bradlee, recently remarried, is a European correspondent for *Newsweek*. He left the embassy for *Newsweek* in 1953, a year before CIA director Allen Dulles authorized one of his most skilled and fanatical agents, former OSS operative James Angleton, to set up a counter-intelligence staff. As chief of counterintelligence, Angleton has become the liaison for all Allied intelligence and has been given authority over the sensitive Israeli desk, through which the CIA is receiving 80 percent of its information on the KGB.* Bradlee is in a position to help Angleton with the Israelis in Paris, and they are connected in other ways as well: Bradlee's wife, Tony Pinchot, Vassar '44, and her sister Mary Pinchot Meyer, Vassar '42, are close friends with Cicely d'Autremont, Vassar '44, who married James Angleton when she was a junior, the year he graduated from Harvard Law School and was recruited into the OSS by one of his former professors at Yale.

Also at Harvard in 1943, as undergraduates, were Bradlee and a man named Richard Ober, who will become Angleton's chief counterintelligence deputy and will work with him in Europe and Washington throughout the fifties, sixties, and early seventies. Both Bradlee and Ober were members of the class of '44 but finished early to serve in the war; both received degrees with the class of '43. Ober went into the OSS and became a liaison with the anti-Fascist underground in Nazi-occupied countries; Bradlee joined naval intelligence, was made a combat communications officer, and handled

---

* Technically, the KGB, the secret police of the Soviet Communist party, was not formed until 1954, a year after Stalin died. It superseded several of Stalin's internal security and intelligence agencies that had been so autonomous as to threaten even the party apparatus. Before 1954 Angleton charted the divisions within Soviet intelligence as well as its activities in foreign countries.

classified and coded cables on a destroyer in the South Pacific. He then worked for six months as a clerk in the New York office of the American Civil Liberties Union, an organization that promotes various progressive causes, including conscientious objection to war. This job, so out of character for the young patriot, may or may not have been an intelligence assignment.

In 1956 Ben and Tony Bradlee are part of a community of Americans who have remained in Paris after having been trained in intelligence during the war or in propaganda at the Economic Cooperation Administration. Many have now addressed themselves to fighting communism, a less visible but more invidious enemy than nazism had been. Some of them, like Bradlee, are journalists who write from the Cold War point of view; some are intelligence operatives who travel between Washington and Paris, London, and Rome. In Washington, at Philip Graham's salon, they plan and philosophize; in foreign cities, they do the work of keeping European communism in check.

Bradlee's childhood friend Richard Helms is part of this group. He has written portions of the National Security Act of 1947, a set of laws creating the Central Intelligence Agency and the National Security Agency, the latter to support the CIA with research into codes and electronic communications. Helms is the agency's chief expert on espionage; his agents penetrate the government of the Soviet Union and leftist political parties throughout Europe, South America, Africa, and Asia.

Angleton and Ober are counterintelligence, and run agents from Washington and Paris who do exactly the opposite: they prevent spies from penetrating American embassies, the State Department, the CIA itself. Head of the third activity, covert operations, is Phil Graham's compatriot Frank Wisner, the father of MOCKINGBIRD, whose principal operative is a man named Cord Meyer, Jr. Meyer was a literature and philosophy major at Yale and is consequently well liked by Angleton, who when at Yale thought himself a poet and edited a literary magazine. Meyer is married to Tony Bradlee's sister, Mary Pinchot Meyer, the woman who later became Kennedy's lover and was murdered in 1964.

Among the fascinating and glamorous Americans of Paris, London, and Rome, the Meyers are more fascinating and glamorous than the rest. Mary was the most brilliant and beautiful girl in her class at Vassar and is now a painter, beginning to be critically recognized. Cord is an attractive, articulate figure whose evolution as an anti-Communist has given him a unique understanding of Communist trends in European trade union and Third World liberation movements. Because of this specialized knowledge, he is, as few men are, considered within the agency to be indispensable.

Meyer served as a marine on Guam and emerged from the war an ardent one-world advocate. He became an aide to Harold Stassen at the San Francisco Conference to form the United Nations, but believed that so loose an association of nations could not succeed; in the late forties he founded United World Federalists, an organization that promotes world government as the way to end war forever. "Within a decade," Meyer predicted, "the world will be organized into one political unit. The only question that remains to be settled is, what form?" The one-world movement was exceptionally strong after the first nuclear bombs were dropped, and the magnetic Meyer became the spiritual leader of it all, overshadowing other people in other groups. He commissioned a film from Pare Lorentz, *The Beginning or the End*, that was to be the definitive statement about the dangers of the atomic age and commanded various organizations to sponsor it, while refusing to accommodate their views in the script.

In 1950 he then began to coordinate with Robert Maynard Hutchins and Elizabeth Mann Borgese of the Committee to Frame a World Constitution, at the University of Chicago, who were about to achieve leadership by organizing a conference of the world's major progressive groups to be held in 1951 in Rome. Meyer at some point strangely had started accepting money from the conservative McCormick family and was, he said, interested in contributing to Hutchins's conference. "You might send all the details to me," he wrote to Mrs. Borgese on World Federalist letterhead. She obliged by providing him with a "plan of action" by which they would try to secure "the cooperation of other not specifically federalist organizations (political parties, trade unions, scientific and religious organizations, etc.) who . . . should be invited to join . . . because to make them work on specific world federalist problems is the best method of penetrating them with federalist propaganda." She gave Meyer a list that included the International Cooperative Alliance, the International Confederation of Free Trade Unions, the Indian Socialist party, and the Congress of Peoples Against Imperialism, which, Mrs. Borgese noted, "represents national democratic and socialist parties in all of the French, British, and Belgian colonies. In the Cameroons alone it counts 300,000."

In 1952 Meyer showed up as a CIA official in Washington knowing the names and activities of these same trade union and national liberation organizations, and the public story was that he had defected from the one-world movement because he had suddenly seen that world government was in danger of being Communistic. This transformation, so out of character for a man of his methodical intellect, caused people within the movement to believe that World Federalism may have been a lengthy intelligence assignment.

It is 1956, then, and Ben Bradlee's brother-in-law is stationed as a covert operations agent in Europe. He travels constantly, inciting "student" demonstrations, "spontaneous" riots and trade union strikes; creating splits among leftist factions; distributing Communist literature to provoke anti-

Communist backlash. This localized psychological warfare is ultimately, of course, warfare against the Russians, who are presumed to be the source of every leftist political sentiment in Italy, France, the entire theater of Meyer's operations. In Eastern Europe his aim on the contrary is to foment rebellion. Nineteen fifty-six is the year the CIA learns that the Soviets will indeed kill sixty thousand agency-aroused Hungarians with armored tanks.

All of this goes on quite apart from his marriage. Mary does not have a security clearance, so he cannot tell her what he is doing most of the time. They begin to drift apart, and Mary draws closer to her sister and to Ben. When in the late fifties her marriage to Cord ends, she goes to live with Tony and Ben in Washington, where *Newsweek* has transferred him, and sets up her apartment and art studio in their converted garage.

The reaction of the intelligence community to Bradlee's presence in Washington is mixed: he is one of them, but he is not. Agency men would not as a rule trust journalists. Bradlee was a particular problem to them because he knew them so well, and they did not trust him to keep a secret.

Helms in 1961 does successfully use Bradlee as a conduit to Phil Graham, to mask the agency's interest in the *Post* buying *Newsweek*; but then Bradlee will not do Angleton the simple favor of recommending to Kennedy that he appoint Cord Meyer ambassador to Guatemala. This does not arise out of journalistic honor but is because he has made the prior judgment that Kennedy does not like Meyer and will refuse. (Bradlee is wrong; Kennedy and Meyer later get along well discussing plans for a demonstration in the Dominican Republic.)

And now Bradlee and Kennedy are cavalierly discussing Meyer's former wife. "Mary would be rough to live with," *

* As quoted in *Conversations with Kennedy.*

Kennedy and Bradlee have agreed. At one of those parties that the women, best of friends, are always organizing, Cord cannot restrain himself from lungeing across the table and trying to choke Bradlee. Angleton experiences similar impulses. It is only a matter of time, Angleton feels, until Bradlee makes a serious mistake, as he eventually does with the publication of *Conversations with Kennedy*, in which he mentions that Mary Meyer was murdered, but only in a footnote. A former *Post* editor named James Truitt is enraged at this; according to Truitt, Bradlee has forced him out of the paper in a particularly nasty fashion, with accusations of mental incompetence, and now Truitt decides to get back at Bradlee by revealing to other newspapers his belief that Bradlee's story on the Cord Meyers in *Conversations with Kennedy* was not the whole story; that Mary Meyer had been Kennedy's lover and that the day of her murder, James Angleton of the CIA searched her apartment and burned her diary. Their feud unnecessarily implicates Angleton, to his disgust and bitterness.

The remarkable thing about Katharine hiring Bradlee was that she was able to sacrifice her personal feelings for the sake of the newspaper. She had decided to try him on the advice of Walter Lippmann, who had known Bradlee's parents and had tutored him in the fundamentals of journalism. Lippmann had suggested Bradlee, so three months after he was hired, Katharine wanted Lippmann to tell Al Friendly that Bradlee was going to have his job. "Have you thought about returning to writing?" Lippmann asked him gently one day, as they were eating lunch together. No, Friendly hadn't, and he was not pleased. The hurt was all the greater because Bradlee had once been his underling at ECA. Later that afternoon he confronted Katharine, who had hoped to avoid just such a scene. "Is this what you want?" he asked her mournfully, standing at the door of her office, while she stared unhappily at her desk. "I would rather have heard it from you."

Katharine was preoccupied with the paper's corporate, political, and journalistic problems, as well as with moving into a position to be able to solve them, but she lacked the force of a comprehensive vision (even her determination to have an executive shake-up had disintegrated with Friendly's tears); and Bradlee, who did indeed have a vision, began to spend long nights at her R Street mansion, working out his ideas with her. He was coming in only five months after the Newspaper Guild had bullied Katharine into the $200-per-week wage settlement, and she told him that she wanted a man to control the newsroom the way Jack Patterson controlled the truckers. Reporters, she said, had to be broken of their union mentality ("Unions interfere with freedom of the press"), editors had to be made to respect her; whereupon Bradlee, whose own loyalty, he knew, was by no means as clear to her as Patterson's, put forth the all-encompassing proposition that she could become as powerful in Washington as the president.

After settling the matters of salary (estimated at $150,000) and stock (with an estimated value of half a million dollars), Bradlee informed his wife that the dedication required of him in this venture was going to "cost you a year" of marriage. It was a marriage already traumatized by Mary Meyer's death, and Bradlee threw himself into his work with frenzy, not only because of ambition, but to escape the anger and guilt that hung over him at home. The year stretched into two, then three, his relationship with Tony deteriorating as the one with Katharine improved, until by 1969 the marriage was not worth saving, and Bradlee moved into an apartment in the expensive Watergate complex on the Potomac River and asked Katharine to make him president of the Washington Post Company, replacing former Secretary of the Navy Paul Ignatius. Katharine by this time understood him as well as he thought he knew her, and she refused. "He is not the kind of man," she commented to eighty-two-year-old Agnes, "who should be given everything he wants."

Ben Bradlee was not generally a theorist, but he had an original theory of "creative tension" that was so brilliant and to the point that it enabled him to achieve simultaneously three crucial and seemingly unrelated objectives at the *Post*: authority over other editors (management), control of the reporters (labor), and his own unique journalistic tone.

Creative tension was most immediately a technique of business, the idea that if a worker can't keep up, he is replaceable. The tension, in Bradlee's construct, would be that people competing for their jobs, or for career advancement, have a hard time holding together a union. The second condition follows from the first: if one is working well enough not to be fired, he is by definition working cost-effectively. The relationship between such methods and the news was obvious to Bradlee. "I have an answer" to improving the paper "that's so revolutionary and anti-union," he liked to say. "I'd have the power to get rid of people. . . . If I had the power to get rid of people, I could put out a hell of a lot better newspaper." The issue was not whether analytical, well-researched, intelligent stories could be produced at all under great stress, but rather who would be in and who would be out with Ben Bradlee, who would write his kind of stories.

Bradlee was a showman; the newsroom was his theater. Once in possession of Friendly's job, he spent time every day strutting up and down the aisles, stopping to talk with certain favored reporters and pointedly ignoring others, conferring status or revoking it on the basis of yesterday's work. The *Post* had always been an enclave of masculine gentility; it now became less genteel, more masculine in the sense of ruthless competitiveness; and many of the older men, Phil Graham's men, became unhappy, as was Bradlee's intention. Because the Newspaper Guild contract did not permit firings, he tried to make them feel uncomfortable, insecure, outdated, while hiring modern young men at better salaries for the choicer assignments. All this was in the way of solidifying his control, and in the first year, aside from Friendly, he was able to drive out John Hayes, the radio and television manager, whom President Johnson then appointed ambassador to Switzerland, a position that allowed him to continue his participation in the project that the CIA had initiated the previous year to broadcast propaganda to Communist China. Bradlee reached accords with Alan Barth and Chalmers Roberts, who stayed on; he asked Katharine to limit the authority of editor-in-chief Russell Wiggins to the editorial pages, which he felt were less influential than news pages.

Bradlee also asked her to raise his budget by half a million dollars a year, until it reached over $7 million. She agreed: Bradlee suited her purposes.

In accordance with business theories of correct executive behavior, Katharine learned not to want to know every horror story of corporate and personnel management. Once she had found Bradlee and other managers whom she trusted, she preferred rather to be informed selectively about problems of implementing her policies (profit efficiency, acquisitions,* wide readership, Bradlee's journalistic "impact" upon the city) and to save herself, as publisher, for issues concerning the soul of the newspaper. These fell into three categories: her relationship with the president of the United States and his advisers, and how the *Post* could communicate their political views; labor, of course, because labor was the enemy of the

---

* In the 1960s the Post Company gained control of several strategic properties in the news industry that were central to its rise as a major communications corporation. The most important of these were the Bowater Mersey Paper Company of Nova Scotia, which ensured the *Post* a permanent supply of newsprint and gave it control over the supplies of other newspapers; and the *International Herald Tribune*, owned jointly with Whitney Communications and the *New York Times*, which brought *Post* writers published in it international prestige, as well as increasing the *Post*'s access to a network of outstanding foreign correspondents.

Meyer family; and finally how to maintain the *Post*'s character as a benevolent family-run institution and convince employees that nothing had changed.

The irony of her executive approach was that it freed her from the complexities of journalism itself; it cut her off from the soul of the news business. As Bradlee maneuvered every day with delicate questions of emphasis (when should a story become the headline story, and how will that affect events?), attitude (what ought to be accomplished with this story, whom should it help or hurt?), accuracy (whom do you believe, the reporter or the official who denies the reporter's account?)—as the news product visibly improved under his touch, as the paper grew fatter and handsomer—Katharine was able to indulge her proclivity for the personal. Most stubbornly she believed Johnson, McNamara, and later Henry Kissinger, who didn't tell her the truth about the war. She continued to run her seminar lunches for reporters. She walked along picket lines (as well as through them) during strikes, shaking hands and asking about the men's families, so that for years the unions thought her to be unaware of her own managers' harsh policies ("If that nice Mrs. Graham only knew . . ."), when in fact she directed and was torn by them.

In relations with the "talent," as distinguished from other labor, she expected, despite creative tension, to enjoy their friendship. She wanted to know their wives, to be consulted on family problems; in turn she wanted them to understand: she had been hurt by Phil, the newspaper was everything to her, she was not simply a woman of power, she was more significantly a woman alone. The self-pity here was just a part of her general self-consciousness and did not dominate her, except once in a while. At such moments she displayed the most irrational, unfair, bitchy sort of behavior, driven by her painful memories, and did the sort of damage that a woman in her position can do.

Two men in particular stirred up her deep anger, and saw

their careers suffer, because they were divorcing their wives, and in one case because she also feared (Phil's) insanity. James Truitt, an editor and a vice-president of the Post Company, was hospitalized for exhaustion early in 1969, after having worked feverishly for several months on the *Post*'s experimental Style section. Katharine called his doctor, an internist, to ask if the problem might be mental. As a result of her inquiry, Truitt was placed under psychiatric observation; Katharine said he could return to the *Post* when cleared. The psychiatrist certified his mental health three months later, and Truitt came back to the paper in May. A day after his return he was terminated without explanation.

Katharine had a similar, if less extreme, reaction to Ben Bagdikian's divorce. Bagdikian was a press critic from the RAND Corporation whom Katharine hired as national affairs editor in 1969, after he had published an article describing the *Post* as "the most frustrating newspaper in America because it is almost great." * He was a serious, thoughtful man quite incapable of mistreating women, yet he and his wife had decided to end their marriage, and Katharine, in a very short time, had become friendly with the wife. "When a man leaves a woman it tears the guts right out of her," she pleaded with him one day. "It's different with a woman. I saw her. She doesn't look good at all." Katharine could not comprehend Bagdikian for other reasons: he declined dinner invitations on the excuse that the "dinner circuit" was journalistically unproductive; he turned down her offer of stock as being a "conflict of interest" with his function as internal press critic † ("I think you're being nitpicking," Katharine told him in a frosty note, "but if you don't want it . . ."); he began living with a

* "What Makes a Newspaper Nearly Great?" *Columbia Journalism Review*, Fall 1967.

† The role of internal press critic, or ombudsman, had been created by Bradlee, on Bagdikian's suggestion, in 1970, in response to attacks by Nixon, Agnew, and Ehrlichman. Bagdikian left his job as national affairs editor to become the paper's second ombudsman in 1971.

reporter, Betty Metzger, who had filed a complaint with the Equal Employment Opportunity Commission alleging that the *Post* discriminated against women. He wanted to come to Katharine's parties with Betty, who in retaliation for her suit had been transferred to the night shift, but he was offended when she allowed herself to comment, "I hope you're not going to do anything to hurt your wife." He and Betty were planning to marry but were being treated like children, which eventually caused them to leave the paper; and all of this in spite of the fact that Bagdikian had directly contributed to Katharine's sudden heroism during the Pentagon Papers crisis, when Ben Bradlee was desperate to get the same secret documents that were being run by the *New York Times*. Bagdikian located a former RAND Corporation colleague who was then living in Boston and was able to obtain a set of them from him. The man's name was Daniel Ellsberg.

☆ ☆ ☆

Although the Pentagon Papers, published to compete with the *Times*, established Katharine Graham as a great American woman in the 1970s, a leader of the moral opposition to the Nixon administration, the truth of the matter was that her newspaper had done a bad job handling the moral issues of the 1960s, as bad as that of the politicians themselves. The significance of the Pentagon Papers was that they put her belatedly on the right side of the issues. They marked the reluctant beginning of her open battle against Nixon, after she had endured his attacks rather meekly for two years. And they formed the link between the enduring American crisis of Vietnam and Nixon's seventh and most terrible crisis, Watergate.

Among the Washington elite, to whom the *Post* was something of a house organ, Katharine had throughout the 1960s represented order. A widow thrust into the public arena and offended by the ideas she found there, the most serious political and ethical challenges to governmental authority in several decades, she allied herself with Lyndon Johnson, the highest authority of all. She decided, as Johnson had, that dissidents were confused youngsters who were being manipulated by the Communists. This profound unspoken conviction applied equally to the antiwar movement and to civil rights, neither being, in the minds of our aristocrats, the result of legitimate political frustration. Manipulation, on the other hand, was very real to them. They engaged in it themselves.

Johnson had always known that the Negroes had grievances and was more willing to respond than were most of the political elite living in the predominantly black capital city, where blacks acted as the servant class. His main concern, though, and one of the reasons he became champion of the 1964 Voting Rights Act, was that the movement might grow, because of government indifference, and attract the more ideological, dangerous kinds of radicals. Extremism, not injustice, was the problem, and the recurring theme in Johnson's speeches, in *Post* editorials ("Let them ask themselves with some humility what action . . . they are entitled to take"), in Katharine's private conversation. "The students will be used by extremists who want very much to see the state occupied by federal troops," she said in 1964 about the Mississippi Freedom Riders. The theoretical basis for this comment, for the *Post*'s "voice of reason," was that Communists were working in America to try to create chaos, a belief that Katharine shared not only with the president, but with the directors of the FBI and the CIA, army intelligence and navy intelligence, all of whom a few years later blamed the Soviets for the rise of Black Power.*

The preoccupation with Vietnam, by militarists of both the Democratic and Republican parties, began in 1950, the year the Communists took power in China, which borders Vietnam on the north. With the Chinese revolution came the secret American decision to pay 70 percent of France's military costs in Vietnam; † also there came to America, under CIA sponsorship, a student named Ngo Dinh Diem, a member of one of Vietnam's prominent Roman Catholic families. Diem's brother was a Catholic bishop whose mentor was Cardinal Francis Spellman, a priest formerly from Boston, then head of the New York archdiocese. Spellman introduced Diem to political circles in New York and Washington as the young hope of his beleaguered country.

By 1954 the French were on the verge of defeat, and the emperor, whom the French had installed to oppose nationalist leader Ho Chi Minh, appointed Diem his prime minister, not in small part because of Diem's powerful American friends. The following year Diem deposed the emperor, which the

---

* "Communists are in the forefront of civil rights, antiwar, and student demonstrations, many of which ultimately become disorderly and disrupt into violence," J. Edgar Hoover testified before the National Commission on the Causes and Prevention of Violence in September 1968.

† The French had been fighting in Southeast Asia almost continuously since 1887, when they began their efforts to consolidate Vietnam, Cambodia, Thailand, and Laos into a French-dominated federation which they called Indochina. In 1946, after the defeat of Japan in World War II, the French signed an agreement with Ho Chi Minh, the leader of the coalition of Vietnamese Nationalist and Communist groups that had been fighting for liberation, promising to allow Vietnam, under Ho, to exist as a free state within Indochina. Later that year, though, the French attempted once again to assert their domination, and thus began the French-Indochina war of 1946–1954, with France, subsidized by the United States, battling Ho Chi Minh's Nationalist forces.

Americans did not mind, but he also began repressing the Buddhists, which made them uneasy. To ensure continued support for Diem, Cardinal Spellman asked an American Catholic leader, Joseph P. Kennedy, to organize a propaganda campaign for Diem among newsmen and members of Congress. Three politicians emerged as crucial to Joe Kennedy's effort: his own son John, a senator on the Foreign Relations Committee, which voted on foreign aid; Senate majority leader Lyndon Johnson, whose advocacy of military preparedness had earned him the chairmanship of the Preparedness Investigating Subcommittee of the Armed Services Committee and a place in the secret group that had sole authority for oversight of the CIA;* and Vice-President Richard Nixon. Nixon in those years was speaking for Joint Chiefs of Staff chairman Admiral Arthur W. Radford and Secretary of State John Foster Dulles, both of whom had long been angry about "losing" China to the Communists and wanted to contain China by bombing Vietnam. In 1954 he had presented the idea of bombing Vietnam in a speech before the American Society of Newspaper Editors, where politicians frequently test the political waters. The editors had not encouraged the bombing, but they had not opposed it and had not criticized the vice-president's suggestion in their newspapers.

President Eisenhower withstood the pressure and refused to attack the little country, but in 1955 Nixon joined forces with Joe Kennedy, lending his name to Kennedy's appeals to editors of *Life* and *Time, Look,* the *New York Times,* the *New York Herald-Tribune.* Nixon was not on good terms with Philip Graham of the *Washington Post,* but John Kennedy and Lyndon Johnson were, and soon the editorial line emerged

* This Senate group was replaced in 1956 with the President's Board of Consultants on Foreign Intelligence Activities (now the President's Foreign Intelligence Advisory Board), one of whose original members was Joseph P. Kennedy.

and (supported by Arthur Schlesinger's American Friends of Vietnam committee)* blanketed the country, so that the first news that a reader received at all about Vietnam was alarmist: Ho Chi Minh wants to take over Vietnam, he is directed by China, the United States must come to the aid of the democratic Diem, if we cannot get rid of Ho at least we can contain China.

By the time Kennedy was elected president, the public relations myth of Vietnam was the truth of the marketplace; the lies used as political tools to settle old grievances, to promote a favorite dictator, had become the basis for military action. Kennedy's inability to overthrow Castro in the Bay of Pigs gave him additional reason to enter Southeast Asia: it was going to be a laboratory for training Americans in techniques of counterinsurgency, including "pacification" of Communist-leaning populations. In Vietnam that meant, since reality did not fit the theory, that people who were being "used" by Ho were to be surveilled by internal security police, just in case they actually supported him.

The distorted reasoning that enabled three future presidents to participate in the creation of a war through public relations and then, as presidents, to continue the war because they had come to believe their own propaganda—that reasoning also permitted them, particularly Johnson, to think that the antiwar movement was essentially a problem of selling the story better. This was what Katharine tried to help Johnson do. But the movement soon became too serious for advertising theory. Unable to admit error, or to understand grass-roots political sentiment, and accustomed and committed to the

---

* American Friends of Vietnam was formed in 1956 in order to help get Americans accustomed to the idea of increased involvement in Vietnam. One of its executive members was a man named Elliot Newcomb, a partner in the publicity firm of Newcomb-Oram, which earlier had signed a contract for $3,000 a month plus expenses to represent the Diem government in the United States.

notion that people believe what they are deceived into believing, the president began to think that Communists were
manipulating the American youth, rather than that they were
unwilling to fight his badly conceived war. "Ho Ho Ho Chi
Minh" was their slogan, "NLF [National Liberation Front] is
gonna win." The movement was a battleground for their
"hearts and minds."

As preposterous and desperate as this idea was, Johnson
acted on it. He began ordering up regular reports from the
intelligence agencies, FBI, CIA, army, and navy, who were
already reporting to him on civil rights/Black Power activities.
The assignment, for both movements, was to find evidence of
foreign influence. Johnson became increasingly frustrated as
they could not find it and insisted that their methods were de-
ficient, that the evidence was there. As a result of this pressure,
CIA director Richard Helms, through his deputy Thomas
Karamessines, authorized counterintelligence chief James
Angleton, on August 15, 1967, to establish an "intelligence
collection program with definite domestic counterintelligence
aspects" and "some sort of system by [Angleton's deputy] Dick
Ober for the orderly coordination of the operations" among
all the intelligence agencies.*

The agencies buried their long-standing rivalries to cooperate on mail intercepts, phone taps, monitoring meetings,
the use of LSD to pump people for information, and surveillance of "U.S. Negro expatriates as well as travelers passing
through certain select areas abroad. Objective is to find out
extent to which Soviets, Chicoms [Chinese Communists] and
Cubans are exploiting our domestic problems in terms of
espionage and subversion." Ober's organization, which reported, in priority, to the CIA, the FBI, the president, and

* Karamessines's memorandum to Angleton, August 15, 1967, reprinted in
the "Supplementary Detailed Staff Reports on Intelligence Activities and the
Rights of Americans" (the Church Commission Report), p. 690.

the National Security Council, whose chairman was the secretary of state, had the code name Operation CHAOS. "High sensitivity is obvious." *

Supremely competent as a businesswoman, working at nothing except building a powerful news machine, Katharine reflected no more deeply upon the purpose of such an instrument than to want it to express her loyalty to the politicians toward whom she felt like a sister or a wife. This vulnerability, and the sublimation of her feelings into intellectual, emotional, and political alliances, seemed to be a fundamental aspect of her widowhood.

She retained the prejudices imparted to her by Phil, which reinforced her natural fear and arrogance. If Johnson, on a strictly political level, saw Communists in the civil rights movement, she did not doubt that there were Communists; but her point of understanding was that "Phil [had been] too much of a Southerner for me not to have a heavy sense of the . . . resentment of the Southerners. I don't mean the thugs but the decent ones." She told Johnson that "my heart bleeds for you" as the victim of antisouthern sentiment.

If she knew that Robert McNamara was torn by the war, and resented the public portrait of him as a warmonger because it hurt him deeply, she was more affected by McNamara as a father who blamed himself for driving his young son Craig into the antiwar movement. Was Craig being used? McNamara's unenviable dilemma was that with every political or military decision that he made, he had to bear the guilt of knowing that his son was a tool for the organizers working fervently against him. Katharine's own guilt was that she was not suffering along with McNamara, that she had somehow been spared. Her son had volunteered for the army in the summer of 1966, immediately upon graduating magna cum

* Cable to field offices describing the collection requirement, August 31, 1967, reprinted in the Church Committee's Report, p. 691.

laude from Harvard (English history and literature). "Vietnam" and not the opposition to it "is the experience of my generation," Donny thought.

Don's strange rebellion against his peers in favor of his class possessed elements of the romantic. The oldest male in his family, he could have requested a deferral from McNamara himself but decided to follow in the footsteps of his father. Donny left behind a new wife, as his father had done; and a mother and a grandmother who as women had nothing of value to say to him about it, although his mother had seen another generation go to war, and his grandmother had seen two generations in two world wars and was now (a war every generation, indeed) "quite weary of it all."

Phil Graham had never seen battle and neither did Donny. A former president of the Harvard *Crimson* (his father had headed the *Law Review*), he became a public information officer, handling newsmen for the famous 1st Cavalry, which was fighting in the Central Highlands, and spending time in Tokyo publishing the division's internal magazine and newspaper. He learned to use a camera and did some simple photography. At night he pored over *Lie Down in Darkness*, which his mother had sent him, and spoke about the war in the manner of William Styron's poetic, rhetorical prose. Donny considered the marines to be the real butchers of the war; they found people with rifles, packs, and fighting gear, he once noted, and killed them with fantastic precision. They shot anyone who looked vaguely suspicious, who tried to run when they flew overhead. His own unit was a parody of Americans fighting a war, he thought: killing Vietnamese whom they never saw, stopping the war at night and living comfortably, throwing c-ration cans out of helicopters.

Donny was visited at his base by Joseph Alsop, the *Post* columnist, whose long affiliation with the China lobby let him see this war as merely a tactic in America's larger war against communism in Asia. Because of his support, the army brought

Alsop into the country by military plane, put helicopters at his disposal for tours of the countryside, provided liquor and the finest accommodations, and briefed him at the embassy in Saigon. Donny thought Alsop was quite brave to go over there, and he wrote his mother that he (Alsop) was smart in the way he was covering the war, that he was doing a good job for her. Donny was temporarily taken out of action when a truck ran into the car he was driving and he had to have three stitches in his cheek.

If the finest quality in a woman is to stand firm with her men during wartime, Katharine in another war would have been exemplary. Faithful to her friends by inclination and by class, so sensitive to loyalty, or lack of it, in Washington's political theater (as members of her class have always been) that she interpreted criticism as betrayal, Katharine could not accept the fact that in this war there were different rules. She was gifted with a penetrating, nontheoretical, noncontemplative intelligence that should have served her well here. But being remote and shy, and profoundly untrusting since her early days with Phil (which is what his condescension and his womanizing had done for her), she preferred to maintain her distance in all aspects of her life. This she did by defining herself as a tycoon. There is no question that such a posture enabled her to laugh at sexual or romantic advances, for which she had no use, glamorous and alluring as she had learned to be. ("You'd really like to fuck a tycoon, wouldn't you?" she has admitted to thinking, when a brave male presumes to make an overture.) More to the point, though, her conceit became a very clear part of her personality at the newspaper. It was known that she expected her powerful attachments to the president and defense secretary to be translated into her news pages; and when a reporter put together a story or an editorial writer drafted an essay, trying to be both fresh and exciting while holding to company line, there was always the additional factor of not upsetting Mrs. Graham.

Her moods could be felt throughout the building and corresponded to the progress of the war. She was anxious and irritable with every troop escalation, every bombing raid, and furious when any criticism of Johnson or McNamara crept into her paper, coming downstairs to confront Bradlee about it. She was appalled when late in 1967 Johnson humiliated McNamara by suddenly nominating him for the presidency of the World Bank, thus revoking his authority for the war. That McNamara had lost heart for the war upset her further. "It seems that the burdens you bear," she wrote emotionally to Johnson, ". . . are almost too much for one human being. The only thanks you ever seem to receive is . . . criticism. Unlike Phil, I find it hard to express [my feelings]. I can't write in the eloquent words he used. But I want you to know [that I] . . . believe in you and [am] behind you with trust and devotion." *

As Johnson's presidency was eroded, and her editors began to think that 1968 might be his final year in politics, Katharine was able to transform her confusion and anger into an unsentimental concern about preserving the machinery of state. That did not mean abandoning Johnson; on the contrary, McNamara's weakess required Johnson's strength. This was particularly true after the beginning of the Tet offensive, an orchestrated attack on one hundred towns and cities in the South, which the North Vietnamese began in January, Donny's last month in Southeast Asia, and finished in February, while McNamara remained impotently in office until Clark Clifford was sworn in on the first of March.

Tet was a devastating blow to Johnson and created new difficulties for him, not the least of which was Eugene Mc-

* Katharine Graham as quoted in Roberts, *The Washington Post*, p. 392.

Carthy, whose campaign for the 1968 Democratic presidential nomination was built entirely upon his opposition to the war. McCarthy was in Katharine's opinion a distasteful character, who pretentiously recited poetry in public and claimed to be above politics, but who had nevertheless found within himself the pragmatism to exploit the Tet disaster for his own gain, precisely at the time the nation most needed to be unified. The courage that McCarthy showed in defying the Democratic party apparatus, which then was very strong; his willingness to jeopardize a twenty-year career in Congress for a principle —these were not the issues for her. She refused, until he almost won the influential New Hampshire primary early in March, to take his candidacy seriously (indeed, McCarthy had a difficult time with the *Post*'s label of him as a frivolous candidate).

When he did nearly win, she personally selected the *Post*'s comment. Printed more than two weeks before Johnson announced on March 31 that he would not run again (at which time he "lanced the boil of faction and opened the abscess of partisanship on the body politic"),* the McCarthy column seemed to be informed by the publisher's knowledge of the president's plans: McCarthy was "nakedly opposed to the Administration," it said. His supporters had, of course, "deserted the President." Richard Nixon, who was clearly going to be the Republican candidate, would be preferable to him, although Nixon ought now to "moderate his position on Vietnam" or McCarthy would retain the youth vote and Nixon would lose the election "by default." †

In that harrowing year of Johnson's political destruction, of the Martin Luther King, Jr., and Robert Kennedy assassinations, of the ghetto riots so dreadful that the army had to be called up to quell them, of the shootings and beatings at the

* "In the Name of Unity," *Washington Post* editorial, April 1, 1968.
† Joseph Kraft, "Vote Shows LBJ Is Vulnerable but Nixon Can't Capitalize on It," *Washington Post*, March 14, 1968.

Democratic convention in Chicago, of the My Lai massacre, Richard M. Nixon was Katharine Graham's candidate of choice. She appeared with Don at the Republican convention in Miami in August and ordered an editorial upon his nomination which praised his "admirable understanding and restraint in his public approach to Vietnam," his "commendable comprehension of some aspects of the Nation's social ills." Nixon was painted as wise and calm, the right man to solve the domestic problems created by Vietnam, though the war itself was left unmentioned.

And then, after his election, he increased troop strength to half a million men, having promised to deescalate, and began secretly to bomb Cambodia, which was neutral. The demonstrations grew increasingly violent, and he placed "internal security" wiretaps on the movement leadership, which his attorney general, who thought that the demonstrations looked like "a Russian Revolution," publicly said he had a right to do. Operation CHAOS was not exposed as the source of the taps. In this way things went from bad to abysmal in 1969, and Katharine supported him more solidly. After Johnson had appointed Russell Wiggins his ambassador to the United Nations in September 1968, as payment for his editorial loyalty, she had started to check every editorial before it went into the paper, having the writer bring it to her house for her to read if she was not at the office.

On October 7, 1969, she approved a silly, snide piece about the first Moratorium, which CHAOS estimated was going to produce two hundred and fifty thousand people in Washington the following week. "If there are any smart literary agents around these days," the editorialist observed, "one of them will copyright the title 'The Breaking of the President' . . . for it is becoming more obvious with every passing day that the men and the movement that broke Lyndon B. Johnson's authority in 1968 are out to break Richard M. Nixon in 1969. . . . There is still a vital distinction . . . between the constitutionally protected expression of dissent . . . and mass movements aimed at breaking the President . . . the one man who can negotiate the peace. . . . The orators who remind us that Mr. Nixon has been in office for nine months should remind themselves that he will remain for 39 more months—unless, of course, they are willing to put their convictions to the test by moving to impeach him. . . . And what a wonderful chapter it would make for Volume 2 of 'The Breaking of the President.' " *

As frantic as Katharine was about the political deterioration and the social upheaval, as eager as she was to establish her moral authority in relation to it, and to prove to Nixon that her family and her corporation shared his interests, Ben Bradlee remained calm. He was, it has been said, "irritated and bored with serious ideas but quick and contemporaneous in his tastes."† He represented himself as a man who did not need political opinions because he had a social vision. But in truth, the claim to no ideology is itself an ideology; it was the means by which Bradlee created the illusion of liberalism in the paper, in spite of its conservative editorials, while doing nothing to upset further the existing order.

That the counterculture was a reaction to the war was so obvious that Bradlee favored reporters who avoided mentioning the fact, but who instead glorified its most innocuous aspects (flower children, drugs, rock music, denim fashions) while rarely giving the antiwar point of view the benefit of a straightforward analysis. The same applied to coverage of the war itself. The Vietnam correspondent whom he most liked was Ward Just, a promising novelist (more promising than Donny Graham), whose reportage consisted of "vignettes about men in the field." § Just was sent to Vietnam in January

* David S. Broder, "The Breaking of the President," *Washington Post*, October 7, 1969.
† Ben Bagdikian.
§ Roberts, *The Washington Post*.

1966 and remained until June 1967, when Bradlee decided that the war effort was in trouble and replaced him with an honest hawk named Peter Braestrup, who consistently produced stories assuring the reader that the United States was winning the war.

One of the ways to get ahead in an atmosphere of creative tension was to be a "new journalist." Bradlee's best new journalists, other than Just, were Nicholas von Hoffman, former assistant to Saul Alinsky, who became a confidant of Mrs. Graham's, an adviser to her on her youngest son's fascination with hippyism; and Sally Quinn, who lived with and seven years later married Bradlee. Such were the rewards of good (entertaining) writing. Von Hoffman and Quinn became the most important of the writers on Style, the section of the *Post* that was Bradlee's ultimate sociological vision and which he started in January 1969, two weeks before Nixon's first inaugural. One of the first things that Washington readers learned about Nixon from Style was that his favorite dish was cottage cheese and ketchup.

The second way to succeed within Bradlee's system was to possess an old-fashioned understanding and mastery of news as intelligence. This, the ability to cultivate sources in the government and eventually to get leaks, scoops, even classified information from them, all of which were considered to be newsworthy by definition, supplemented the sophisticated, hip tone that Bradlee wanted with the political "impact" (his word) that he also wanted.

Its most astute young practitioner was a reporter named Bob Woodward, who came to the *Post* in 1971 with a background almost identical to Bradlee's own: he too had been a communications officer for naval intelligence. Woodward had enlisted in 1965 after graduating from Yale and had handled coded cables on a guided-missile ship. Later he had been transferred to the Pentagon and during the first year of the Nixon presidency had been an intelligence liaison between the Pentagon and the White House. It does not have to be said that Bradlee took a special interest in this unusual young man, who, like Donny Graham, was so unlike others his age. While Woodward was still on probation at the Metro desk, developing his first contacts with the police department and the FBI, not yet trusted with the national news, Bradlee began assigning him stories that he felt might bring Woodward a Pulitzer Prize.

By contrast there were those reporters who did neither new journalism nor intelligence journalism, and they had a very different experience with their editor. Two cases in point were Ben Bagdikian, who wrote thoughtful press criticism, and Betty Metzger, the woman Katharine did not want him to marry. She had spent ten months on a series about the role of black churches in black community politics and then had been relegated to the night shift. Such were the ideas with which Bradlee was bored.

And then there was the matter of Carl Bernstein, the house misfit, who was talented enough to be a new journalist and wrote in the dramatic prose that Bradlee enjoyed, but whose insistent pieces on ethnic neighborhoods, alternative politics (the missing link between the war and the counterculture), the movement as a movement, not a fashion, were a continual source of annoyance to him. Bernstein was not part of Bradlee's scheme; he killed a good number of his stories, and he cursed the guild for standing in the way of firing him.

There is a certain convenience in having a company scapegoat, and Bernstein served the purpose well. He was the child of Jewish labor organizers, allegedly Communists ("Al and Sylvia Bernstein, Communist labor leaders," was the title of a McCarthy-era file that Carl accidentally found in the *Post*'s morgue, years later). He, with his long hair and political commitments and his infamous parents, embodied all that was myth about Jews/Communists/hippies/radicals. No doubt this was part of his self-image. The terror of McCarthyism had forced his family to hide with relatives for months after

Julius and Ethel Rosenberg had been executed. They feared the beginning of a wave of persecution of Jews, and their fear had left its mark on Carl. If it was easy enough at the *Post* to dismiss him as childish or dangerous, and either way to ridicule his causes, it was also true that Mrs. Graham was embarrassed by him. She blamed Bernstein for Spiro Agnew's attacks on the "left-leaning" media and for his views of the Jewish influence in it, which she understood to be a reference to her own Jewish blood.

The assault began without warning in November 1969, a year after the election, while Katharine was still straining to achieve a rapport with the man she felt she had helped to elevate to the high office. Superficially, and belatedly, it seemed to be Agnew's wounded response to an editorial that the *Post* had published after Nixon chose him as a running mate, fifteen months before. Ward Just, back from Vietnam, had self-indulgently written: "You can view Agnew with alarm, or you can point to him with pride, but for now we prefer to look on with horrified fascination. . . . Nixon's decision . . . to name Agnew . . . may come to be regarded as perhaps the most eccentric political appointment since the Roman emperor Caligula named his horse a consul." * Cruel as this characterization was, though, it had little political significance; if it was the reason that Agnew, rather than another man, was allowed to deliver the initial blows, it was certainly far too trivial to have been the original cause of the problem. The irrationality and self-destructiveness of Nixon's media hatred has been analyzed at length elsewhere and need not be repeated here; it is important only to say that Katharine Graham offered him her friendship, and that he rejected her.

He did this although she was with him on the war, which was most important, and on questions of domestic unrest. She

* *Washington Post*, September 25, 1968.

had joined a Special Committee on Crime Prevention and Control at the invitation of Edward Bennett Williams, its chairman (one of his innumerable gestures toward her since the episode with her husband's wills), and had been meeting with District police about methods for handling antiwar demonstrators.

The police had for some time been recruiting men directly from the military bases as they returned from Vietnam, telling them that the war was not won unless it was won at home.* And though he had not signed up then, Don had thought about it and had joined the District force in January 1969. He had taken Civil Disturbance Unit training, where he had learned to use a gun, to negotiate with terrorists, to control crowds with nightstick and gas pellets (trainees were required to breathe the gas in order to understand its effects); and by June he had gone undercover, four months before the first Moratorium.† The Graham family involvement with the problem was therefore substantial, Don being in physical danger from it, and when Katharine went to the White House in October, after the "Breaking of the President" editorial, to ask Nixon for National Guard protection for the *Post* building during the Moratorium (something that Johnson would have

---

* "The cop on the beat . . . is on our side in the war against crime. His uniform is the uniform of our troops. A policeman's badge should command the same respect granted a soldier's green beret." This quotation is from Spiro Agnew.

† The truth about Donny's service with the District of Columbia police has been a matter of some confusion. The *Post*'s official information sheet on him says that he was a patrolman from January 1969 until June 1970, eighteen months, with which Chalmers Roberts's official history of the *Post* concurs. Police personnel records, however, indicate something different: that he joined in January 1969 and resigned in June 1969, shortly after finishing academy training. This would be the end of it, except that the payroll office lists him until January 1970. When such a discrepancy exists, according to the personnel office, it is because an officer has gone undercover, into the intelligence unit or the vice squad; a man with Don's Civil Disturbance training most likely would have gone into intelligence. That he claims to have been with the force until June 1970, five months longer than he actually was, remains a mystery.

done for her as a matter of course, without making her ask for it), she was more than insulted when he wanted to know whether she thought her newspaper was a national asset. She was more than insulted, sensing the profoundness of Nixon's contempt for her: she was afraid.

Soon after that, Katharine gave a luncheon for John Ehrlichman in her private dining room. It was to be a routine meeting with Bradlee and several other editors: what were the administration's concerns, what sorts of stories would the president like to see in the paper, what could they expect to happen in the next few months? Things started pleasantly, Katharine seating Ehrlichman next to her at a rectangular table (the round table is more recent), asking how he was, Ehrlichman replying cordially; but the luncheon deteriorated from there. Before the salads had been served, Ehrlichman reached matter-of-factly into his breast pocket and extracted a folded paper. He put on his glasses, assumed his bulldog expression, and slowly began to read a grocery list of the sins that he claimed the *Washington Post* had committed against the president of the United States. The points were trivial, many of them factually incorrect, all contentious. Katharine sat biting her lip and tightly twisting her napkin underneath the table, sad and disturbed. "What can we do to improve ourselves?" she asked him over and over again.

It happened during this time, in late 1969, that Daniel Ellsberg began to visit the paper. He was an analyst, considered to be brilliant, who had worked in the 1960s on the most sensitive of assignments. In 1962, on loan from the RAND Corporation, the elite foreign policy think tank, he had done strategic nuclear war planning for Kennedy during the Cuban missile crisis. In 1965 he took a leave of absence from RAND to become special apprentice to Major General Edward G. Landsale in Vietnam and also worked for the deputy ambassador at the embassy in Saigon. In 1967, again at RAND, he was made a member of the McNamara Study

Group which McNamara, in his disillusionment, had commissioned to write a classified "History of Decisionmaking in Vietnam, 1945–1968." This was the Pentagon Papers, in forty-seven volumes. Ellsberg worked on the Kennedy years.

In 1968, shortly before the traumatic study was finished (traumatic for the analysts, who concluded, and proved, that Vietnam had been twenty years of misjudgment and calculated deception; traumatic for the war makers who read it), he and several colleagues consulted jointly for the National Security Council, Defense, and State on Vietnam "options." From this effort evolved the "two-track method" for trying to settle the war. Ellsberg's approach was so effective that Clark Clifford quickly adopted this theory, that on one track the United States and North Vietnam should negotiate only about military withdrawal from South Vietnam, and on the other track that Saigon and the NLF should negotiate a political settlement. Clifford made this the basic structure for the peace talks opening in Paris on May 10.

The talks were considered within the Nixon campaign to be a grave threat, and there were two things that the future president did to try to damage them: first, he hired Henry Kissinger, Rockefeller's foreign policy adviser, and had Kissinger develop *his* plan for ending the war, which Nixon referred to in all of his campaign speeches as being superior (the plan went largely unexplained); and second, Nixon told South Vietnam's President Thieu that if he would hold back in the talks with Johnson, then he, Nixon, would give Saigon a better deal.* After Nixon won the election, Kissinger worked

* This truly Nixonian incident is related in a light biography of Johnson, *A Very Human President*, by Jack Valenti (New York: W. W. Norton, 1975): "The president . . . beginning in early October felt that all signs pointed to a break in the Paris peace talks. Hanoi began to show a willingness to go forward . . . [and] the South [for the first time was] willing to take part in the peace negotiations, with the proviso that the bombing would stop. . . . Suddenly the South turned bafflingly stubborn, delaying, backing and filling. . . . The president said that hard information had come to him that representatives of Nixon [had] reached President Thieu and

with Ellsberg and the other analysts and in January 1969 published an article in *Foreign Affairs* in which he explained their "two-track method" and claimed it as his own.

In 1969 Daniel Ellsberg was a man tormented. After months of working with Kissinger, having seen his real peace plan, which was to pressure Hanoi through the Soviet Union and Communist China (hence detente and the China initiative), and to destroy Cambodia with bombs, rather than to talk sincerely in Paris; having been invited to San Clemente three times to tell Kissinger about "options" and urging him to read the Pentagon Papers, which, incredibly, he had not looked at, Ellsberg felt he had to repudiate everything he had done for the previous ten years. He became obsessed with breaking the deadly silence (the Cambodia bombing would remain secret until April 1970), with ending the deception and the self-deception of the national security types who were still, in spite of the Pentagon study, keeping that ridiculous war going out of more self-deception, desperation, and pride. In September he and his daughter and son and Anthony Russo (a RAND fellow who had analyzed Viet Cong "motivation and morale" for the government by interviewing prisoners in Saigon jails) made copies of the Pentagon Papers in a small Los Angeles advertising agency. The papers had been in private circulation at RAND, and Ellsberg, one of their authors, had legitimate access to them.

In November he gave several of the documents to Senator J. William Fulbright, a war critic, who could not see their value in ending the war and did nothing with them. He gave

---

urged him not to accept this arrangement. They intimated to Thieu that it would be in his best interests, more than intimating that if Nixon won, the South would get a better deal . . . [but] that the U.S. would sell out Saigon [if] Humphrey took office. . . . Johnson said that he had kept both Nixon and Humphrey informed of every turn in the negotiations, and both . . . said they would back LBJ in his every move. But the president said it was clear to him that Nixon [was] nervous and fidgety over the prospect of a full bombing halt and the inclusion of the South in the talks."

a complete set to Marcus Raskin at the Institute for Policy Studies, a prestigious left-wing think tank in Washington, and Raskin, with two colleagues, immediately started work on a book based upon them, *Washington Plans an Aggressive War.* *

And he began testing the waters at the *Post,* showing up to see editorial page editor Phil Geyelin, talking passionately about how important it was that the paper change its position. On one occasion Ellsberg asked Geyelin if it were true that he could not always write as he wanted because of Mrs. Graham's relationship with Kissinger, who had been cultivating her, taking her to movies, confiding his well-known "anguish of power." In fact Kissinger had warned her about Ellsberg being "unbalanced," which was all he had needed to say. "That's not true," Geyelin blurted; "we ran a critical editorial the other day and now Kissinger stopped seeing her and won't return her phone calls and things are very tense around here." Geyelin walked with Ellsberg into the lobby, where they saw Katharine and Bradlee. There were introductions all around. Katharine shook Ellsberg's hand coldly and walked away. Bradlee wordlessly followed her.

The *New York Times* broke the Pentagon Papers on Sunday, June 13, 1971, with six pages of news stories and documents that told a different version of the war: that Truman and Eisenhower had committed the United States to Indochina through France, that Kennedy had turned that commitment into a war by using a secret "provocation strategy" that led eventually to the Gulf of Tonkin incidents, that Johnson had planned from the beginning of his presidency to expand the war, that the CIA had concluded that the bombing was utterly ineffective in winning it. One of the documents was a memorandum written in 1964 by assistant

* By Raskin, Stavins, and Barnet, previously cited. The book presented a serious argument that those responsible for the Vietnam war were guilty of war crimes; this issue was lost when the publication of the papers became identified with freedom of the press.

secretary of defense John T. McNaughton. American goals in South Vietnam, he had said, are "70 pct.—To avoid a humiliating U.S. defeat . . . 20 pct.—to keep SVN [South Vietnam] territory from Chinese hands. 10 pct.—To permit the people of SVN to enjoy a better, freer way of life. Also— To emerge from crisis without unacceptable taint from methods used. NOT—To 'help a friend,' although it would be hard to stay in if asked out." Daniel Ellsberg went into hiding.

Katharine and Ben Bradlee were humiliated that the *Times* broke the story first and felt that the *Post* now had to catch up. On Monday morning, when the *Times* headline read "Vietnam Archive: A Consensus to Bomb Developed Before '64 Election, Study Says," Bradlee met with Marcus Raskin and expressed interest in reading his manuscript. He received a copy of it by noon, but refused to publish excerpts because "they [the authors] were in the war criminal racket," having concentrated on the Kennedy years.* That the papers told of war crimes became clear to him by Tuesday, when the *Times* headline read "Vietnam Archive: Study Tells How Johnson Secretly Opened Way to Ground Combat." Tuesday night the Nixon administration took the *Times* to court and won a temporary restraining order on the basis of the Espionage Act. By the time Ben Bagdikian had located Ellsberg in Boston on Wednesday and flown up to get a set of the papers, Bradlee was excited about defying Nixon for the cause of freedom of the press. On Thursday he felt differently. The papers were in his den, and his face was gray at the prospect of publishing them. Suddenly there were other considerations: legal issues, national security issues, the fact that two days before, the *Post* had become a public corporation, and its stock might suffer.

* Raskin's book became the basis of an essay by the eminent political theorist Hannah Arendt, which she called "Lying in Politics," in *Crises of the Republic* (New York: Harcourt Brace Jovanovich, 1972).

Bradlee and the *Post* lawyers finally decided to notify Attorney General John Mitchell that the papers were in their possession, at which point Bagdikian said angrily, "You're going to have a full-scale revolt from the staff." Bagdikian had obtained the papers from Ellsberg on Bradlee's word that he would publish them. "You know that you have an obligation to me to publish these papers." Bradlee called Katharine, who was hosting a party for a retiring business manager. "It certainly weighed very heavily in this rush decision that the editors were absolutely wild about this," she reasoned, "and the reporters felt incredibly strongly that we had to go ahead." It would be all over town that the *Post* had gotten the papers but had been afraid to publish them, Bradlee lamented. "OK," Katharine told him, "go ahead." That night, as Jack Patterson was supervising the loading of delivery trucks, he was approached by two FBI agents who ordered him to destroy all of the freshly printed newspapers. Patterson looked levelly at them. "Get the fuck off the loading dock," he said.

Their first story, "Documents Reveal U.S. Effort in '54 to Delay Viet Election," was from the Eisenhower era, although Ellsberg had stipulated that they begin their series with the Kennedy years. One week later, after the Nixon government had sued to restrain the *Post* also, and the *Post* and the *Times* had consolidated their appeals, Katharine sat victoriously in the Supreme Court listening to the justices find in the newspapers' favor, six to three. "The *Washington Post* and other newspapers should be commended for serving the purpose that the Founding Fathers saw so clearly," Justice Hugo Black noted. That was on June 25; from then on Katharine Graham was famous.*

But when the excitement faded, she was not at all happy to be openly at war with the president. The next time she saw

* For a fine, complete account of the Pentagon Papers case, see Sanford J. Ungar, *The Papers and The Papers* (New York: E. P. Dutton, 1972).

Bagdikian she stopped him. "Well, what kind of trouble have you gotten us into today?" she demanded. She began to fear for her television licenses, and the "*Post* want[ed] to return all sensitive documents" * by July 6.

That summer and fall, a series of meetings took place within the White House that included Nixon, Kissinger, H. R. Haldeman, and Ehrlichman. Their purpose was threefold: to plan how to ruin Ellsberg by painting him as another Alger Hiss; how to increase security in their ranks (Ellsberg had worked with Kissinger's staff); and how to turn the Pentagon Papers to their advantage, by pressuring the CIA, the FBI, and former Johnson advisers to reveal additional documents that would prove that the war had been the fault of the Democrats.†

June 6, 1971—Nixon, Mitchell, Ehrlichman:

PRESIDENT: It's treasonable.

PRESIDENT: I went through all this on the Hiss case and we won that.

June 17—Nixon, Kissinger, Haldeman, Ehrlichman:

KISSINGER: Ellsberg—genius, best student I ever had, shot at peasants, always a little unbalanced, drugs-flipped, hawk to peacenik in early '66.

PRESIDENT: Like [Whittaker] Chambers.

KISSINGER: McNamara in tears, won't betray Pres. Johnson; Bundy wants to come clean regarding Johnson.

June 23—Nixon, Kissinger, Haldeman, Ehrlichman:

KISSINGER: Go on the attack.

July 1, 10:30 A.M.—Nixon, Haldeman, Charles Colson, Ehrlichman:

PRESIDENT: 6 Crises—Hiss chapter—it was won in press, Truman, Hoover wouldn't help me.

* Senate Watergate hearings, Appendix III, John Ehrlichman's handwritten notes, p. 128.
† The following comments are selected from Ehrlichman's notes, pp. 90–203. The conversations from which they are excerpted took place between June 6 and October 8, 1971, and they appear here in chronological order.

July 1, 1:30 P.M.—Nixon, National Security Study Group, William Rehnquist, Ehrlichman:

REHNQUIST: Ellsberg says 10 years is a small price to pay.
PRESIDENT: Yes, & he'll pay it.

July 2—Nixon, Haldeman, Ehrlichman:

PRESIDENT: Brookings—pull clearances of people—Council on Foreign Relations also.
PRESIDENT: CIA, FBI—Military Espionage—use.

July 6—Nixon, Mitchell, Haldeman, Ehrlichman:

PRESIDENT: Need Hoover's cooperation. Must be tried in the paper. Get conspiracy smoked out through the papers. Hiss & Bentley cracked that way.
PRESIDENT: Domestic communist ties to Ellsberg.
JOHN MITCHELL: Post wants to return all sensitive documents; fear effect of conviction [in threatened criminal prosecution] on TV licenses.
PRESIDENT: Leak the evidence of guilt. Tell Hoover.
PRESIDENT: Keep one step away from me.

July 9—Nixon, Haldeman, Ehrlichman:

EHRLICHMAN: [General Vernon A.] Walters into CIA as #2.
PRESIDENT: Kissinger's staff must be cleaned out. Don't bother Kissinger.

July 10—Nixon, Haldeman, Ehrlichman, Rose Mary Woods:

HALDEMAN or EHRLICHMAN: Ellsberg [is talking to reporters about] McNamara tapes [McNamara had been taped without his knowledge through the war room, while he was a consultant to the Joint Chiefs of Staff after he left office].
PRESIDENT: Rogers should be tapping more.
PRESIDENT: Goal—Do to McNamara, Bundy, JFK elite the same destructive job that was done on Herbert Hoover years ago.

July 20—Nixon, Haldeman, Ehrlichman:

PRESIDENT: [Ellsberg] conspiracy.

July 24—Nixon, Haldeman, Ehrlichman, Kissinger:

PRESIDENT: Anyone with access to top secret—sign a prior agreement to take polygraph—put fear into these people!

July 28—Nixon, Ehrlichman:

PRESIDENT: Push [Ellsberg trial] *past* October election [November 1972 presidential election]. Dent Rusk.

August 11—Nixon, Ehrlichman:

EHRLICHMAN: The presidential [taping] system has been inaugurated—a personal system.

PRESIDENT: Position Rehnquist—Don't discuss presidential system.

EHRLICHMAN: Speak to Kissinger re: political use of intelligence.

September 18—Nixon, Mitchell, Haldeman, Ehrlichman, EK (probably Egil Krogh):

PRESIDENT: Make the Democrats squabble about it [the origins of the war].

PRESIDENT: LBJ can be with us on this [that Kennedy started the war by killing Diem].

PRESIDENT: Let CIA take a whipping on this.

EK: President wants entire Diem file by next Friday.

PRESIDENT: Speed up Walters to CIA.

EHRLICHMAN: Bay of Pigs—order to CIA—President is to have the FULL file *or* else—nothing withheld.

EHRLICHMAN: President was involved in Bay of Pigs—must have the file—theory—deeply involved—must know *all.*

EHRLICHMAN: Keep President out of it—use Tom Huston [coordinator of security affairs for the White House] to read it—Liddy & Hunt.

October 8—Nixon, Ehrlichman, Richard Helms:

HELMS (to President): Cooperation of FBI with intelligence community is extremely delicate.

PRESIDENT: Purpose of request for documents: must be fully advised in order to know what to duck; won't hurt Agency, nor attack predecessor.

HELMS: Only one president at a time; I only work for you.

PRESIDENT: Ehrlichman is my lawyer—deal with him on all this as you would me.

EHRLICHMAN: I'll be making requests for additional material.

HELMS: OK, anything.

An indictment was brought against Daniel Ellsberg and Anthony Russo, and on August 16, 1971, they pleaded guilty to espionage, theft, and conspiracy. Their trial opened in Los Angeles, the scene of the "crimes," early in 1973. It was a scene reminiscent of the Hiss case, except that the case against Ellsberg was even weaker: photocopying is not theft; espionage is spying for a foreign government, and foreign diplomats had been allowed to see the Pentagon Papers when the American public had not. Conspiracy, on which the trial really hung, was so transparently political a charge (conspiracy is a crime even when the acts committed are not themselves criminal) that the government tried to disguise the fact by concentrating on proving the other charges. Things were going badly for the government in the Ellsberg trial, so one Sunday Nixon brought the presiding judge, Matthew Byrne, down to San Clemente in a limousine, took him for a walk on the beach, and asked him to become director of the FBI, as Byrne immediately told the newspapers. From then on things began to get worse.

Late in April, Judge Byrne heard, from the prosecutors of a case called Watergate, that Ellsberg's psychiatrist's office had been burglarized by Howard Hunt and Gordon Liddy, two White House "Plumbers," on September 3, 1971. The Plumbers had been formed the previous July, two weeks after the Pentagon Papers were published. On May 11, 1973, the judge also learned from the Watergate prosecutors that Ellsberg's phone had been tapped. To Nixon's horror, Byrne dismissed the case "with prejudice," because of governmental misconduct.

In the scant year that passed between the publication of the Pentagon Papers, in June 1971, and the Plumbers' first and second burglaries of the Democratic National Committee headquarters at the Watergate in May and June 1972, Nixon had indeed "put fear" into all of his "enemies," as he had planned that summer of 1971: they included not only Katharine Graham, but the intelligence community (Helms and Hoover) and the national security managers who had run and were running the war. By the time of the break-ins, much of Washington was seething with hatred for Nixon; his enemies would bring about his destruction, just as he had always known they would.

Katharine's mother died in September 1970, having told her daughter to the end, as she had been saying from the time of Nixon's HUAC hearings in the late 1940s, that Nixon was plainly "an outlaw." Frederick Beebe, chairman of the board of the Washington Post Company and Katharine's treasured father figure, was ill with cancer; he died in 1973. The loneliness and sorrow that she suffered during the long, brutal fight with the president are not part of the Watergate legend, nor is the incapacitating fear that in that fight she would lose the corporation (beginning with her television licenses) that her dead parents had entrusted to her care. The legend is that Katharine Graham used her newspaper to destroy Richard Nixon, that she is therefore the strongest and wisest and most courageous publisher in recent history, and that her name is synonymous with the power and the possibilities of the press.

Not to diminish the value of legend, it had long been established practice at the *Post*, by the time Watergate erupted, for Katharine not to interfere with Bradlee's newsroom (as he once informed her, "I can't edit when you have your fucking finger in my eye"). She and he had well-defined areas of authority, and hers was business. The only legitimate reason that she had, in the minds of both, for questioning Bradlee's judgment was if the health of the corporation were at stake. She was asked to make major decisions, such as "going ahead" with the Pentagon Papers, only after Bradlee had guided a situation into its crisis stages, and without exception she approved what Bradlee wanted to do.

The Watergate investigation was Bradlee's operation. By

the time Katharine had formally been asked to let the reporters track obscure and explosive leads, to undertake more
thorough, time-consuming, expensive, and analytical work
than Bradlee had ever before demanded, or wanted, the hunt
had already gotten started. Nixon and everyone else in the
city knew it, and Katharine had little choice but to go along.
Bradlee and the reporters believed, from two days after the
break-in, when Deep Throat confirmed to Bob Woodward
the significant and leading fact that Howard Hunt was connected with the White House, that the trail would take them
to the president. In the oppressive air of Nixon's Washington,
where intimidation had become the rule (Katharine bullied;
McNamara reduced to tears; William Rogers forced to wire-
tap the *Post*, his long-time client; Clark Clifford denied a
security clearance, although he had been chairman of the
Foreign Intelligence Advisory Board since 1963), where the
presidency was not as it should have been, but was an alien
camp, Katharine hoped that it was true. It fell to her, after
Deep Throat's intervention, to shine the light on the evils of
Richard Nixon: she allowed it to be done.*

In that remarkable book *All the President's Men*,† in
which Woodward and his partner Carl Bernstein chronicle
the development of the case against Nixon almost day by day,
there are only eleven page references to Katharine. An appointment is made with her by the head of the Committee to
Re-elect the President but is canceled. John Mitchell tells Bernstein that "Katie Graham is gonna get her tit caught in a big
fat wringer" if Bernstein writes the story linking him to campaign funds. Bradlee thinks about asking her if they can run
that story, but decides not to ask. Katharine asks Bernstein

* According to Robert Dole, chairman of the Republican National Committee, Katharine's motivation was simply "because I hate him." This quote,
however, was denied by Katharine: see Roberts, *The Washington Post*, p.
436.
† Carl Bernstein and Bob Woodward (New York: Simon and Schuster,
1974).

after it has run if he has any more messages for her. Katharine is told by a "close friend who had ties to the administration," William Rogers, that her phones are tapped, and she spends $5,000 on an electronic sweep. Henry Kissinger says to her unkindly, "What's the matter, don't you think we're going to be re-elected?" and she tells Woodward that Kissinger thought they were being "terribly, terribly unfair." Managing editor Howard Simons telephones her in Singapore in March 1973 to let her know about the McCord letter, which ends the reporters' agonizing dry spell after Nixon's reelection. The letter charged that "political pressure had been applied to the defendants [the Watergate burglars, who had gone to jail that January] to plead guilty and remain silent." She watches Nixon announce on television that he has fired Ehrlichman and Haldeman and she says, "This is too much." Nixon's chief of staff, General Alexander Haig, reaches her by telephone in a restaurant and snarls at her for the "scurrilous" story about Nixon's lawyers supplying Haldeman's and Ehrlichman's lawyers with White House documents. She and Howard Simons and Woodward and Bernstein (strangely, not Bradlee) are subpoenaed by CRP in its defense against the $1 million damage suit by the Democratic party, and she takes possession of the reporters' notes and says she will go to jail rather than relinquish them; the subpoenas are thrown out of court.

This, then, was the level and tenor of her involvement: worried, ladylike questions, humorous quips, receipt of telephone threats and Kissinger's insults, one instance of bravado. She went on like that for a full year until the Senate formed the Ervin Committee to investigate Watergate in the spring of 1973, in response to the McCord letter, and for another year at lesser risk until the House Judiciary Committee adopted three articles of impeachment against the president. She went on like that, knowing that the entire affair was orchestrated, at least in part, by a man with the code name

Deep Throat, putting her corporation in jeopardy to publish information provided by him, and never, incredibly, wanting to know his name, not wanting to "carry that burden around with her."

That Woodward was manipulated, or "run," by Deep Throat is very clear from *All the President's Men,* which is another reason that the book is an amazing document. It is evident that Deep Throat has a serious interest in the *Post*'s succeeding with its investigation; he is not merely doing Woodward a favor by meeting him in a dark garage in the middle of the night; he expects results. He will not tell him how he knows what he knows or why he wants to help Woodward implicate Nixon; "I have to do this my way," he says, and Woodward, with his naval intelligence training, "listens obediently." The entire "friendship" seems to consist of Deep Throat's telling Woodward a fraction of what he knows, making Woodward do exhausting legwork and then come begging for more hints; it is a classic counterintelligence operation, of which the exotic flower pot signals, speechless phone calls, clock hands drawn on newspapers, are only the more obvious techniques.

The psychological manipulation is more important: Woodward pursues the story according to Deep Throat's outline, becoming more committed and beholden to him each time he finds evidence that Deep Throat is right. He thinks of Deep Throat as a "wise teacher," he has faith in him, he wants to please him. Deep Throat doesn't like newspapers because he "detest[s] inexactitude and shallowness," and Woodward wants to prove him wrong. When Woodward does not understand a clue, Deep Throat becomes impatient with him: "Don't you get my message?" When he makes a serious mistake, the story that Haldeman was named in front of the Watergate grand jury as one of the men controlling the CRP slush fund, Deep Throat becomes angry and instructive: " 'Well, Haldeman slipped away from you,' Deep Throat stated. He kicked his heel at the garage wall, making no attempt to hide his disappointment. The entire story would never become known now. . . . Deep Throat moved closer . . . 'Let me explain something. . . . When you move on somebody like Haldeman, you've got to be sure you're on the most solid ground. Shit, what a royal screw-up! . . . Everybody goes chicken after you make a mistake like you guys made. . . . It contributes to the myth of Haldeman invincibility. . . . It looks like he really stuck it in your eyes, secretly pulling the strings to get even the *Washington Post* to fuck it up. . . . A conspiracy like this . . . a conspiracy investigation . . . the rope has to tighten slowly around everyone's neck. You build . . . from the outer edges in. . . . You've put the investigation back months.' Woodward swallowed hard. He deserved the lecture." *

The minor deception in the book is that only Woodward knew who Deep Throat was. Bradlee knew him, had known him far longer than Woodward. There is a possibility that Woodward had met him while working as an intelligence liaison between the Pentagon and the White House, where Deep Throat spent a lot of time, and that he considered Woodward trustworthy, or useful, and began talking to him when the time was right. It is equally likely, though, that Bradlee, who had given Woodward other sources on other stories, put them in touch after Woodward's first day on the story, when Watergate burglar James McCord said at his arraignment hearing that he had once worked for the CIA. Whether or not Bradlee provided the source, he recognized McCord's statement to the court as highly unusual: CIA employees, when caught in an illegal act, do not admit that they work for the CIA, unless that is part of the plan. McCord had no good reasons to mention the CIA at all, except, apparently, to direct wide attention to the burglary, because he

* Bernstein and Woodward, *All the President's Men.*

267

had been asked to state only his present occupation, and he had not worked for the CIA for several years.

What matters is not how the connection with Deep Throat was made, but why. Why did Bradlee allow Woodward to rely so heavily upon it, and ultimately, why did the leaders of the intelligence community, for whom Deep Throat spoke, want the president of the United States to fall?

What we have seen so far has been Nixon's attempt, after the Pentagon Papers, to bludgeon CIA director Helms and FBI director Hoover into cooperating with his campaign to use the papers against the Democrats. Actually, Watergate goes back to the early days of the Nixon administration, when Henry Kissinger, the head of the National Security Council, issued NSSM (National Security Study Memorandum) 1 (ironically, Daniel Ellsberg had helped him draft it), which required different intelligence agencies and departments to provide him with independent answers to comprehensive sets of questions about the Vietnam war. The purpose of NSSM 1 was not only to be able to run the war better, for Kissinger was running the war the way he wanted to in Vietnam and Cambodia anyway, but to play the agencies off against each other, with the power, in the confusion, going to Kissinger. He was, of course, understood to be operating for Nixon.

NSSM 1 came out on February 1, 1969, about a week after Nixon took office; in February 1970 Kissinger then formed the infamous 40 Committee, to which the CIA was to submit all plans for covert actions. In December 1970 Kissinger assigned James Schlesinger, assistant director of the budget, the task of analyzing the intelligence budget with an eye to cutting back the department of Thomas Karamessines, Helms's deputy and the director of plans. There were other memos and other major changes until 1973.*

Against this destabilized background, the directors of the

* For a more complete discussion of Kissinger's reorganization effort, see Corson, *The Armies of Ignorance*, pp. 411–33.

agencies were expected, in spite of their antagonism and alarm, to help Kissinger when he needed them, which was all the time. He had not only Vietnam to worry about, and the world-wide spread of communism, but detente, the Arab-Israeli wars, and domestic subversion. In 1969, as part of a solution to the last three problems, all of which he thought were closely related, he moved CIA counterintelligence chief James Angleton into the White House and put him in charge of an Israeli counterintelligence desk that was in theory independent from and more important than the Israeli desk at the CIA.

For years Israeli intelligence, with whom Angleton was the liaison, had been the source of 80 percent of the CIA's information on the Russians. Now in the White House, Angleton provided Kissinger with Israel's information in three areas: detente, of course; Russian military and support activity in the Arab countries; and Russian influence on Al Fatah, the military arm of the Palestine Liberation Organization that was creating nests on American college campuses. In Kissinger's mind the Al Fatah issue merged with the larger one of the Russians' stimulating other campus activism, particularly the antiwar movement; indeed, Angleton's deputy Richard Ober had investigated Al Fatah's Communist ties when he had been looking for Communist influence in the movement prior to 1967, the year that he formed Operation CHAOS for widespread domestic counterintelligence. Angleton worked closely with Kissinger and knew almost everything that he was doing, although Kissinger did not have the same advantage with Angleton. Despite Kissinger's concern about domestic unrest, Angleton did not trust Kissinger enough to inform him of the existence of CHAOS, that unprecedented mechanism by which the rival intelligence agencies were working together against the domestic threat. If Angleton had told him, Nixon would not have tried to achieve the same cooperation in the same illegal activities that he did with the Huston Plan, an idea about which Angleton later said: "All . . .

matters of enlarging procurement within the intelligence community were the same concerns that existed prior to the Huston Plan, and subsequent to the Huston Plan. The Huston Plan had no impact whatsoever on the priorities within the intelligence community." *

The Huston Plan for surveillance, mail interception, wiretapping, burglary, all of which were already being performed by CHAOS, was drawn up by Tom Huston, Nixon's coordinator for security affairs, in June 1970, one month after the invasion of Cambodia, which had caused a fearfully violent reaction in the country, resulting in the shooting of four students at Kent State. Kissinger blamed intelligence for not warning him that there would be this kind of reaction to the Cambodia bombing (although he had not told anyone with official or unofficial responsibility for domestic intelligence anything about the bombing ahead of time); and the attempt at intensified domestic surveillance was his and the president's response to their own failure to understand the national mood.

The Huston Plan was presented at a meeting between Nixon and directors of the FBI (Hoover), CIA (Helms), and army and navy intelligence—the CHAOS group—during which Nixon demanded better intelligence about "revolutionary activism." Hoover afterward leaked the story that he had rejected the order out of hand because it was blatantly illegal, but a black bag operation does not expose another black bag operation because it disapproves of black bag operations. What really happened is that the story was leaked to discredit Nixon; while within the government, Hoover demanded that Nixon personally sign each separate illegal order, which Nixon knew would enable Hoover to blackmail him. Nixon with-

* Angleton's testimony before the Senate Select Committee to Study Government Operations with Respect to Intelligence Activities (the Church Committee), September 24, 1975. A fascinating discussion of the Huston Plan and Operation CHAOS appears in the Church Committee's Final Report, Book 3, "Supplementary Detailed Staff Reports on Intelligence Activities and the Rights of Americans."

drew the Huston Plan, but became more suspicious of the intelligence agencies and more determined to have what he wanted, with or without them. Three months later he authorized John Mitchell to provide Justice Department cover for an Intelligence Evaluation Committee (IEC, for which Hoover refused to provide FBI staff), which monitored civil disturbances and coordinated and evaluated domestic intelligence. The president also began to rely heavily upon the counsel of Richard Ober, Angleton's deputy, the man in the CIA most concerned with domestic counterintelligence, and one of the few whom Nixon trusted. Ober was given a small office inside the White House, where he was known only to Nixon, Haldeman, Ehrlichman, and possibly Kissinger. He had unlimited access to the president, could pass Haldeman at any time without permission and without going on the record (his name was never recorded in White House logs), and was present at many of the meetings that took place after the publication of the Pentagon Papers, when Nixon's obsession with his enemies pushed him to the limits to rational thought. The president, in his confusion, began to equate the Democrats with both the war (the Kennedy Democrats) and the antiwar movement (the McGovern Democrats); decided that a McGovern victory in the approaching presidential election would be a victory for the movement's Communists; and became more firmly convinced than he had always been that his reelection was synonymous with the best interests of the nation. He also knew, and must have complained to his personal intelligence consultant, Ober, that neither the CIA nor the FBI would help ensure that he would win.

Nixon's confidence in Ober did not come automatically; a man like Nixon must have proof of loyalty. He would have had to see, from Ober, the evidence that he did not care for bureaucratic battles, that he put the president's interests above those of the CIA. The most effective way for Ober to have proven himself was to have acted as consultant when Ehrlichman, Nixon's domestic affairs adviser, was ordered to establish (without experience in such matters) the president's personal intelligence unit, the Plumbers, in the summer of 1971. Ober would have found Ehrlichman the right men for the job (men like former CIA operative James McCord); he would have provided equipment, given detailed instructions, helped Ehrlichman to analyze their results. He would have shown Nixon that he was willing to risk his career for him by doing what the CIA would not have done—for example, overseeing the burglary of the office of Daniel Ellsberg's psychiatrist—which more than anything else would have demonstrated Ober's correct state of mind and persuaded Nixon that he could finally trust him.

The essential rule of counterintelligence is to use an enemy's weaknesses against himself, to one's own advantage. Haldeman and Ehrlichman held the authority in the Nixon White House for political intelligence and sabotage, but Nixon, by his nature, needed to keep secrets even from them; he needed to think that certain plans were too sensitive to share with anybody except Ober. This operative, who was next to Angleton the most skilled counterintelligence man in the nation, understood Nixon's fear of the Democrats and did not tell him that with his thirty-point lead in the polls the fear was illogical. Instead, he played upon it; he either persuaded Nixon or agreed with him that the Plumbers ought to stop working on the fringes of the campaign, that they should be sent directly into Democratic National Committee headquarters to plant telephone bugs and steal documents, which they did for the first time on May 1, 1972, the day, coincidentally, before J. Edgar Hoover died.

The first burglary whetted Nixon's appetite, ensuring that he would want the Plumbers to go back again, but it also would serve the purpose, from a counterintelligence point of view, of establishing for the public record that the burglaries were part of a pattern, and that the president knew about them. This point was deliberately obscured during the Watergate investigations, but it is crucially important to the question of Nixon's guilt: the first burglary was reported in the newspapers, and Nixon would have known about it that way, even if, as he claims, he could have known of it no other way. Once aware, he would have been expected to order that nothing of the kind ever be done again; when the second burglary took place on June 17, the inescapable conclusion is that Nixon gave his consent to it.

Watergate was, according to this scenario, a counterintelligence operation of the highest order, carried out for patriotic as well as bureaucratic reasons, which were, in the minds of the intelligence directors, one and the same. It is clear what their motives must have been: Kissinger was pursuing a disastrous policy in Cambodia, disregarding the CIA's advice and blaming the CIA when he failed, all the time adding fuel to the antiwar movement. Nixon's harsh and stupid attempts "to get political control over the CIA," as Watergate burglar James McCord later told the Senate Watergate committee, his intention to have the agency's judgments conform to rather than inform his policies, "smacked of the situation which Hitler's intelligence chiefs found themselves in" before the fall of Germany. But primarily because Nixon seemed at times to be insane, a terrible and a dangerous head of state, double agent Ober, by this logic, arranged for double agent McCord to be arrested during the second Watergate break-in.

And then Richard Ober, the head of Operation CHAOS, the only man in the nation with access to classified information at the White House, the FBI, the CIA, and CRP, became Deep Throat, a favor to Ben Bradlee, an old Harvard chum. Ober's boss, James Angleton, finally had achieved the ultimate dirty trick: Bradlee would take all of the risks, and either Bradlee would succeed in getting rid of Nixon, or Katharine Graham would have to salvage her newspaper by getting rid of Bradlee.

In the spring of 1974, after two years of the *Washington Post*'s Watergate stories, a year-long investigation by the Senate, and the indictment for conspiracy to obstruct justice of Nixon's closest aides, the House of Representatives adopted three articles of impeachment against the president for "high crimes and misdemeanors" against the state. Also during that spring, Katharine gave a breakfast for Robert Redford, who wanted, to her amusement, to immortalize the *Washington Post*, its editors, and two of its reporters in a Hollywood film. It was to be a political detective story, based upon *All the President's Men* by Bernstein and Woodward, which was originally written as a study of John Mitchell and Gordon Liddy; Redford had heard about the book and had called Woodward, whom he had never met, to suggest that the plot be changed to feature the reporters as protagonists. The manuscript was nearly finished before Woodward showed it to Katharine, who told him, "It's wonderful."

When the book was delivered to the publisher early in 1974, half a year before Nixon's resignation, and ending, presciently, with Nixon's desperate promise that he had "no intention whatever of ever walking away from the job that the American people elected me to do," Redford quietly paid $425,000 for the movie rights. Then he asked Woodward to introduce him to Mrs. Graham. Though the request, in Katharine's view, came rather belatedly, after he had assumed her cooperation on his project, she agreed to the meeting. "Fine," she told Woodward; "all of you come to breakfast."

She had initially been nervous, that morning in March, when Redford came to call on her, but then so had he; in fact he felt himself to be in the presence of a greater legend and a greater human being. Hollywood, as Redford knew, created myth that lived on as American culture. Katharine Graham, a woman of authentic power, could do what he could never do; she created myth that lived on as history, as truth.

INDEX

275

Index

Index